International Journal on Advances in Systems and Measurements

2017 vol. 10 nr. 1&2

Printed from e-media with permission by:

Curran Associates, Inc.
57 Morehouse Lane
Red Hook, NY 12571

Some format issues inherent in the e-media version may also appear in this print version.

Printed by Curran Associates, Inc. (2018)

International Academy, Research, and Industry Association (IARIA)
412 Derby Way
Wilmington, DE 19810

Phone: (408) 893-6407
Fax: (408) 527-6351

petre@iaria.org

Additional copies of this publication are available from:

Curran Associates, Inc.
57 Morehouse Lane
Red Hook, NY 12571 USA
Phone: 845-758-0400
Fax: 845-758-2633
Email: curran@proceedings.com
Web: www.proceedings.com

The *International Journal on Advances in Systems and Measurements* is published by IARIA.
ISSN: 1942-261x
journals site: http://www.iariajournals.org
contact: petre@iaria.org

Sponsored by IARIA
www.iaria.org

International Journal on Advances in Systems and Measurements
Volume 10, Number 1 & 2, 2017

Cristina Seceleanu, Mälardalen University, Sweden
Guodong Shao, National Institute of Standards and Technology (NIST), USA
Dongwan Shin, New Mexico Tech, USA
Larisa Shwartz, T.J. Watson Research Center, IBM, USA
Simone Silvestri, University of Rome "La Sapienza", Italy
Diglio A. Simoni, RTI International, USA
Radosveta Sokullu, Ege University, Turkey
Junho Song, Sunnybrook Health Science Centre - Toronto, Canada
Leonel Sousa, INESC-ID/IST, TU-Lisbon, Portugal
Arvind K. Srivastav, NanoSonix Inc., USA
Grigore Stamatescu, University Politehnica of Bucharest, Romania
Raluca-Ioana Stefan-van Staden, National Institute of Research for Electrochemistry and Condensed Matter, Romania
Pavel Šteffan, Brno University of Technology, Czech Republic
Chelakara S. Subramanian, Florida Institute of Technology, USA
Sofiene Tahar, Concordia University, Canada
Muhammad Tariq, Waseda University, Japan
Roald Taymanov, D.I.Mendeleyev Institute for Metrology, St.Petersburg, Russia
Francesco Tiezzi, IMT Institute for Advanced Studies Lucca, Italy
Wilfried Uhring, University of Strasbourg // CNRS, France
Guillaume Valadon, French Network and Information and Security Agency, France
Eloisa Vargiu, Barcelona Digital - Barcelona, Spain
Miroslav Velev, Aries Design Automation, USA
Dario Vieira, EFREI, France
Stephen White, University of Huddersfield, UK
Shengnan Wu, American Airlines, USA
Qingsong Xu, University of Macau, Macau, China
Xiaodong Xu, Beijing University of Posts & Telecommunications, China
Ravi M. Yadahalli, PES Institute of Technology and Management, India
Yanyan (Linda) Yang, University of Portsmouth, UK
Shigeru Yamashita, Ritsumeikan University, Japan
Patrick Meumeu Yomsi, INRIA Nancy-Grand Est, France
Alberto Yúfera, Centro Nacional de Microelectronica (CNM-CSIC) - Sevilla, Spain
Sergey Y. Yurish, IFSA, Spain
David Zammit-Mangion, University of Malta, Malta
Guigen Zhang, Clemson University, USA
Weiping Zhang, Shanghai Jiao Tong University, P. R. China

International Journal on Advances in Systems and Measurements
Volume 10, Numbers 1 & 2, 2017

CONTENTS

Constraint-Based Graphical Modelling of On-Site and Factory-Based Construction Production Systems

Ian Flood
Rinker School, College of Design, Construction and Planning,
University of Florida,
Gainesville, Florida, USA
flood@ufl.edu

Abstract — **Planning and control of a construction project requires the development of an appropriate model of the project's processes. The Critical Path Method (CPM) is the most widely used process modelling method in construction since it is simple to use and reasonably versatile. Discrete-event simulation is the most versatile of existing modelling methods in terms of the type of work and detailed logic that can be represented, but it is not easy to use compared to CPM and for this reason has not been widely adopted in practice. *Foresight* is a new modelling method designed to combine the simplicity of CPM and versatility of simulation. Earlier work has demonstrated the modelling simplicity and versatility of *Foresight* relative to other project planning tools for a range of on-site based processes. This paper continues this investigation, focussing on the relative performance of *Foresight* and discrete-event simulation in terms of modelling both on-site and factory-based (manufactured) process logic. The principles and relative performances of the two approaches are demonstrated in application to three example problems. The study demonstrates the advantages of *Foresight* over simulation hold for both on-site and manufacturing type processes.**

Keywords – discrete-event simulation; Foresight modeling; interactive modeling; process modeling; visualization.

I. INTRODUCTION

This paper extends earlier work comparing the performance of conventional simulation and constraint based modelling techniques in application to both on-site and factory-based construction production [1].

A wide range of methods for modelling construction processes have been developed over the last 100 years since the introduction of the Gantt Chart. An analysis of the genealogy [2] of these tools shows that they can be grouped into three main categories: the Critical Path Methods (CPM); the linear scheduling techniques; and discrete-event process simulation. Most other tools are either an enhancement or an integration of these methods or have a very limited scope of application. For example, 4D-CAD and nD-CAD planning methods [3] [4], where one of the dimensions is time, are strictly CPM models hybridized with 3D-CAD for visualization purposes.

Each of the three main groups of modelling method have, unfortunately, practical limitations in terms of their application to construction planning. The CPM methods (the most popular in construction) are well suited to modelling projects at a relatively general level of detail, but are limited in terms of the types of interactions they can consider between tasks [5]. Moreover, CPM models become cumbersome when used to model repetitive processes, and provide little understanding of the interactions between repetitive tasks. When presented in Gantt Chart format, a CPM model provides some visual insight into how a system's logic affects its performance (thus suggesting more optimal ways of executing work) but this is limited to event-based logical dependencies and their impact on time-wise performance.

Linear scheduling, on the other hand, is targeted at projects where there is repetition at a high level, such as high-rise, tunnelling, and highway construction work (see, for example, Matilla and Abraham [6]). These models are very easy to understand and represent the system's logic and its performance within an integrated framework. Consequently, they provide the modeller with strong visual insight that can help identify more optimal ways of achieving the project's production goals. For example, they show in graphic form how the relative progress of repetitive tasks can lead to conflict, both in terms of time and physical interference between productive resources (such as crews and equipment). However, linear scheduling cannot be used to model non-repetitive work, and it includes some simplistic assumptions which often make it difficult to model real-world repetitive processes. For example, velocity diagrams (a linear scheduling technique) cannot easily represent operations that follow different paths, such as two underground utility lines that interact at a cross-over point but otherwise follow different routes.

Discrete-event simulation (see, for example, Halpin and Woodhead [7]; Sawhney et al. [8]; Hajjar and AbouRizk [9]) is an established tool that is very versatile in that it can in principle model any type of interaction between tasks and any type of construction process (including repetitive and non-repetitive work). However, the relatively high degree of expertise and effort required to develop and validate a simulation model has limited its adoption in the field. In addition, simulation models provide no direct visual indication of how a system's logic determines its performance. That is, performance is an output from the model after it has been fully developed; it is not an integral part of the model and therefore its dependence on the model's logic is not directly apparent.

Most projects include a variety of processes some of which may be best modelled using CPM while others may be better represented by linear scheduling or simulation. However, it is not normally practical to expect planners and plan-users to employ more than one modelling method to manage a project. In any case, using several tools that are not fully compatible makes it impossible to seek a globally optimal solution to a planning problem. On the other hand, the alternative approach of using one tool to model all situations (typically CPM) compromises a user's ability to plan and control work optimally.

The ideal solution would be a single tool that combines the versatility of discrete-event simulation (in terms of modelling the broad spectrum of repetitive and non-repetitive construction work), the visual insight of linear scheduling, and the ease-in-use of CPM. *Foresight* [10] has been developed to meet these objectives, and has been demonstrated capable of modelling all types of work covered by CPM, linear scheduling and discrete-event simulation. Construction processes are traditionally performed on-site; however, some are performed within a controlled environment such as a factory, and in recent years there has been a slowly growing interest in manufactured and modular component production. The logistics of manufactured processes can be quite different from on-site processes, often characterized by a job-to-process flow of work (as opposed to process-to-job flow), and batch processing of multiple component types. This paper compares *Foresight* with *CYCLONE* [7] (a commonly adopted simulation modelling system designed specifically for construction) in application to a variety of construction processes including a factory based production system.

Section II introduces the principals of the *Foresight* modelling system. Sections III to V provide three case studies: a multiple-cycle earthmoving operation that includes an intermediate storage facility, a tunnelling operation; and a factory-based process that produces batches of various types of prefabricated reinforced concrete components. The paper concludes in Section VI with a summary of the findings and an identification of continuing research.

II. PRINCIPAL MODELING CONCEPTS OF FORESIGHT

The goal in developing the new approach to modelling was to attain the simplicity of CPM, visual insight of linear scheduling, and the modelling versatility of simulation. In addition, hierarchical structuring of a model (see for example, Huber et al. [11] and Ceric [12]) and interactive development of a model were identified as requisite attributes of the new approach since they facilitate model development and aid understanding of the organization and behaviour of a system.

The three principle concepts of the *Foresight* modelling approach are as follows and illustrated in Figure 1:

(1) *Attribute Space.* This is the environment within which the model of the process exists. Each dimension defining this space represents a different attribute involved in the execution of the process, such as time, cost, excavators, skilled labour, number of repetitions of an item of work, permits to perform work, and materials. The attributes that make-up this space are the resources that are used to measure performance and/or that could have a significant impact on performance.

(2) *Work Units.* These are elements that represent specific items of work that need to be completed as part of the project. They are represented by a bounded region within the attribute space. A unit can represent work at a high level (such as 'Construct Structural System'), a low level (such as 'Erect Column X') or any intermediate level. Collectively, the work units must represent all work of interest but should not represent any item of work more than once. Work units may exist in different or overlapping subsets of attribute space.

(3) *Constraints and Objectives.* Constraints define the relationships between the work units and the attribute space, either directly with the attribute space (such as constraint 'a' in Figure 1) or indirectly via relationships with other work units (such as constraints 'b', 'c', and 'd' in Figure 1). These constraints effectively define the location of the edges of the work units. A constraint can be any functional relationship between the borders of the work units and/or the space within which they exist. Practical examples include: (i) ensuring that crews at different work units maintain a safe working distance; (ii) ensuring that the demand for resources never exceeds the quantity available; (iii) determining the duration for a work unit based on the number of times it has already been repeated; and (iv)

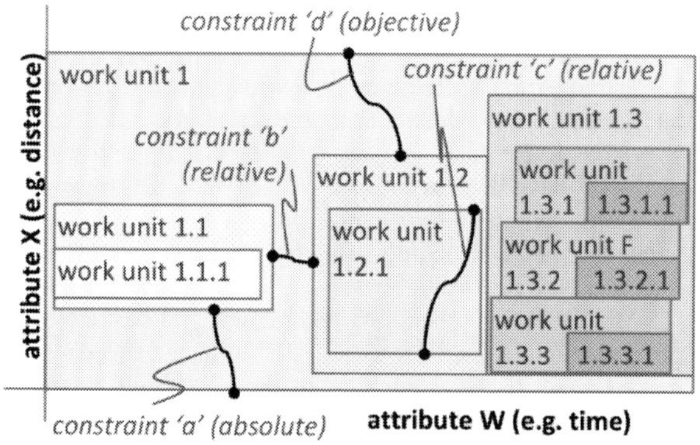

Figure 1. Schematic illustrating the three principal concepts of Foresight.

ensuring that idle time for a task is kept to a minimum. The objectives are the specific goals of the planning study, such as to maximize profits or to complete work by a deadline (such as constraint 'd' in Figure 1). Fundamentally, they are the same thing as constraints, albeit at a higher level of significance, and therefore are treated as such within the proposed new modelling system.

There are two secondary concepts of the *Foresight* modelling system, both concerned with its structure:

(1) *Nesting*. Work units can be nested within other work units (such as work unit '1.2.1' in Figure 1 which is shown to be within work unit '1.2' which is respectively part of '1'). Nesting of work units is defined explicitly, allowing the model to be understood at different levels of abstraction, increasing its readability, reducing the likelihood of errors in the design of the model, and reducing the amount of work required to define and update a model.

(2) *Repetition*. Work units can be repeated (such as occurs within work unit 1.3 in Figure 1) and can be implemented at any level within the nesting hierarchy, thus minimizing the amount of work required to define a model. Repetition of a work unit will include a repetition of all relevant constraints and its nested work units and their constraints.

A standard specification of *Foresight* is that model development be implemented interactively. That is, the visual presentation of a model is updated and all constraints are resolved as the work units and constraints are either edited or added to the model. This way, the modeller can see immediately the impact of any changes or additions that are made. Another point to note is that these models are presented as a plot of the work units within at least two dimensions of the attribute space. This form of presentation allows the progress of work to be visualized within the model's functional structure. This is an extrapolation of the way in which linear scheduling models are presented, and has the advantage of allowing the user to visualize directly how the performance of the model is dependent on its structure. These points will be illustrated in the following three example applications.

It should be noted that *Foresight* is, strictly speaking, a simulation system in that it requires the use of a three-phase simulation algorithm to resolve its constraints.

III. EARTHMOVING OPERATION

The first system to be modelled is that of an earthmoving system comprising a bulldozer used to push dirt from the cut area into a stockpile, and an excavator used to load dump trucks which, in turn, haul the dirt to a fill area. Figure 2 shows the *CYCLONE* [7] simulation diagram of this system for a situation where there is 1 bulldozer that can push 3 cu-m of dirt on each cycle, a loader with a 1 cu-m bucket, and 3 dump trucks of 5 cu-m capacity each. The loader must therefore perform five cycles to load a truck.

This model, once defined within the computer and validated, would be run several times to gain measures of performance of the system, such as production rates and queue length distributions. To the lower left of Figure 2, for example, is a measure of the amount of dirt in the stockpile plotted against time resulting from a single simulation run. Similarly, to the lower right of the figure is a measure of output from the system against time, measured as truck loads at the "dump" activity.

The *Foresight* representation of this system is presented in Figure 3. The first part of this figure shows the hierarchical form of the model (without the main constraints added) whereas the second part shows the model in its normal format with all constraints included representing, for example, work unit durations, and precedence. In this case, the model is displayed within the attribute dimensions of "quantity of dirt" and "time". The model is shown for the first 10 cu-m of dirt removal.

Inspecting the second part of Figure 3, it can be seen that the bulldozer (yellow) and loader (blue) cycles are well balanced, operating at a similar rate of performance. The loader and trucks, however, are not well balanced leaving the loader in an idle state for much of the time. It can be seen from the second part of this figure that the addition of one or two more dump trucks would improve this situation.

One of the benefits of the Foresight mode of representation is that it is possible to see how the performances of different sections of a model are related. For example, the growth in the amount of dirt in the stockpiles (the green bars) can be seen in terms of both the input rate (the leading edges defined by the performance of the bulldozer) and the output (the trailing edge defined by the performance of the loader and dump trucks). However, sometimes it is helpful to isolate a part of a model and inspect that on its own terms. This can be at any level in a model hierarchy; for the stockpiles, this is shown in part 3 of Figure 3. Alternative filtering could have been undertaken to monitor the utilization of any item of equipment, time-wise variance in the length of a queue, or output from the system. Other attributes that may have been included to impose additional constraints on the system or to monitor performance, include cost and location.

Several important differences between *CYCLONE* and *Foresight* can be understood by comparing the model representations of Figures 2 and 3. First, it should be understood that *CYCLONE* requires the complete logic of the model (as represented by the *CYCLONE* diagram of Figure 2) to be finalized before the system's performance can be predicted in a simulation run. In contrast, the *Foresight* model integrates the structure and logic of the model and the estimated performance of the system within a single format as represented by the second part of Figure 3. This gives *Foresight* a couple of significant advantages. First, as work units are added to a model and their parameters altered, the impact of these edits on the estimated performance of the system are seen immediately - the model does not have to be

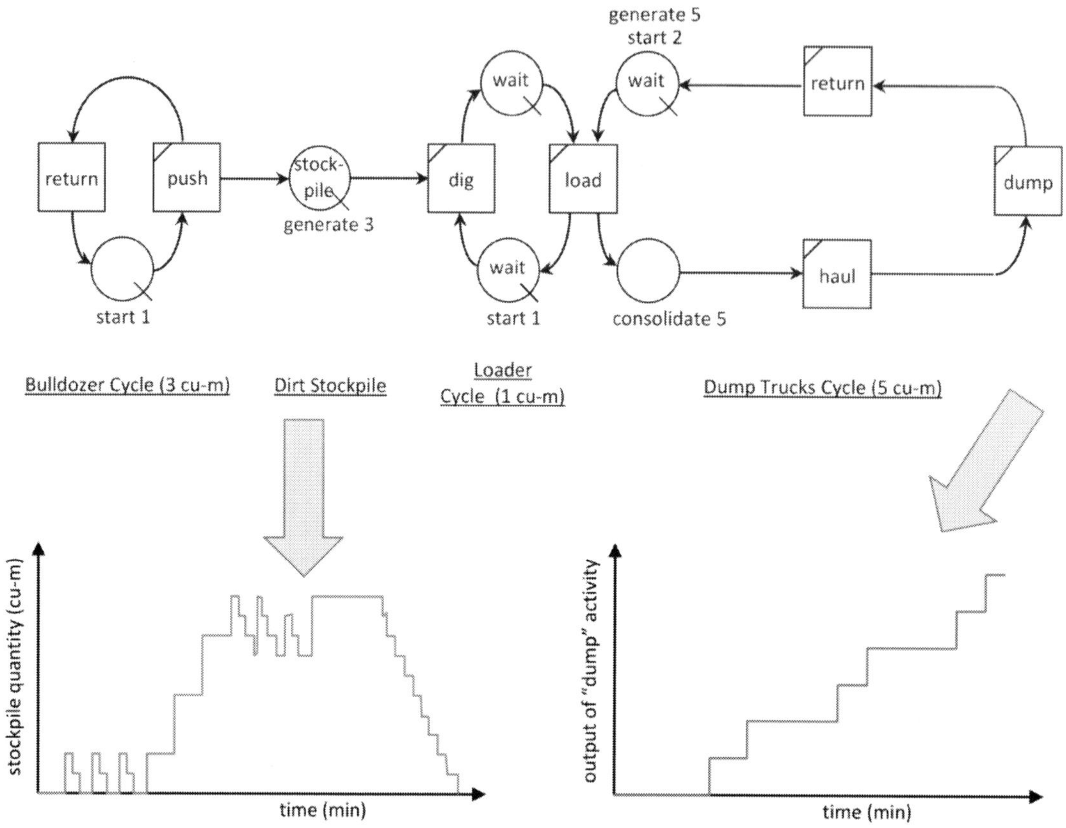

Figure 2. CYCLONE simulation model of an earthmoving operation.

completed before the simulation results are produced. This is a similar advantage to that seen in other graphically based planning tools such as linear scheduling. The second advantage is that in a *Foresight* model, the way in which the logic and structure of the model affect the performance of the system is directly visible, which in turn assists in the optimization of the design of the system - this point will be illustrated in the next case study of a sewer-tunneling operation.

IV. Tunnelling Operation

The second study is concerned with modelling the construction of a 2 m internal diameter sewer, where tunnelling is through a stiff clay and the lining is formed from concrete ring segments grouted in place. The example is used to illustrate the steps in developing a *Foresight* model for a problem that, given its complexities, would best be modelled using simulation methods.

A component oriented approach should be adopted when developing a *Foresight* model, such that each work unit represents the construction of a physical component or sub-component of the facility under construction. A top-down, hierarchical approach is an effective strategy for developing these models, starting with the highest level component (the complete facility) and then breaking it down into its constituent components. The first part of Figure 4 shows the hierarchical structure of the *Foresight* model of the tunnelling operation. At the lowest level in this breakdown are the work units "excavate" representing the cutting of 1 m length of the tunnel, and "line tunnel" which involves placing and grouting concrete ring segments in the 1 m cut. The work units "excavate" and "line tunnel" are repeated 3 times to construct a 3 m length of tunnel. These are followed by "lay track" which adds a 3 m length of track used to carry a manually propelled train for removal of spoil and delivery of materials. If two crews are used for the project then the model shown in Figure 4 would be duplicated (once for each crew) and placed within a parent work unit.

The work unit at the second highest level represents the process of constructing a 3 m section of tunnel, and will be repeated for the length of the tunnel.

Addition of constraints can occur as work units are added to the model. For this tunnel model, the main constraints were as follows:

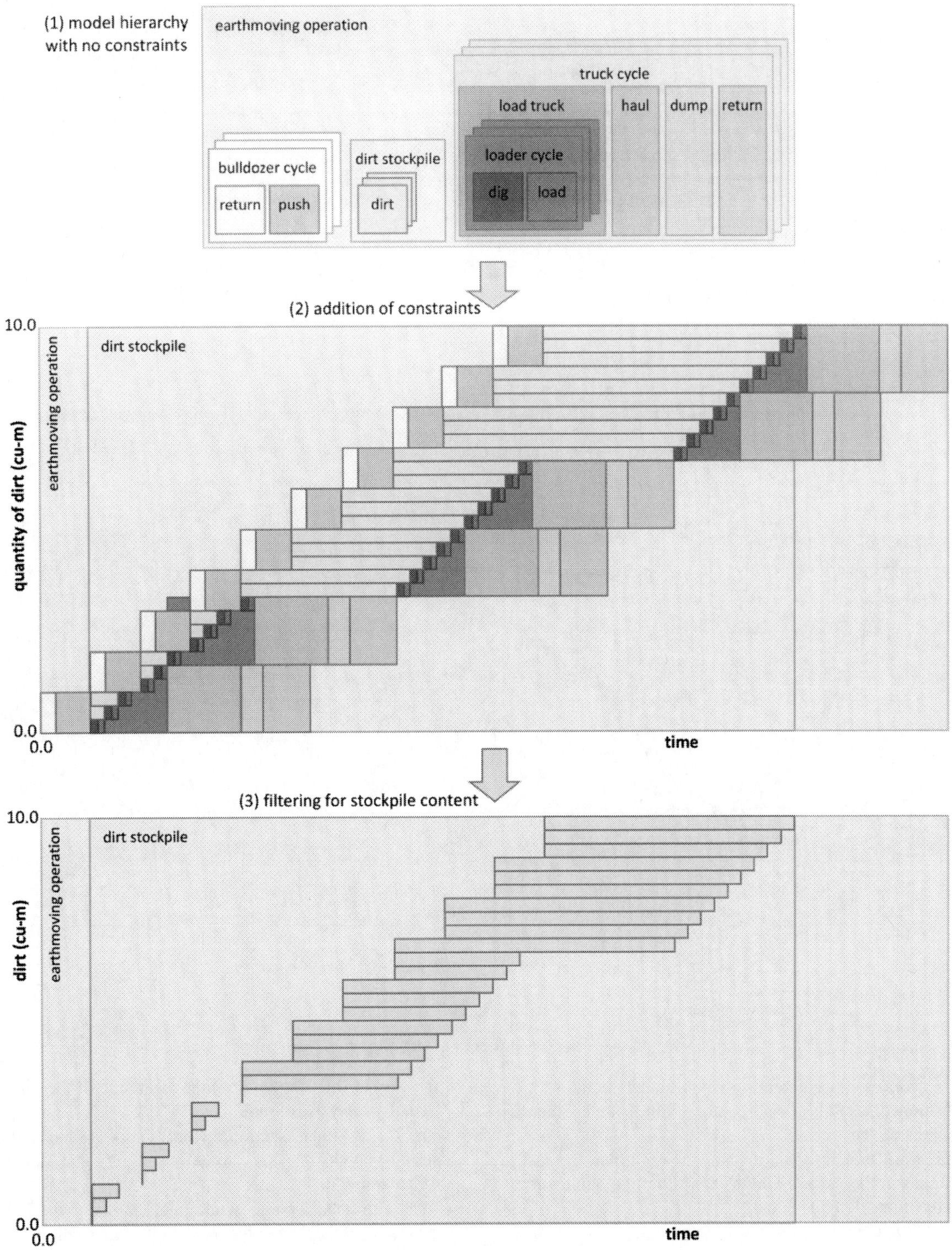

Figure 3. Foresight model of a simple earthmoving operation.

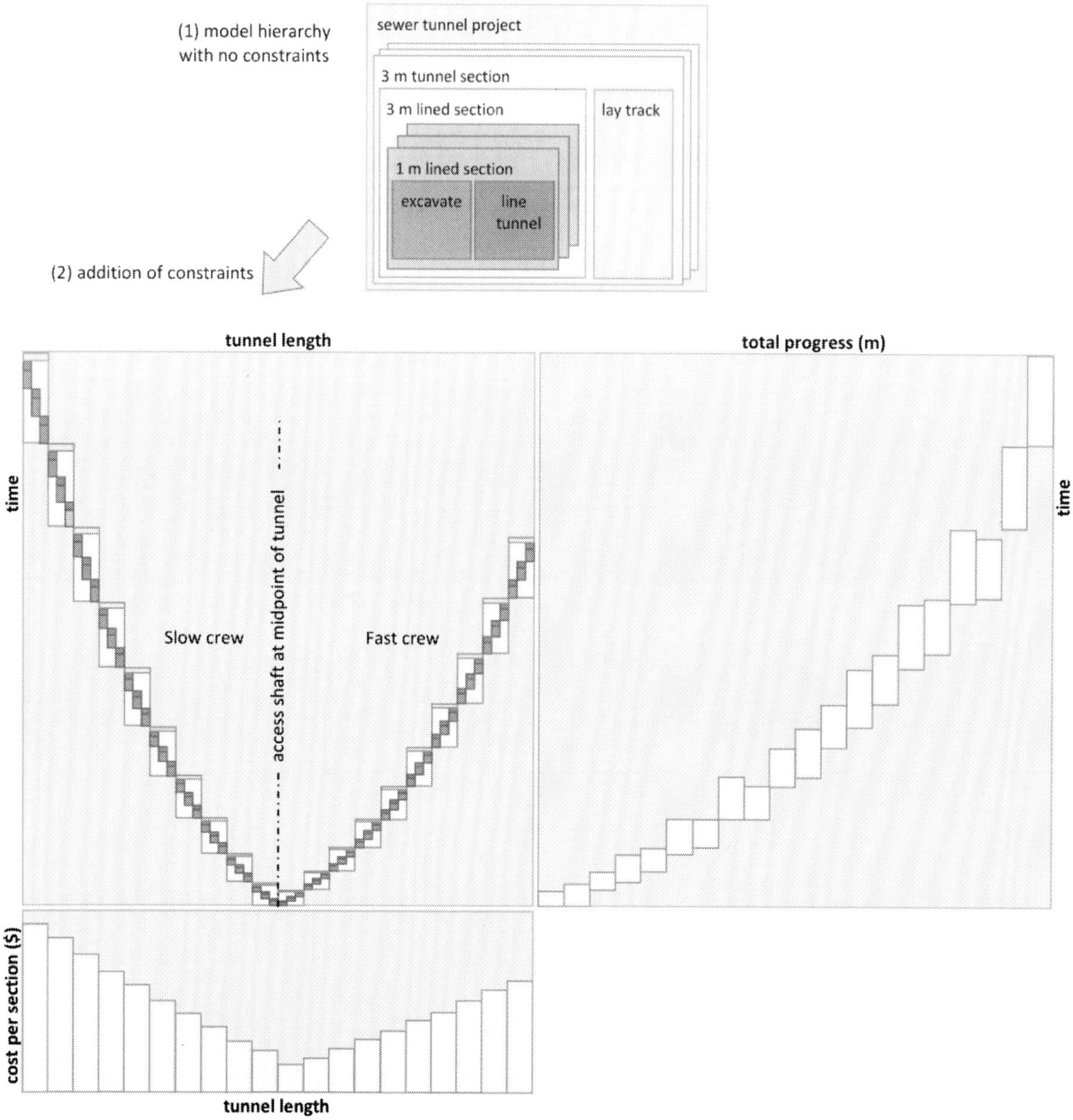

Figure 4. Foresight model of a sewer tunneling operation.

- The work units representing "3 m tunnel sections" are positioned serially both in the "time" and "tunnel length" dimensions.
- The work unit representing the "sewer tunnel project" extends in the "tunnel length" direction to a value equal to the tunnel length.
- The "3 m tunnel section" work units start at the left side of the "sewer tunnel project" work unit and extend all the way to (but not beyond) the right side of the "sewer tunnel project" work unit.
- The "1 m lined section" work units are positioned serially both in the "time" and "tunnel length" dimensions.
- The "1 m lined section" work units span from the left to right side of their "3 m tunnel section" work unit.
- The work units "excavation" and "concrete lining" are positioned sequentially in the "time" dimension.

Completion of any *Foresight* model requires addition of the constraints. For the tunnelling model, this includes adding functions specifying the individual durations of the "excavation", "concrete lining", and "light track" work units, the result of which is shown in the part 2 of Figure 4, specifically the upper left quadrant of the diagram. In this model, two tunnelling crews have been added by duplicating the highest level work unit. The crews are started at the access shaft located at the midpoint of the tunnel, then head in opposite directions but with different rates of production. For convenience, only the first 60 m of tunnel construction is shown. Note, the progress of the crews follows a curve (reducing with time) which results from the fact that the duration to remove spoil and bring concrete ring segments to the tunnel face increases with tunnel length. This dependence was established by making the duration for a work unit a function of its position along the length of the tunnel.

There are many refinements that may be made to this model to provide more accuracy and/or greater detail to allow decisions to be made about equipment types to be employed. Additional detail may involve, for example, further decomposition of the "excavate", "line tunnel" and "lay track" works units. Furthermore, "excavate" may contain work units representing digging at the tunnel face, loading the light train, hauling the spoil from the tunnel, dumping the spoil, and returning the light train. Other attributes may be added, such as crew members, allowing these to be shared between different work units concurrently.

The visual power of these models is apparent by inspecting the upper left quadrant of the second part of Figure 4, which shows clearly the relative performances of the two crews across the length of the tunnel. In this case crew-performance records had indicated that 1 crew operated about 50% faster. From the *Foresight* model it is apparent that, for a 30 m tunnel, the optimum position for the access shaft would be 3 m to the left of its current position, giving the slow crew just 27 m of tunnel to construct and the fast crew 33 m of tunnel.

Alternatively, an additional attribute could be added to the model representing starting the crews at different positions along the tunnel length, thus providing an automated sensitivity analysis of project duration versus starting point for the crews.

V. Manufacture of Reinforced Concrete Prefabricated Components

This third case study compares the performance of *Foresight* with *CYCLONE* based simulation for modelling a manufacturing process. Specifically a prefabricated reinforced concrete component production system was considered comprising job-to-process flow logic, multiple batch production, a constraint on storage space for components in mid-process, and a dependence on an external material supply line.

Figure 5 shows the *CYCLONE* diagram of this system where production starts with a batch of 10 type A components, followed by a batch of 6 type B components, and finishes with a second batch of 3 type A components. The system is also dependent on the supply of steel reinforcing (rebar) which is delivered to the factory in three lots at different points in time. Finally, there is a limit of 3 components allowed within the curing room at any time (a high humidity space), which is implemented by a permitting resource "cure space". Note, the model would be set-up with a component numbering system that gives priority to the batches in the required order of manufacture.

Figure 6 shows the equivalent *Foresight* model for this manufacturing process. The first part of Figure 6 shows the hierarchy of work units involved in the batch production of the types A and B prefabricated reinforced concrete component, and the supply of rebar. At the third level in the hierarchy are work units representing stations in the factory where tasks such as setting-up forms are executed or temporary storage is provided such as for the curing of the cast concrete components. At the fourth level are the individual repetitions of these tasks.

The second part of Figure 6 shows this section of the model with all constraints added, and is plotted for: Units (counting the number of components produced); and Time. The constraints, which would be added as the work units are added, include:

- The durations of each third level work unit which are defined as the difference between the start and end of a work unit measured in the time dimension.
- Two batches of 10 and 3 units respectively for the Type A components, interposed with a batch of 6 Type B components. The limits on each batch are defined in a similar way to the durations, as difference between the limits of the parent work unit.
- The time dependences between the finishes and starts of Set-Up Forms, Cut & Fix Rebar, Place Concrete, Cure Concrete, and Remove Forms.
- Place Concrete precedes Cure Concrete for each component.
- Cure Concrete precedes Remove Forms for each component. This is implemented by introducing a new attribute Curing Space Permits, assigning all fourth level work units within Place Concrete and Cure Concrete a value of 1 in the Curing Space Permits dimension, and setting the first level work unit for the system to a value of 3 in this dimension. The impact of this limit can be seen in the second part of Figure 6 whereby every 3rd component experiences a delay to Place Concrete.
- The final constraint is concerned with the delivery of rebar. This may be constrained in another dimension, measuring say weight of steel, although for convenience here it is measured in components. The constraint limits the start of Cut & Fix Rebar and is shown in green in Figure 6. The impact of the scheduled delivery is also indicated within this figure.

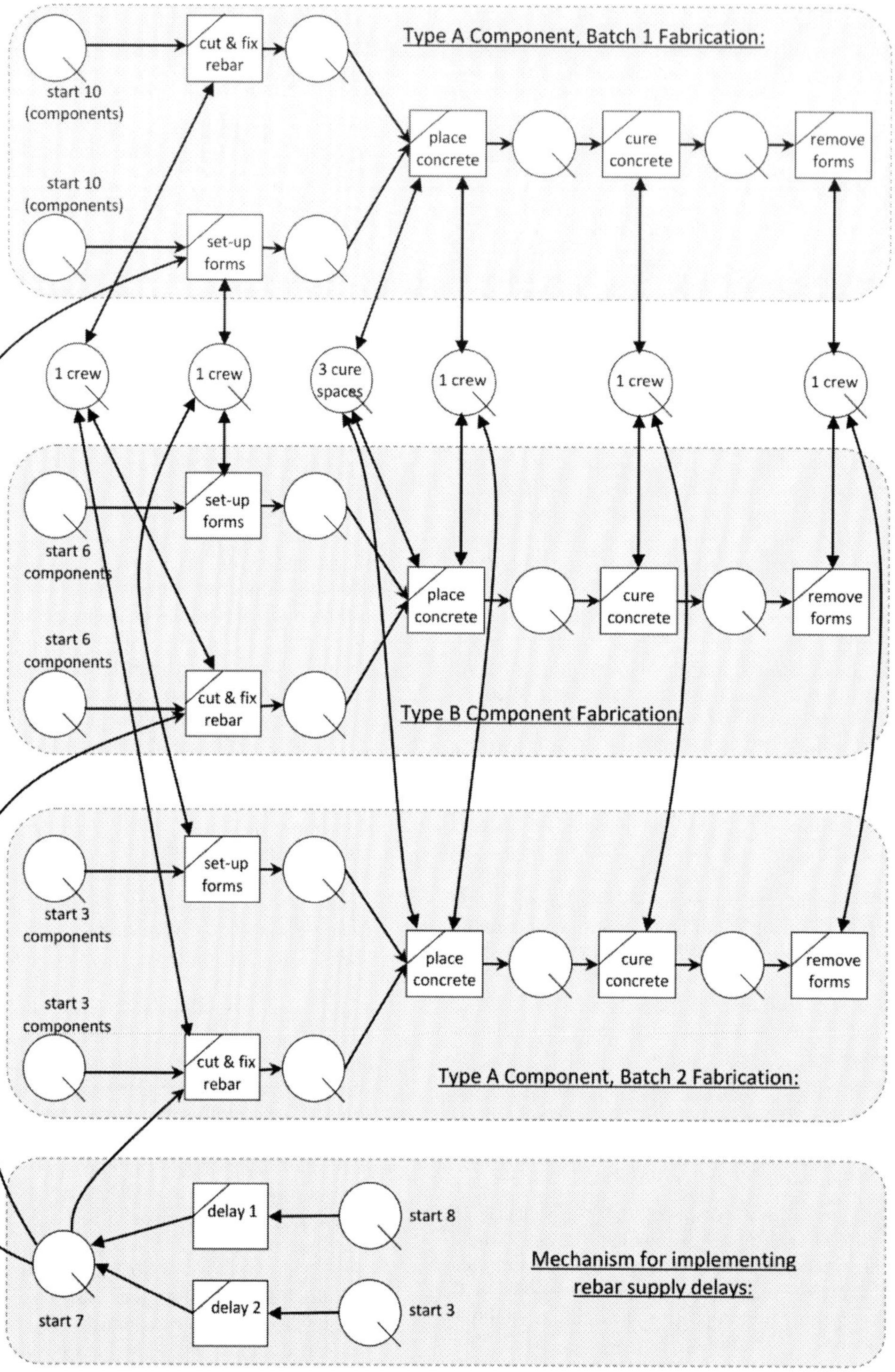

Figure 5. CYCLONE model of manufacture of RC prefabricated components (*adapted from Flood [13]*)

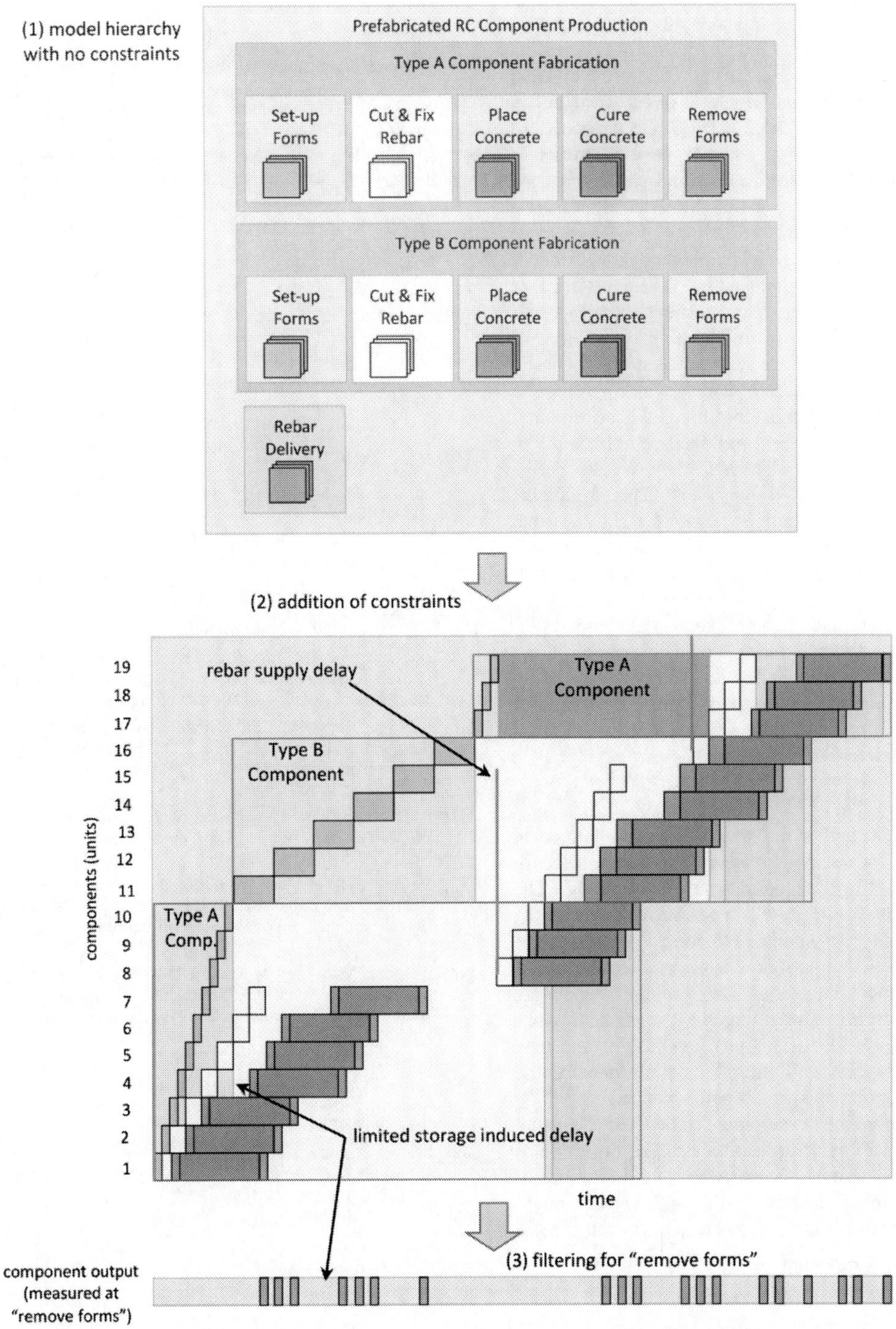

Figure 6. Foresight model of manufacture of RC prefabricated components (*adapted from Flood [13]*)

An important advantage of Foresight over *CYCLONE* is the relative simplicity of the models. A total of 95 terms are required to define the *CYCLONE* model shown in Figure 5 while just 30 terms are required to define the Foresight equivalent. This is similar to the findings made by Flood and Nowrouzian [14] where they made a direct comparison between Foresight and *STROBOSCOPE* [15] (a derivative of the *CYCLONE* modelling system) for construction operations and found that Foresight required around one third of the number of terms to define a model. It was also shown that while *STROBOSCOPE* may employ 25 or more modeling concepts for a relatively simple model, the number of basic modeling concepts employed in *Foresight* will never exceed 5 (the work unit, constraint, attribute, nesting, and repetition). This comparison is for deterministic versions of both the *CYCLONE* and *Foresight* models; if stochastic factors were considered then both models would require the input of additional information describing the uncertainty. For *CYCLONE* these parameters would define uncertainty in the activity durations, for *Foresight* they would define uncertainty in the value of a constraint. This highlights another advantage of *Foresight* over *CYCLONE* that uncertainty can be applied to any model parameter not just activity duration, although simulation in general is also capable of this.

It can be seen visually from Figure 6 that delays in production due to limited curing room space could be removed by expanding this facility to enable storage of an additional 4 components. However, it is also apparent that the most significant cause of poor performance results from the delays to the delivery of rebar.

VI. CONCLUSIONS

In this paper the author has proposed a new approach, named *Foresight*, for modelling construction processes built on concepts relevant to contemporary project planning. The principles upon which *Foresight* is based provide it with the versatility necessary to model the broad spectrum of construction projects that until now have required the use of several different modelling tools. The resultant models are highly visual in form, representing the progress of work within the model structure. This provides insight into how the design of a process will impact its performance, and suggests ways of optimizing project performance.

Research is on-going developing detailed models using this method for a variety of project types. The objective of these studies is to determine the successes and limitations of the proposed planning method in the real-world, and to determine refinements that will increase its value as a modelling tool.

REFERENCES

[1] I. Flood, "A Constraint-Based Graphical Approach to Modelling Construction Systems: An alternative to discrete-event simulation," 4th International Conference on Advanced Communications and Computation, INFOCOMP 2014, July 20 - 24, 2014, Paris, France, pp. 168-174.

[2] I. Flood, R.R.A. Issa, and W. Liu, "A New Modeling Paradigm for Computer-Based Construction Project Planning," Proc. Joint Intnl. Conf. on Cmptg. and Decision-Making in Civil and Building Engineering, Montreal, Canada, ASCE, June 2006, pp. 1-11.

[3] B. Koo and M. Fischer, "Feasibility Study of 4D CAD in Commercial Construction," Journal of Construction Engineering and Management, ASCE, 126(4), 2000, pp. 251-260.

[4] R.A. Issa, I. Flood, and W. O'Brien, (Eds.), 4D CAD and Visualization in Construction: Developments and Applications, A. A. Balkema Publishers, Steenwijk, 2003.

[5] R.B. Harris and P.G. Ioannou, "Scheduling Projects with Repeating Activities," Journal of Construction Engineering and Management. ASCE, 124(4), 1998, pp. 269-276.

[6] K.G. Matilla and D.M. Araham, "Linear-Scheduling: past research efforts and future directions," Engineering, Construction, and Architectural Management, Blackwell Science Ltd, 5(3), 1998, pp. 294-303.

[7] D.W. Halpin and R.W. Woodhead, Design of Construction and Process Operations, John Wiley and Sons, Inc., New York, NY, 1976.

[8] A. Sawhney, S.M. AbouRizk, and D.W. Halpin, "Construction Project Simulation using CYCLONE," Canadian Journal of Civil Engineering, 25(1), 1998, pp. 16-25.

[9] D. Hajjar and S.M. AbouRizk, "Unified Modeling Methodology for Construction Simulation," Journal of Construction Engineering and Management, ASCE, 128(2), 2002, pp. 174-185.

[10] I. Flood, "Foresight: A Structured Graphical Approach to Constraint-Based Project Planning," Proc. 2nd International Conference on Advances in System Simulation, SIMUL 2010, IEEE CSDL, Nice, France, August 2010, 6 pp.

[11] P. Huber, K. Jensen, and R.M. Shapiro, "Hierarchies of Coloured Petri Nets," Proc. 10th Int. Conf. on Application and Theory of Petri Nets, (LNCS 483), Springer-Verlag, 1990, pp. 313-341.

[12] V. Ceric, "Hierarchical Abilities of Diagrammatic Representations of Discrete-Event Simulation Models," Proc. 1994 Winter Simulation Conference, (Eds. J. D. Tew, S. Manivannan, D. A. Sadowski, and A. F. Seila), 1994, pp. 589-594.

[13] I. Flood, "Modeling Construction Processes: A Structured Graphical Approach Compared to Construction Simulation," International Workshop on Computing in Civil Engineering, Austin, TX, ASCE, June 2015, 8 pp.

[14] I. Flood and V. Nowrouzian, 2014, "Discrete-Event Simulation versus Constrained Graphic Modelling of Construction Processes," Australasian Journal of Construction Economics and Building, 2 (1), 2014, pp. 13-22.

[15] J.C. Martinez, "STROBOSCOPE, State and Resource Based Simulation of Construction Processes," PhD. Dissertation, University of Michigan, 1996.

Evaluation of Response Capacity to Patient Attention Demand in an Emergency Department

Eva Bruballa
Tomàs Cerdà Computer Science School
Universitat Autònoma de Barcelona
Barcelona, Spain
eva.bruballa@eug.es

Alvaro Wong, Dolores Rexachs, Emilio Luque
Computer Architecture and Operating Systems Department
Universitat Autònoma de Barcelona
Barcelona, Spain
alvaro@caos.uab.es, dolores.rexachs@uab.es, emilio.luque@uab.es

Francisco Epelde
Short Stay Unit
Parc Taulí Hospital Universitari
Institut d'Investigació i Innovació Parc Taulí I3PT
Universitat Autònoma de Barcelona
Sabadell, Spain
fepelde@tauli.cat

***Abstract*— The progressive growth of aging, increased life expectancy and a greater number of chronic diseases contribute significantly to the growing demand of emergency medical care, and thus, on saturation of Emergency Departments. This is one of the most important current problems in healthcare systems worldwide. This work proposes an analytical model to calculate the theoretical throughput of a particular sanitary staff configuration in a Hospital Emergency Department, which is, the number of patients it can attend per unit time given its composition. The analytical model validation is based on data generated by simulation of the real system, based on an agent based model of the system, which makes it possible to take into account different valid sanitary staff configurations and different number of patients entering the emergency service. In fact, we aim to evaluate the response capacity of an ED, specifically of doctors, nurses, admission and triage personnel, who make up a specific sanitary staff configuration, for any possible configuration, according to the patient flow throughout the service. It would not be possible to test the different possible situations in the real system and this is the main reason why we obtain the necessary information about the system performance for the validation of the model using a simulator as a sensor of the real system. The theoretical throughput is a measure of the response capacity to patient's attention in the system and, moreover, it will be a reference in order to make possible a model for planning the entry of non-critical patients into the service by its relocation in the current input pattern, which is an immediate future goal in our current research. This research offers the availability of relevant knowledge to the managers of the Emergency Departments to make decisions to improve the quality of the service in anticipation of the expected growing demand of the service in the very near future.**

Keywords—Emergency Department (ED); Agent-Based Modeling and Simulation (ABMS); Decision Support Systems (DSS); Response Capacity; Lenght of Stay (LoS); Knowledge Discovery.

I. INTRODUCTION

The current research focuses on the field of modeling and simulation of a Hospital Emergency Department (ED) and, specifically, on the use of simulation as a source of data for the extraction of information. This information, finally, must provide us with an extensive knowledge of the behavior of the system in any situation.

We proceed with the main objective of providing a methodology that allows the managers of an ED to be able to make decisions to improve the quality of the service provided to patients who use the service.

With this objective in mind, in a previous paper, we explained the idea of characterizing the system through an analytical model based on the definition of a set of indexes, indicators of its attention capacity and its performance, given different possible scenarios [1]. The given model in [1] presents some limitations, since it does not take into account all possible combinations of the healthcare staff, as it's already mentioned in the referenced article. The generalization of this model is presented here.

Currently, given the growing demand for emergency medical care, mostly due to the progressive growth of aging, increased life expectancy and greater number of chronic diseases, the management of EDs is increasingly important. Particularly, how to manage the increasing number of patients entering into the service is one of the most important problems in EDs worldwide, because it requires a substantial amount of human and material resources, which unfortunately are often too limited, as well as a high degree of coordination between them [2][3]. A major consequence of the increase in patients entering the service is its saturation [4]. This results in an increase in the total time a patient spends in the service, from their entry to their discharge, called *Length of Stay* of patients in the service (*LoS*). This can produce a general discontent among patients for reasons such as being abandoned without receiving care, limited access to emergency care and an increasing patient mortality [5].

Some studies in the related literature try to analyze the factors that influence patients' long periods of stay of in the ED and its saturation [6] [7]. Others show that saturation and long waits increase the proportion of patients who leave the service without being seen by a doctor (LWBS) [8] [9]. The aim of some others is to reduce the *LoS*, and therefore, the total time the patient is waiting to be attended, or length of waiting for patients (*LoW*), and some of the solutions that have been found and have been implemented are called Fast Tracks [10] [11], or other measures known as See and Treat [12]. Finally, we highlight those references using simulation to test the effectiveness of the proposed measures for improvement in the *LoS* of patients in the ED [13] - [17].

The ED service is one of the most complex areas of the hospital due to its dynamism and variability over time. The operation of the system is the result of the interaction between the different elements of which it is composed, and all this makes it a complex real system.

Modeling and simulation of complex real systems, such as an ED, is one of the most powerful tools available for their description. Simulation provides a better understanding of their operation and of the activity of their elements, and it can help decision-making to establish strategies for an optimal system operation [18][19].

The final objective of modeling and simulation of a real system is to find additional knowledge about it. This can be achieved by inference processes on the variables of interest of the system in order to make predictions about the behavior of these variables under different conditions, based on information obtained from the generated data [20].

As a result of an intensive previous research, we have an ED simulator available, based on an Agent-Based Modeling (ABM) design of the system, which has been developed, verified and validated within our research group, the "High Performance Computing for Efficient Applications and Simulation" Research Group (HPC4EAS) of the Universitat Autònoma de Barcelona (UAB), in collaboration with the ED Staff Team of the Short Stay Unit of Hospital de Sabadell (one of the most important hospitals in Spain, which provides care service to a catchment area of 500,000 people, and attends 160,000 patients per year in the ED). The model describes the ED's behavior from the actions and interactions between agents, and between them and their physical environment. The input parameters that characterize each different scenario in the simulation of the real system are the healthcare staff configuration, the number and type of incoming patients each hour, and the period of time simulated. As output, given that the most widely used and accepted parameter in the literature as an indicator of the quality of service is the total *LoS* of patients in the service, each simulation provides data of this index of all patients in all locations in the ED. In addition, the simulator includes sensors to obtain fully temporalized information about the agents, in such a way that data on the number of patients per hour and location are also available for each iteration. The implementation of the simulator has been done with NetLogo, an agent-based simulation environment well-suited for modeling complex systems [21][22].

An initial application of the simulator, with interesting results, was carried out by analyzing the effects of different derivation policies over the ED performance, particularly by analyzing how these changes modify the *LoS* of patients in the service [23].

Another study in the same research line consisted of trying to find the optimal healthcare staff configuration to minimize the *LoS* of the patients in the service, taking into account a constraint related to the cost of the configurations and the amount of available resources [24].

There are a great number and variety of simulated agents, and different possible values for the input parameters in the simulator. This results in a large number of different possible scenarios to be simulated. Thus, the use of High Performance Computing (HPC) was necessary in both experiments, due to the high number of executions required and the amount of data to be computed.

The main purpose of these previous researches was to provide some understanding of specific variables affecting the normal system performance. This could support decision-making (DSS), aiding the administrators and heads of the ED to choose the policies that could permit them to achieve a better quality of service with the available human and technical resources.

Our current work tries to obtain further and different knowledge concerning the performance of the system. We propose a model for system characterization with respect to the sanitary staff available configuration in it. It is an analytical model based on a set of equations that allow us to obtain the necessary information to obtain knowledge regarding the theoretical capacity to patient care of the system with respect to its staff resources, given a specific staff configuration and according with the patient flow in the system.

The content of the paper is organized as follows: Section II presents the research objectives and methodology of the research; Section III briefly describes the ED process and the simulation model; Section IV presents the analytical model proposed; and the experimental results for model validation are showed in Section V. Finally, Section VI closes the paper with discussion and future work.

II. RESEARCH OBJECTIVES AND METHODOLOGY

It is a fact that saturation of the ED service is mostly due to admission of patients with lower acuity level. Based on historical real data from the Hospital de Sabadell, these patients represent a high percentage of the admitted patients and most of them are non-critical (see Figure 4 in Section III.B). We hypothesized that a redistribution of these non-critical patients in the input pattern initially planned by historical data (Figure 1), can lead to an improvement in waiting times for all patients, and therefore, to an improvement in the quality of service from the point of view of the users of the service, as it could avoid long waiting times in the service.

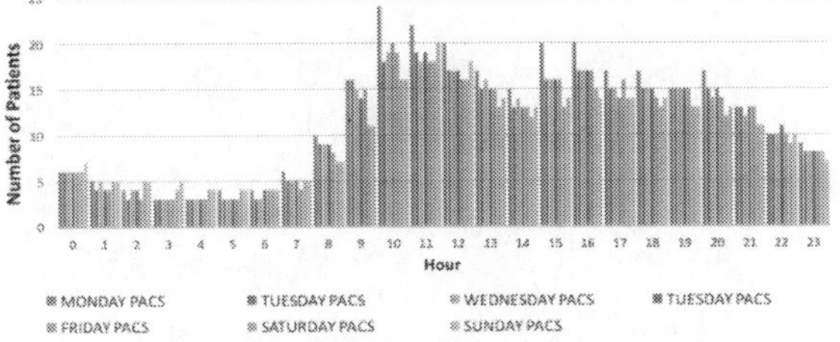

Figure 1. Input pattern of patients per hour and day of the week (historical data of 2014 of the Hospital de Sabadell).

In fact, the real starting point of this research was to understand the simulator as our main source of data. These data are the raw material for the analysis and they become information when we assign them some special meaning. When a model is found or designed, in order to interpret this information, and the model represents an added value, we refer to it as knowledge.

Moreover, simulation allows us to obtain data from situations, which cannot be proved in the real system, therefore any experimental limitation in the real system can be overcome through computer simulation. This idea suggested to us the hypothesis of the ability to gain knowledge about the ED service behavior from the data provided by the simulation of any possible reality.

From the analysis of the data from simulation, we can obtain information concerning patient's *LoS* in the service. The research we are conducting aims to improve the quality of service provided in a ED, trying to reduce the *LoS* of patients, through a model for scheduling the entry of non-critical patients into the service. The model will be based on the prediction of the *LoS* of patients in the ED by simulation. Simulation would also be the way to demonstrate the effectiveness of the scheduling model for patient admission, in which we are currently working on.

Specifically, the goal of the work presented in this paper is the first step on the way to the definition of this scheduling model. It consists of developing an analytical model to determine the *theoretical throughput* (*T_ThP*) of a particular healthcare staff configuration, which we define as the number of patients it can take care per unit time given its composition. It is a reference to measure the performance of the system and the capacity of the healthcare staff configuration to absorb the demand for the service, so it is an indicator of the response capacity of the system to patient attention.

It should be clarified that we propose a simplified model for the calculation of the system capacity, considering the system in a steady state. It is a continuous flow model, with regular admission and no queues. With this, we want to obtain, analytically, a reference value of the productivity of the system for its characterization in an ideal situation. This reference value will allow us to evaluate the effects on the behavior of the system against different measures through simulation. Specific changes in the input parameters of the simulator, in particular, referring to the patient input and the configuration of the sanitary staff, simulating different possible real situations, will modify the actual productivity of the system. The theoretical value obtained through the analytical model will be a reference to guide these changes.

The corresponding value for the *T_ThP* is an appropriate indicator for system characterization and it will indicate whether the considered healthcare staff configuration will generate endless queues for a specific scenario, or in another way, the number of patients attending the service is below its response capacity, and so the occupancy of the staff is not at its limit.

In the experimental results for the validation of the model in Section V, we conduct a sensitivity analysis on the effect of an increase or a decrease in the number of patients entering the service every hour, with respect to the theoretical value obtained as reference for the *T_ThP*. This analysis shows how the number of patients waiting to be attended in each phase of the process, which we call *Waiting Queue Length* (*WQL*), reaches endless values when the input for patients reaches and surpasses the obtained *T_ThP* with the model. It is also observed how the percentage of time in which the corresponding healthcare staff is attending or treating patients for each phase (occupancy) reaches 100% when this happens.

Once the system is characterized by this value, we can take it into account to act in order to avoid long waiting times through the admission scheduling of non-critical patients, and ultimately improve the *LoS* of all patients in the service.

The final aim of the complete research will be to obtain an input distribution of patients, which is as homogeneous as possible, so that the flow of patients in the service shall be in accordance with the response capacity of the system according to the healthcare staff resources at any time.

Moreover, the simulator will again be the main source of data for the model validation.

III. DESCRIPTION OF THE EMERGENCY DEPARTMENT OPERATION PROCESS

We divide this section into three subsections in which we describe the basic operation of the ED, the different types of patient and the functionality of the ED simulator.

A. Emergency Department Process

The operation of the ED is based on a process consisting of different steps or phases in which each patient is passing from their entry into the service until they are discharged, referred to another service or admitted to the hospital (Figure 2).

The ED is divided into different areas, which correspond with the different process phases:

- *Admissions Area*: Administrative staff carries out the registration of the patient's arrival and the reasons for their visit to the emergency service.
- *Triage Area*: Professional sanitary staff identifies the priority level with which the patient should be treated.

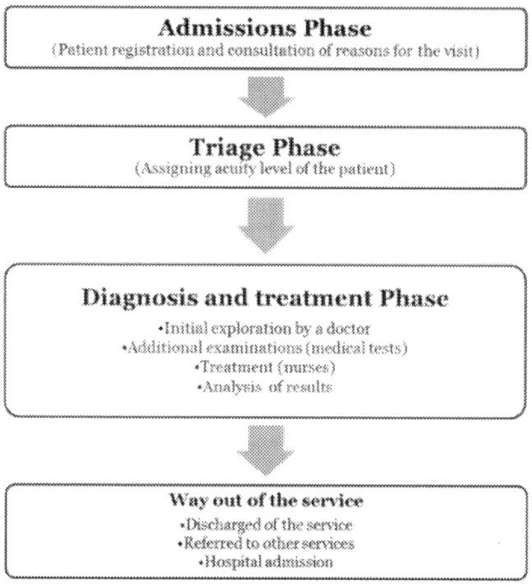

Figure 2. Operation of the Emergency department.

- *Diagnosis-Treatment Zone*: Healthcare staff (doctors, nurses and specialist technicians) try to identify the causes of the patient's health problem and, as far as possible, try to solve it. This area is in turn divided into different areas (medical room, nursing room, care boxes and X-ray laboratories).
- *Waiting Rooms*: Distributed in different zones of the ED, where patients wait to be treated at the different stages of the process.

B. Classification of patients

Real data from *Hospital de Sabadell* corroborate that the majority of patients attending the service are not critical patients and, therefore, they do not require immediate valuation or can be outpatients (Figure 3). If these non-critical patients had the possibility of getting information about when it is more advisable to go to the service, depending on the waiting time estimated for them, they would probably do it when the prevision for waits were lower. These are the patients suitable for a possible relocation in the current pattern of patients entering the service.

In the triage phase, patients are classified according to their acuity level and they are assigned a priority. The scale of priority and urgency to be applied in Spanish hospitals (Spanish Triage System) is based on the Andorran Triage Model (MAT) [25] (Figure 4).

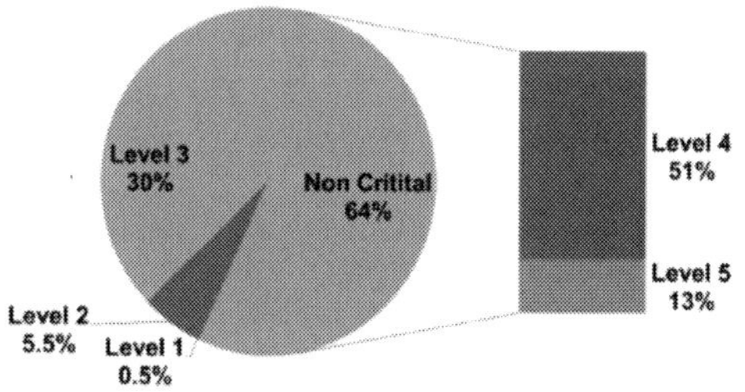

Figure 3. Percentage of patients by acuity level (historical data of 2014 of the Hospital de Sabadell).

TRIAGE	TYPE OF ATTENTION	DESCRIPTION
LEVEL 1	REVIVAL	Extreme health condition life-threatening. It requires IMMEDIATE ATTENTION.
LEVEL 2	EMERGENCY	Health condition life-threatening. It requires IMMEDIATE ATTENTION. BUT NOT PRIORITY.
LEVEL 3	URGENCY	Acute condition but not life threatening. Requires NOT IMMEDIATE EVALUATION.
LEVEL 4	MINOR URGENCY	Acute condition, not life threatening. Requires DEFERRED VALUATION.
LEVEL 5	NOT URGENT	Symptomatic condition, not life threatening. DOESN'T REQUIRE URGENT ATTENTION. OUTPATIENT.

Figure 4. Classification of patients according to their level of urgency (Spanish Triage System).

C. Functionality of the Simulator

From the moment when the patient enters the service, the simulation runs according to the patient flow shown in Figure 5. The admission and triage phases are common to all patients entering the service, and there is a percentage, although low, of patients being referred to other services after the triage stage and also others who leave the service without being seen. After triage, patients with acuity level 1, 2 and 3 are treated separately from those with acuity level 4 and 5 for the diagnostic and treatment phase. In the simulation model, patients 1, 2 and 3 are treated in a specific area called Area A for diagnosis and treatment, and patients 4 and 5 are treated in a separate area identified as Area B. The admissions and triage phase share the same healthcare staff, but doctors and assistant nurses are different for Area A and B.

For our work, we are interested in tracking patients 4 and 5, those who are non-critical patients, and can be relocated in time for their arrival to service. So, we will consider all patients for admissions and triage phases, but only patients 4 and 5 (Area B) for diagnosis and treatment.

In the diagnostic and treatment phase, all patients generated by the system go through an initial medical exploration phase, which we will identify hereafter as *IE*. A percentage of them are directly discharged and leave the ED after the *IE* phase (showed by a continuous line in Figure 5). The rest remain in the ED and they go through a phase of complementary examinations and/or treatment carried out by technical staff and/or nurses. After this, they return to see the doctor, who analyzes the test and/or treatment results (we will use *AR* onwards to refer to this phase). Finally, they are discharged from the service (showed by a dashed line in Figure 5).

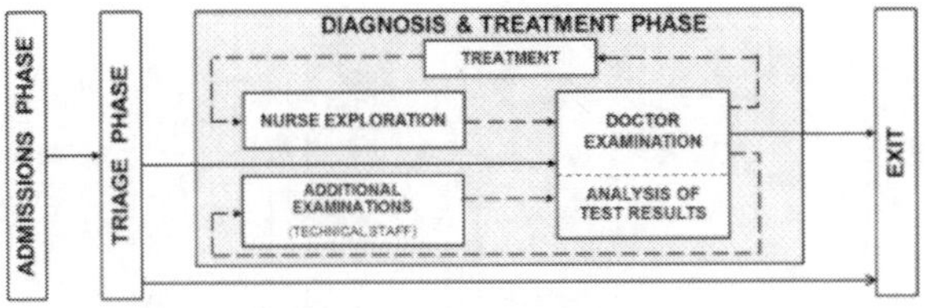

Figure 5. Patient flow in the Emergency Department.

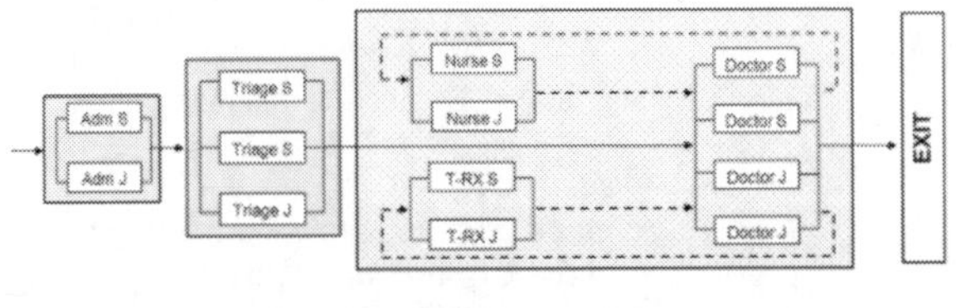

Figure 6. Sanitary staff working in parallel on each phase.

The simulator includes the following agents: patients, admissions staff, triage nurses, assistant nurses, doctors and radiology technicians. In the case of agents representing healthcare staff (all except patients), we consider two levels of experience (Junior/Senior) and all of them can work in parallel in each phase (Figure 6). The level of experience has an effect on the amount of time required for patient attention, which is different depending on their condition of junior or senior staff (hereafter *SS* and *JS*).

The actions and interactions between the involved agents at each process step result in changes of state of the agents, which ultimately result in the global operation of the system.

Each scenario of simulation is identified by an input healthcare staff configuration and a specific input of patients into the service, and the output of the simulation brings data concerning the number of attended patients, attention time and waiting time for each patient in all phases in their way through the service.

IV. ANALYTICAL MODEL

The quality of service, from the point of view of the user, is reflected in the time spent on patient attention and waiting times between different phases of the process. Moreover, from the point of view of service management, performance is directly related to the number of patients treated per unit time and an efficient use of resources.

We propose a model for system characterization, which should give us information and knowledge in order to make possible changes in the system to improve it. The model is based on the definition of a set of indicators of the quality of service, and a set of equations that allow us to measure some intrinsic characteristics of the system given a specific healthcare staff configuration, and the patient flow presented in Figure 5.

These equations will allow us to have information, and so knowledge, about the system capacity regarding its resources. We aim to use this knowledge to find an algorithm for the relocation of non-critical patients, modifying their current arrival pattern, such that their arrival at the service should be in accordance with the calculated system capacity.

A. Definition of indexes

As an indicator of the quality of service from the point of view of the user, we define an index called *Patient attention Time (PaT)* as the total time a patient is receiving attention throughout all stages in the service for a given configuration. This index is calculated from the summation of the values for the attention time in each stage, which are obtained from the simulator calibration, based on the corresponding values provided by the hospital:

$$PaT = \sum_{i=1}^{Stages} PaT_{stage\ i} \tag{1}$$

$PaT_{stage\ i}$ indicates the *Patient Attention Time in stage i*, and it is independent of the number of patients entering the service. Notice that *PaT* is not a fixed value for all patients, as it depends on the followed way by each patient (not all patients are required for additional examinations or receive some treatment).

Another parameter widely used and accepted in the literature as an indicator of the quality of service is the *Length of Stay (LoS)*. It is defined as the total time a patient spends in the service. Unlike the previous one, the value of this index depends not only on the healthcare staff configuration, but also on the number and type of patients admitted to the service, as it includes the waiting time.

Finally, the *Length of Waiting (LoW)* is the total waiting time of a patient throughout the service. Note that,

$$LoS - PaT = LoW \text{ and always } PaT \leq LoS. \tag{2}$$

Moreover, the *Equivalent Patient attention Time* for stage *i* ($EpaT_{stage\ i}$) is defined as the attention time of a patient taking into account the possibility of working in parallel for the agents in that stage, and (3) shows how it is calculated:

$$EPaT_{stage\ i} = \frac{1}{\frac{SS_i}{PaT_{SS}^{i}} + \frac{JS_i}{PaT_{JS}^{i}}} \tag{3}$$

where SS_i and JS_i in (3) and (5) stand for the total number of senior/junior health workers in the stage *i* respectively, and the calculation is the corresponding one for parallelization on a pipeline model.

The slowest stage of the configuration will fix the speed at which patients can be attended in the service and also is the one which can saturate the system. It is, therefore, the inverse of the equivalent attention time of the slowest stage, which will determine the number of patients that a given configuration can treat per unit of time given its composition. We call this index *Theoretical Throughput (T_ThP)*, which is the indicator we will use to measure the patient attention capacity of the configuration, that is, its response capacity for a specific situation. Expression (4) gives its calculation:

$$T\_ThP = \frac{1}{Max\ EPaT_i} \tag{4}$$

In fact, the *Theoretical Throughput* for a specify stage i will be obtained by the inverse of (3):

$$T\_ThP_{stage\ i} = \frac{SS_i}{PaT^{i}_{SS}} + \frac{JS_i}{PaT^{i}_{JS}} \qquad (5)$$

B. Theoretical throughput for the diagnosis and treatment phase.

Unlike other stages of the process for a patient along his path through the ED, this is the most complex stage due to its non-linearity. All patients first go through an initial medical exploration (*IE*), which is their first contact with the doctor. There is a percentage p_1 of patients who require additional tests after the initial exploration phase with the doctor, and also a percentage p_2 of patients who require some treatment. Treatment is administered and controlled by assistant nurses. The return of these patients for the doctor's final diagnosis (after completing the complementary examinations requested by the doctor after his first contact with the patient (*AR*)) must be taken into account, as the time the doctor uses to see these patients again cannot be used to see new patients. The rest of patients will be discharged from service directly after their first contact with the doctor.

Figure 7 shows in detail patients' flow along this phase, in accordance with all these preliminary considerations.

The total number of assistant nurses, senior or junior, in the considered configuration is represented by *NS/NJ* respectively. The total number of doctors, also senior or junior, are represented by *DS/DJ*, and it is necessary to distinguish between:

- DS_{IE}/DJ_{IE}: Senior/Junior doctors attending patients in the Initial Exploration stage.
- DS_{AR}/DJ_{AR}: Senior/Junior doctors attending patients in the Analysis of Results stage.

We consider that doctors prioritize the attention of patients who have already gone through the *IE* (initial exploration stage), and therefore, these patients will be treated in the time the doctor is available for *AR* (analysis of results). This prevents endless queues on the return of patients from their requested complementary examination or treatment.

The *Theoretical Throughput (T_ThP)* has been defined as the number of patients which can be treated by the healthcare staff configuration working in each stage of the process, being so an indicator of the response capacity of each phase or stage. For its calculation in the diagnosis and treatment phase, it is necessary to consider the average attention time of each type of doctor depending on their experience (Junior or Senior), and depending on the type of care they are providing, either in the first step of initial exploration (*IE*), or in the second, consisting of the analysis of the results of a requested supplementary examination (*AR*). These times are known, determined by the calibration of the simulator, and denoted by PaT_i^j, which represents the average *Patient Attention Time* for a doctor type i doing j.

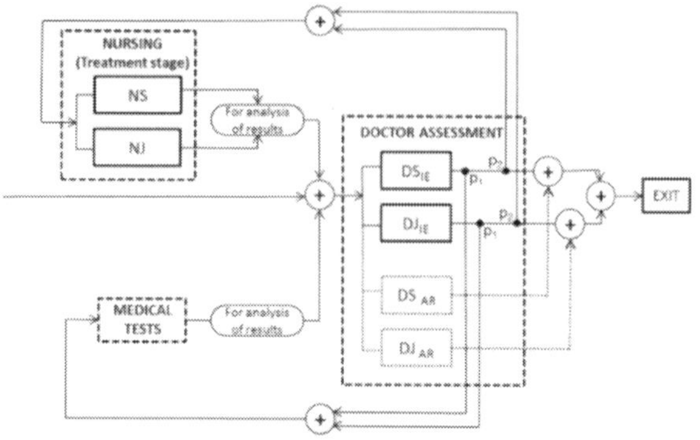

Figure 7. Patient flow in diagnosis & treatment phase.

Then we consider:

- PaT^{IE}_{DS} : Average attention time of a senior doctor (*DS*) in the Initial Exploration stage (*IE*).
- PaT^{AR}_{DS}: Average attention time of a senior doctor in the Analysis of Results stage (*AR*).
- PaT^{IE}_{DJ} : Average attention time of a junior doctor (*DJ*) in the Initial Exploration stage (*IE*).
- PaT^{AR}_{DJ}: Average attention time of a junior doctor in the Analysis of Results stage (*AR*).

Given these times, their inverse will give us the number of patients that each doctor can treat per unit time considered:

$$P^{IE}_{DS} = \frac{DS_{IE}}{PaT^{IE}_{DS}} = \text{Patients per minute for a } DS \text{ in } IE \text{ stage;}$$

$$P^{IE}_{DJ} = \frac{DJ_{IE}}{PaT^{IE}_{DJ}} = \text{Patients per minute for a } DJ \text{ in } IE \text{ stage;}$$

$$P^{AR}_{DS} = \frac{DS_{AR}}{PaT^{AR}_{DS}} = \text{Patients per minute for a } DS \text{ in } AR \text{ stage;}$$

$$P^{AR}_{DJ} = \frac{DJ_{AR}}{PaT^{AR}_{DJ}} = \text{Patients per minute for a } DJ \text{ in } AR \text{ stage.}$$

where DS_{IE}, DS_{AR}, DJ_{IE}, DJ_{AR} are unknown values.

From the historical real data provided by the *Hospital de Sabadell* we know that patients can go once, twice or more times for tests and/or treatment, and so see the doctor more than once (Figure 8). Anyway, for patients 4 and 5, the percentage of patients that require more than one test or treatment is very low.

There is a percentage p_1 of patients who, after their first contact with the doctor, require additional tests, and a percentage p_2 who require some treatment. Then, there is a percentage $1-(p_1+p_2)$ of patients who are discharged from the service directly after their initial exploration with the doctor, those who do not require any additional test nor any treatment.

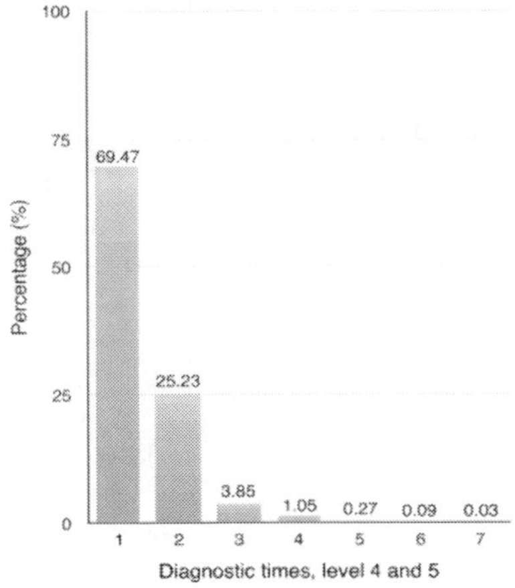

Figure 8. Percentage of number of diagnostic times (doctor care) for non-critical patients (Area B).

By observing the data represented in Figure 8, we can see that around 70% of patients 4 and 5 are discharged from the service directly after their initial exploration with a doctor. Therefore, only 30% of patients in Area B require some test or treatment ($p_1 + p_2$). Thus, given these percentages and the patient flow of Figure 7, we obtain the following relations of continuity:

$$P_{DS}^{IE} \cdot (p_1 + p_2) = P_{DS}^{AR} \quad (6)$$

$$P_{DJ}^{IE} \cdot (p_1 + p_2) = P_{DJ}^{AR} \quad (7)$$

$$DS_{IE} + DS_{AR} = DS \quad (8)$$

$$DJ_{IE} + DJ_{AR} = DJ \quad (9)$$

The solution of this linear system of equations gives us the values for DS_{IE}, DS_{AR}, DJ_{IE}, DJ_{AR}, and therefore, the values for P_{DS}^{IE}, P_{DS}^{AR}, P_{DJ}^{IE}, P_{DJ}^{AR}, for the considered configuration of doctors.

Now, we can obtain the *theoretical throughput* for the doctors' stage in the diagnosis and treatment phase by the summation of patients who have only been attended once by the doctor ($P_{only\ IE}$), those who have been required for additional testing (P_{Test}), and those who have gone to the nurses stage for some treatment (P_{Treat}), as shown in (10):

$$T\_ThP_{Doctors} = P_{only\ IE} + P_{Test} + P_{Treat} \quad (10)$$

where:

$$P_{only\ IE} = (P_{DS}^{IE} + P_{DJ}^{IE}) \cdot (1 - p_1 - p_2) \quad (11)$$

$$P_{Test} = (P_{DS}^{IE} + P_{DJ}^{IE}) \cdot p_1 \quad (12)$$

$$P_{Treat} = (P_{DS}^{IE} + P_{DJ}^{IE}) \cdot p_2 \quad (13)$$

When we introduce equations (11) to (13) on (10) we find:

$$T\_ThP_{Doctors\ stage} = P_{DS}^{IE} + P_{DJ}^{IE} \quad (14)$$

so,

$$T\_ThP_{Doctors\ stage} = \frac{DS_{IE}}{PaT_{DS}^{IE}} + \frac{DJ_{IE}}{PaT_{DJ}^{IE}} \quad (15)$$

Moreover, the *theoretical throughput* for the assistant nurses in the treatment stage, inside the diagnosis and treatment phase, will be calculated as shown in (5):

$$T\_ThP_{treatment\ stage} = \frac{NS}{PaT_{NS}} + \frac{NJ}{PaT_{NJ}} \quad (16)$$

Finally, the *theoretical throughput* for the diagnosis and treatment phase will be the lowest value of (15) and (16), and this value will be the indicator for the response capacity to patient attention in the ED, assuming that the admission and triage phases do not limit this value.

V. EXPERIMENTAL VALIDATION

Once we have defined the equations for the calculation of the theoretical throughput (*T_ThP*), we must validate them. For this validation we have used the simulator to see if the obtained values for the *T_ThP* for each stage in the ED process are in accordance with the generated data by the ED simulator. We consider a sufficient rate of patients entering into the service, the same each hour, to ensure that the system is running continuously and we assume the system is in a steady state, after a time of warm up.

We have used two different healthcare staff configurations (Staff I and II), and we only consider Area B for the diagnosis and treatment phase. The corresponding obtained values for the *T_ThP* calculated from the equations of the model are presented in Tables I and II, respectively.

TABLE I. THEORETICAL THROUGHPUT FOR EACH PHASE OF THE ED PROCESS CORRESPONDING TO STAFF I

		STAFF I				
		Healtcare Staff		*PaT* (minutes)		*T_ThP*
		Junior	Senior	Junior	Senior	(pat/hour)
ADMISSIONS PHASE		3	0	8.00	6.00	22.50
TRIAGE PHASE		1	2	12.00	8.00	20.00
DIAGNOSIS & TREATMENT	Nursing	5	7	30.00	27.00	25.56
	Doctors *IE*	5	2	23.89	21.74	14.68
	Doctors *AR*			19.17	15.25	

TABLE II. THEORETICAL THROUGHPUT FOR EACH PHASE OF THE ED PROCESS CORRESPONDING TO STAFF II

		STAFF II				
		Healtcare Staff		*PaT* (minutes)		*T_ThP*
		Junior	Senior	Junior	Senior	(pat/hour)
ADMISSIONS PHASE		1	1	8.00	6.00	17.50
TRIAGE PHASE		2	1	12.00	8.00	17.50
DIAGNOSIS & TREATMENT	Nursing	4	3	30.00	27.00	14.67
	Doctors *IE*	3	2	23.89	21.74	10.63
	Doctors *AR*			19.17	15.25	

The values for *PaT* in Tables I and II are the average values for each phase that result from the calibration of the simulator according to real data from the hospital. Moreover, it is important to point out that the simulator considers a random exponential distribution to model the real behavior of the *PaT*, depending on the type and age of patient.

We run the simulation for four different values for the number of patients entering the service per hour, around the theoretical value obtained as reference for the *T_ThP* for each phase from the equations of the model. Next, we conduct an analysis of the effect of the number of patients entering the service every hour, firstly on the percentage of time, which the corresponding healthcare staff spend on attending or treating patients (Occupancy) for each phase of the whole process, and secondly, on the number of patients waiting to be attended in each phase of the process, which we call *Waiting Queue Length* (*WQL*).

These are the indicators we use to validate our theoretical values. Therefore, we consider that the theoretical value obtained from the model is a good approach to the real throughput value, when the occupancy of the considered staff is below its maximum limit of capacity, and no queues are observed for this value, but they are generated when we add more patients per hour entering the service and the staff in this phase is at 100% of its capacity.

The analysis presented in the following sections shows how the *WQL* reaches endless values when the input for patients reaches and surpasses the obtained *T_ThP* with the model. The obtained results show how this situation inevitably leads to over-saturation of the system when we increase the simulation time. It is also observed how the occupancy of the corresponding staff in each stage reaches 100% when this happens.

A. Simulation results for admission phase.

We first go for the experiments for the validation of the *T_ThP* calculated value for the admissions phase. Once fixed, the input parameters for the configuration of the Staff I, and according to the results in Table I, we generate a constant and homogeneous patients input to ensure a steady state for the validation of the obtained values for the *T_ThP* for each phase. The results are shown in Figures 9 and 10.

The diagram in Figure 9 shows the results for the Staff I occupancy in the admissions phase for four different inputs of patients around the calculated *T_ThP*. We observe that the bar corresponding to the input of 21 patients per hour for admissions staff occupancy goes up to nearly 100% of occupancy, which is reached for 22 patients. This means that, with 22 or more patients, the admission phase has surpassed its limit of capacity, so this simulation result is in accordance with the *T_ThP* obtained with the analytical model for admissions phase in Table I. This first check validates this value.

On the other hand, Figure 10 shows the evolution on *WQL* with time, that is, the number of patients in the queue in the waiting room for this phase of the ED process depending on the number of simulated days, and for the

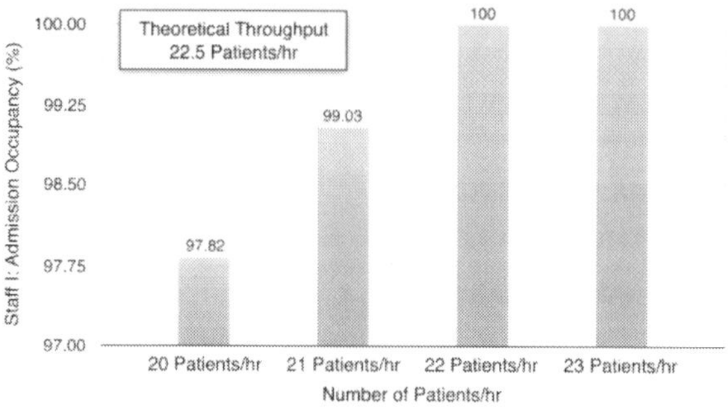

Figure 9. Occupancy percentage for admission phase (Staff I).

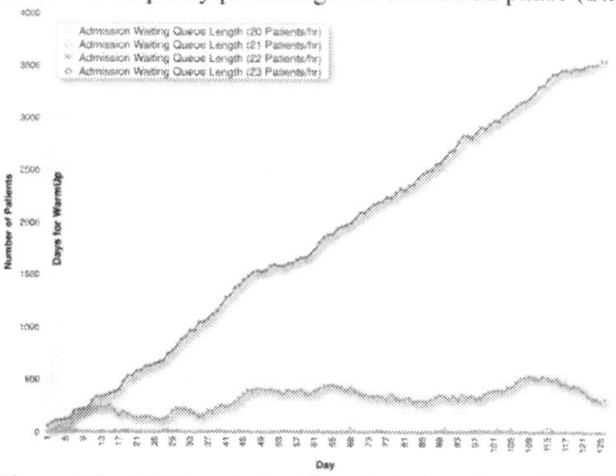

Figure 10. *WQL* evolution for admission phase (Staff I).

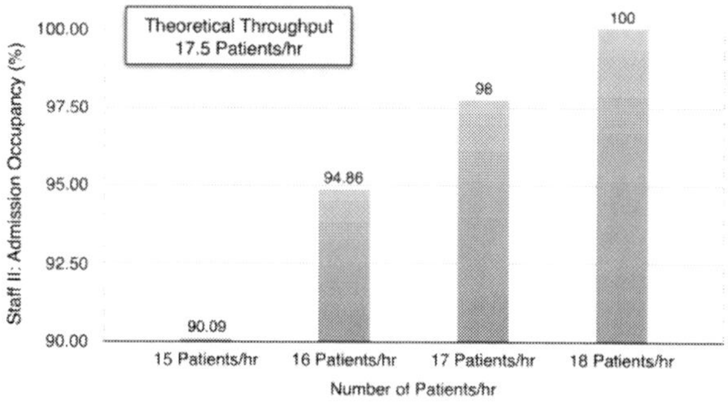

Figure 11. Occupancy percentage for admission phase (Staff II).

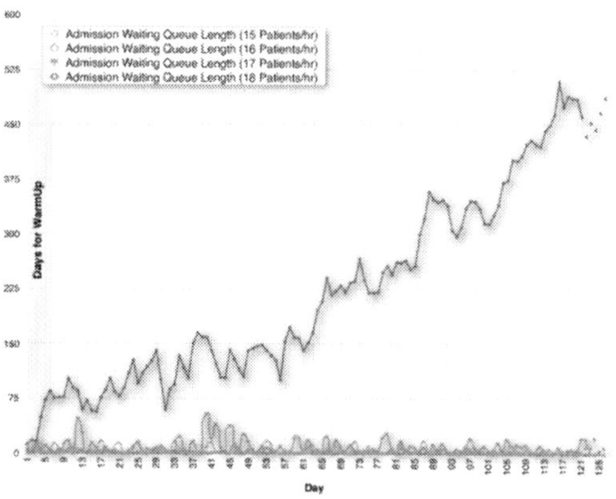

Figure 12. *WQL* evolution for admission phase (Staff II).

same four different input values for the number of patients entering the system.

The *WQL* is under control until the number of patients reaches and exceeds the obtained 22 patients for the *T_ThP* with the model, when it reaches endless values.

We proceed now with the validation of the admissions *T_ThP* value for the configuration in Staff II (see now Table II). Figures 11 and 12 show the results for the Staff II occupancy in the admissions phase and the *WQL* evolution again for four different inputs of patients around the calculated value for *T_ThP*.

When the input is 17 patients per hour, the admissions staff occupancy almost reaches its limit of capacity, and no important queues are generated. See how the bar of 17 patients/hr in the diagram in Figure 11 goes up to nearly 100% of occupancy, and temporal lines in Figure 12 for 17 or less patients per hour do not lead to saturation of the system, but only one more patient per hour entering the service produces endless queues. This simulation result is in accordance with the *T_ThP* obtained with the model (17.5 patients per hour) and so, it validates this value.

The fluctuations observed in the temporal lines in Figures 10 and 12 are due to the distribution used by the simulator to consider the variation of *PaT* depending on both the type and age of patients. The simulator uses an exponential distribution to model this fact, as a result of its calibration with the available real data from the hospital. These variations in the random values assigned to *PaT* for each generated patient can produce some queues, which appear anytime but, which the system can finally absorb if the number of patients entering the service per hour is below the system's capacity of attention.

Hereinafter, we proceed in the same way for validating the remaining values for *T_ThP* corresponding to the other stages: triage, doctors and nursing for treatment in the diagnosis and treatment phase.

B. Simulation results for triage phase.

The simulation results for the validation of the *T_ThP* value considering Staff I for the triage phase are shown in Figures 13 and 14. The bar chart of Figure 13 shows that the maximum attention capacity for this phase is 20 patients per hour, since it is for this value when 100% occupancy of the healthcare staff responsible for this stage is reached.

In Figure 14, we can observe the evolution of the *WQL* for the triage phase, again for four different inputs of patients. Endless queues are formed when 20 or more patients per hour enter the service, which is its limit of capacity. Meanwhile, there are no queues for values under the *T_ThP* calculated in Table I. This simulation result is again in accordance with the *T_ThP* obtained with the model, so it validates this value for the triage *T_ThP*.

Figures 15 and 16 show the *WQL* for the triage phase for Staff II and the corresponding staff occupancy respectively, for four different inputs of patients. When the input is 17 patients per hour, the triage staff occupancy nearly reaches the 100%, so it is almost at its limit of capacity. Only one patient more per hour collapses the system in this stage, as

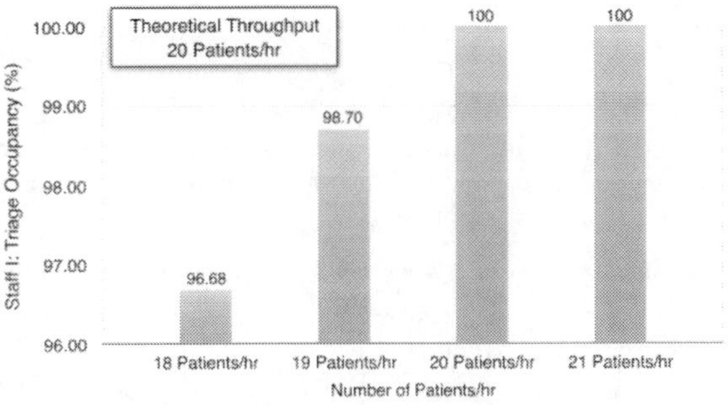

Figure 13. Occupancy percentage for triage phase (Staff I).

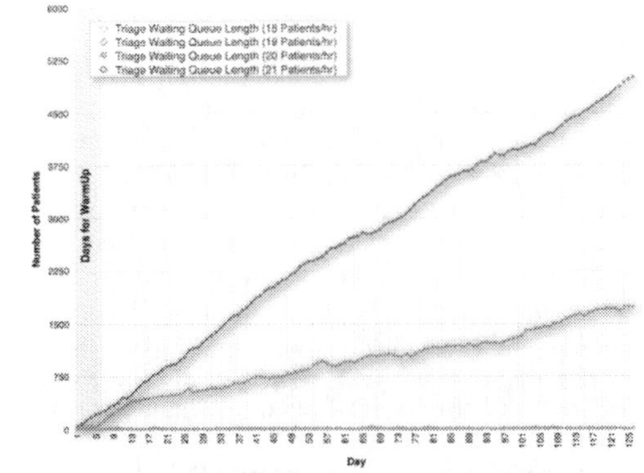

Figure 14. *WQL* evolution for triage phase (Staff I).

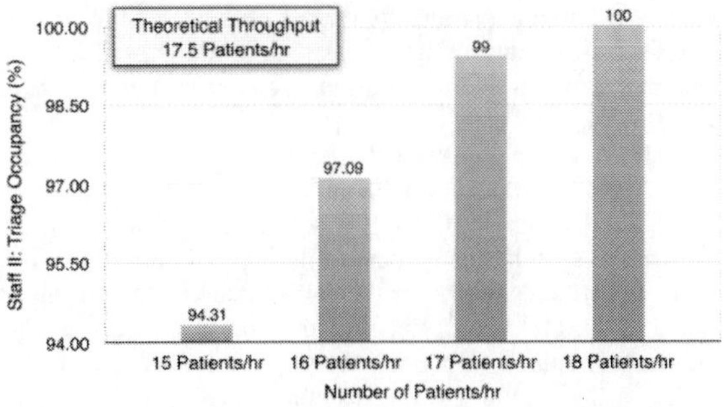

Figure 15. Occupancy percentage for triage phase (Staff II).

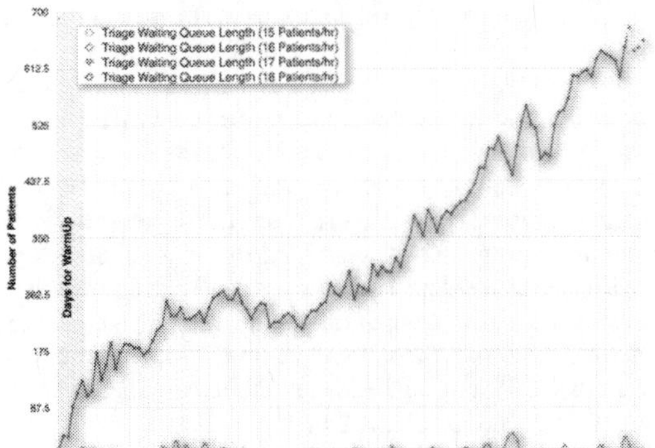

Figure 16. *WQL* evolution for triage phase (Staff II).

the temporal line shows in Figure 16 for 18 patients per hour entering the system.

This simulation result is in accordance with the *T_ThP* obtained with the analytical model (Table II), so it validates this value for the triage *T_ThP* for staff configuration II.

Once again the fluctuations observed in Figure 16 are due to the random exponential distribution used by the simulator to consider the variation of *PaT*.

C. Simulation results for diagnosis and treatment phase.

Here only patients 4 and 5 are considered, since we are analyzing the behavior in Area B, where non-critical patients are treated. According to data presented in Figure 8, the probability of these patients requiring some additional test or treatment has been fixed at 30%.

Figures 17 and 18 show the simulation experimental results for the doctor's stage of the diagnosis, considering the staff I configuration in Table I. In Figure 17, we can see the corresponding staff occupancy for this stage, for four different inputs of patients. Here, the *T_ThP* value obtained from the equations is 14.68 patients per hour. The simulation data shows how the occupancy for 14 patients per hour is almost at 100%, and also the analysis for the *WQL* shows how doctors are saturated when only one more patient per hour enters the service. Once again the *T_ThP* is at its limit of capacity and when this value is surpassed, the system collapses in this phase. These results are in accordance with the doctors' *T_ThP* obtained with the model and hence validate it.

In the same way, Figures 19 and 20 show the staff occupation rate and the *WQL* tendency for the doctors' stage, within the diagnosis and treatment phase for Staff II, again for four different inputs of patients. The probabilities for patients to require some additional test or treatment have also been fixed at 30%.

The *T_ThP* is between 10 and 11 patients, and we can see how when the input is of 11 patients per hour, medical staff occupancy reaches 100%. Therefore, this simulation result shows the system has surpassed its limit of capacity and this is in accordance with the *T_ThP* obtained with the model. Long and non-ending queues also collapse the service for 11 or more patients. Once again, this validates the obtained value for the Doctors *T_ThP* in this case.

Finally, we try to validate *T_ThP* for the for treatment stage, carried out by the assistant nurses inside the diagnosis and treatment phase. Figures 21 and 22 show the simulation results for this stage when we consider the specific configuration for the healthcare staff specified in Table I.

The obtained values by simulation for the occupation rate are in accordance with our theoretical value of 25.56 patients per hour (Figure 21), when the number of patients waiting for treatment grows dramatically and the *WQL* becomes very large (Figure 22). Also, with the staff II configuration, the obtained values for occupation in the nursing stage are in accordance with our theoretical value of 14.67 patients per hour (Figure 23), and again the number of patients waiting for attention grows dramatically (Figure 24).

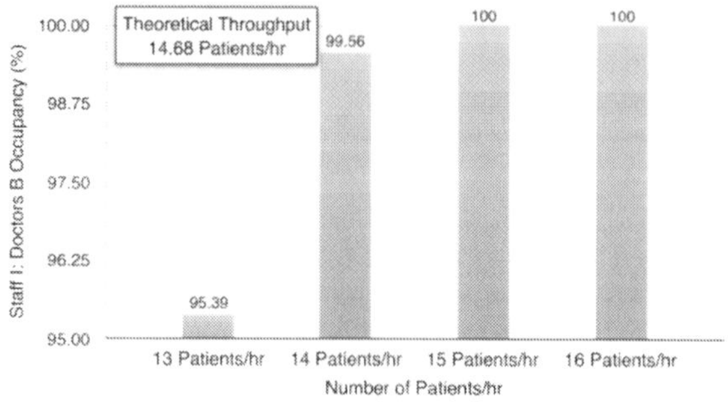

Figure 17. Occupancy for doctors phase (Staff I) in Area B.

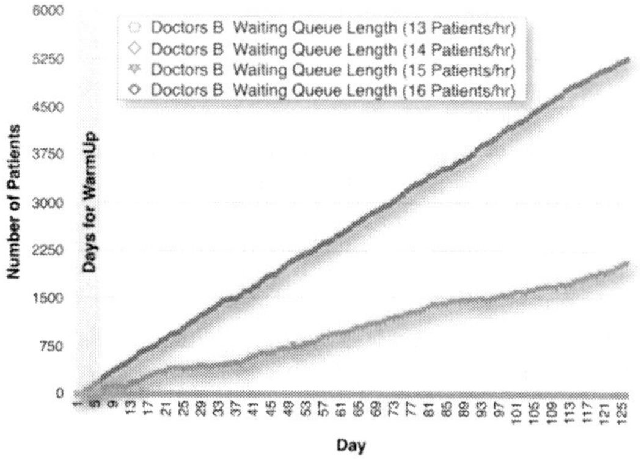

Figure 18. *WQL* evolution for doctors phase (Staff I) in Area B.

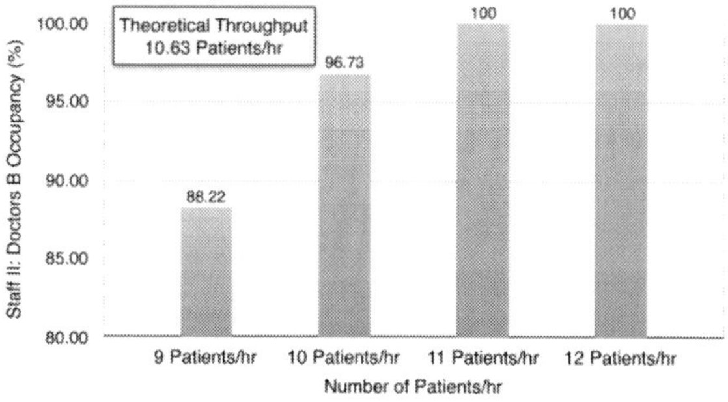

Figure 19. Occupancy for doctors phase (Staff II) in Area B.

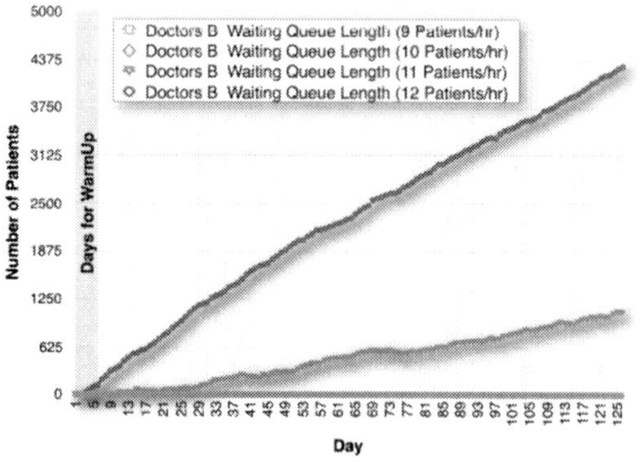

Figure 20. *WQL* evolution for doctors phase (Staff II) in Area B.

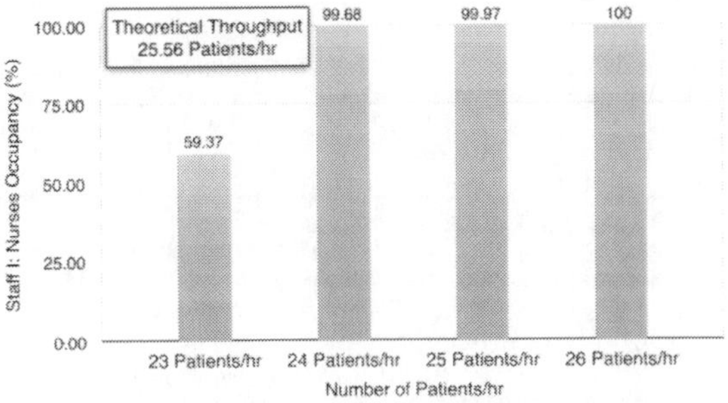

Figure 21. Ocupancy percentage for nursing phase (Staff I).

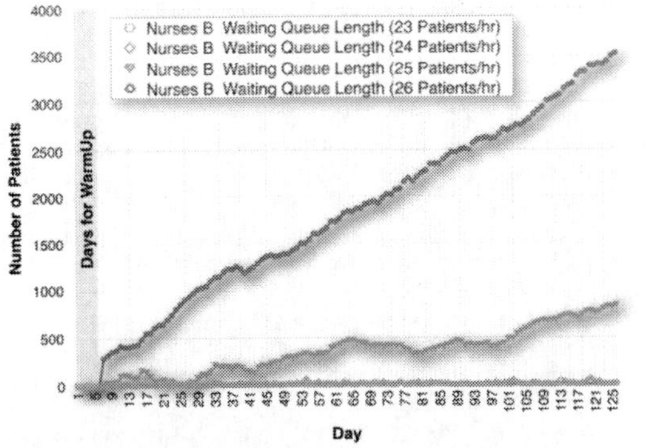

Figure 22. *WQL* evolution for nursing phase (Staff I).

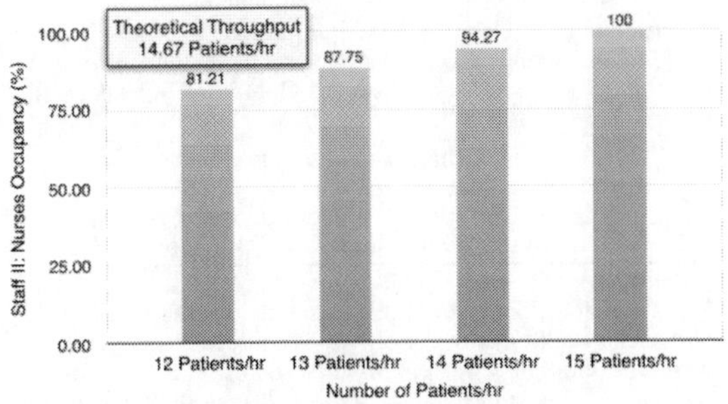

Figure 23. Occupancy percentage for nursing phase (Staff II).

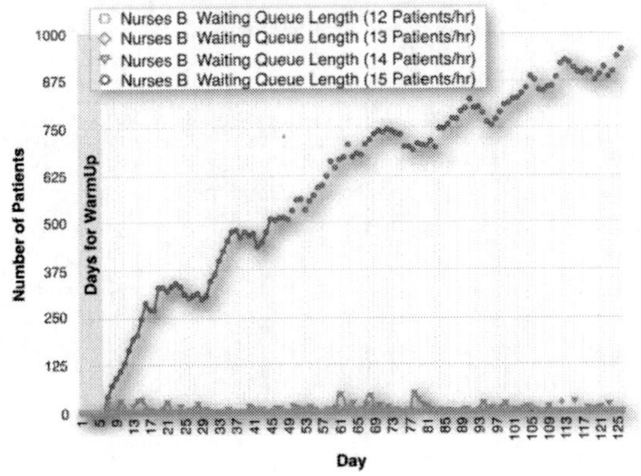

Figure 24. *WQL* evolution for nursing phase (Staff II).

In Figures 23 and 24 we can see how the simulation results for the nursing stage are once more in accordance with the model when we modify the staff parameters to Staff II configuration.

All the values of *T_ThP* for admission, triage, doctors and nurses have been validated, and they are in accordance with the simulation results with a very good approximation. The simulator is our sensor of the real system, so these results validate the proposed analytical model.

VI. Conclusion and Future Work

The main contribution presented in this paper is the ED's healthcare staff characterization, through its capacity, named theoretical throughput, which is the number of patients that the system should be able to absorb per unit time, given the staff composition.

We have defined an analytical model to determine the theoretical throughput of a particular healthcare staff configuration based on the number of admission staff, triage, assistant nurses, and doctors, and their respective attention times for patients.

The analytical model of equations to calculate the values of the *T_ThP* for admissions phase, triage phase, nursing and medical exploration stages in diagnosis and treatment phase, according to the actual patient flow in the ED process, has been validated. For the validation of the model we have used an ED simulator based on an agent based model of the system, as a sensor of the real system. Output data from simulation of different possible real situations have been analyzed to obtain the information for the model validation.

We have seen how the theoretical throughput is a reference to measure the performance of the system, and the capacity of the healthcare staff configuration to absorb the demand of the service, so it is an indicator of the response capacity of the system to patient attention.

The analytical model for the *T_ThP* calculation will give us information to relocate non-critical patients, so that the theoretical throughput will be the reference indicator for the redistribution of non-critical patients. The idea is to try to modify their current arrival according to system capacity at any time, which is our current research in progress. This relocation may improve the time patients stay in the service, and therefore the service quality.

Our future work will consist of designing a admission scheduling model for non-critical patients in the service, using the ED simulator for their *LoS* prediction.

The historical data provided by the hospital, the defined analytical model for the evaluation of the response capacity of the system, and the information obtained from the analysis of the data from simulation, will all enable the possibility of planning admission of non-critical patients into the service.

This proposed future model for relocation of patients will be efficient to the extent that a supposed "self-triage and recommendation system" is effective on patient entry, so that patient input curve gets flatter and approaches the value corresponding to the maximum capacity of the system, and therefore, an improvement in performance is expected.

A good relocation of non-critical patients and a significant improvement in the quality of service mean a reduction on *LoS* of patients in the service, without removing patients, which in some cases, could make the reduction of under-utilized resources possible.

Finally, and more generally, our global proposal aims to improve the ED service, which is the main entry of patients in the healthcare system in relation to access, quality of service, user satisfaction and efficiency.

ACKNOWLEDGMENT

This publication is based upon work supported under contract TIN2014-53172-P, funded by the MINECO Spain.

REFERENCES

[1] E. Bruballa, M. Taboada, A. Wong, D. Rexachs, and E. Luque, "An Analytical model to evaluate the response capacity of emergency departments in extreme situations," The Seven International Conference on Advances in System Simulation (Simul 2015), pp. 12-16, 2015.

[2] F. Kadri, S. Chaabane, T. Berger, D. Trentesaux, C. Tahom, and Y. Sallez, "Modelling and management of the strain situations in hospital systems using ORCA approach," IEEE IESM, Rabat, Morocco, pp. 202-210, October 2013.

[3] F. Kadri, S. Chaabane, and C. Tahon, "A simulation-based decision support system to prevent and predict strain situations in emergency department systems," Simulation Modelling Practice and Theory, vol. 42, pp. 32-52, March 2014.

[4] A. Boyle, K. Beniuk, I. Higginson, and P. Atkinson, "Emergency Department Crowding: Time for interventions and policy evaluations," Emergency Medicine International, Article ID 838610, 2012.

[5] P.C. Sprivulis, J.A. Da Silva, I.G. Jacobs, A.R.L. Frazer, and G.A. Jelinek, "The association between hospital overcrowding and mortality among patients admitted via Western Australian emergency departments," Medical Journal of Australia, vol. 184, num. 5, pp 208-212, 2006.

[6] Ph.Yoon, I.Steiner, and G. Reinhardt, "Analysis of factors influencing length of stay in the emergency department," Canadian Journal of Emergency Medicine (CJEM), vol. 5, issue 03, pp. 155-161, 2003.

[7] N.R. Hoot and D. Aronsky, "Systematic review of Emergency Department Crowding: causes, effects and solutions," Annals of Emergency Medicine, vol. 52, Issue 2, pp. 126-136, 2008.

[8] L.M. Stock, G.E. Bradley, R.J. Lewis, D.W. Baker, J. Sipsey, and C.D. Stevens, "Patients who leave emergency departments without being seen by a physician: magnitude o the problem in Los Angeles County," Annals of Emergency Medicine, vol. 23, pp. 294-298, 1994.

[9] C.M. Fernandes, A. Price, and J.M. Christenson, "Does reduced length of stay decrease the number of emergency department patients who leave without seeing a physician?," The Journal of Emergency Medicine, vol 15, pp. 397-399, 1997.

[10] M. Sanchez, A. Smally, R. Grant, and L. Jackobs, "Effects of a fast-track area on emergency department performance," The Journal of Emergency Medicin, vol.31, pp. 117-120, 2006.

[11] S. W. Rodi, M.V. Graw, and C.M. Orsini, "Evaluation of a fast track unit: alignment of resources and demand results in improved satisfaction and decreased length of stay for emergency department patients," Quality Management in Health Care, vol 15, pp. 163-170, 2006.

[12] R. Davies, ""See and Treat" or "See" and "Treat" in an Emergency Department," Proceedings of the Winter Simulation Conference, pp. 1519-1522, 2007.

[13] S. Samaha, W.S. Armel, and D.W. Starks, "The use of simulation to reduce the length of stay in an Emergency Department," Proceedings of the winter Simulation Conference, pp. 1907-1911, 2003.

[14] J. Wang, J. Li, K. Tussey, and K. Ross, "A simulation study to reduce length of stay in Emergency Department at a large community hospital," IIE Annual Conference. Proceedings. Institute of Industrial Engineers-Publisher, pp. 1-6, 2011.

[15] J. Wang, J. Li, K. Tussey, and K. Ross, "Reducing length of stay in emergency department: a simulation study at a community hospital," IEEE Transactions on Systems, Man, and Cybernetics- PART A: Systems and Humans, Vol. 42, No 6, pp. 1314-1322, 2012b.

[16] K.W. Tan, H.C. Lau, and F. Lee, "Improving patient length of stay in Emergency Department through dynamic queue management," Proceedings of the Winter Simulation Conference, December 2013.

[17] D.J. Medeiros, E. Swenson, and C. DeFlitch, "Improving patient flow in a hospital emergency department," Proceedings of the winter Simulation Conference, pp. 1526-1531, 2008.

[18] A. M. Mancilla, "Simulation: A tool for the study of real systems," Ingenieria y Desarrollo, Universidad del Norte, vol. 6, pp.104–112, 1999.

[19] J. Pavón, M. Arroyo, S. Hassan, and C. Sansores, "Simulation of social systems with software agents," CMPI-2006, Actas del Campus Multidisciplinar en Percepcion e Inteligencia, vol. 1, pp. 389-400, 2006.

[20] L. R. Izquierdo, J.M. Galán, J.I. Santos, and R. Del Olmo, "Modeling complex systems using agent-based simulation and system dynamics," Empiria: Revista de metodología de ciencias sociales, vol. 16, pp. 85–112, 2008.

[21] M. Taboada, E. Cabrera, M. L. Iglesias, F. Epelde, and E. Luque, "An agent-based decision support system for hospitals emergency departments," Procedia Computer Science, vol. 4, pp. 1870–1879, ICCS 2011.

[22] L. Zhengchun, E. Cabrera, D. Rexachs, and E. Luque, "A generalized agent-based model to simulate emergency departments," The Sixth International Conference on Advances in System Simulations, IARIA, pp. 65-70, Nice, France, October 2014.

[23] M. Taboada, E. Cabrera, and E. Luque, "Modeling, simulation and optimization of resources management in hospital emergency departments using the agent-based approach," Advances in Computational Modeling Research, pp. 1–31, 2013.

[24] E. Cabrera, M. Taboada, M. L. Iglesias, F. Epelde, and E. Luque, "Simulation optimization for healthcare emergency departments," Procedia Computer Science, vol. 9, ICCS, pp. 1464–1473, 2012.

[25] W. Soler, M. Gómez Muñoz, E. Bragulat, and A. Álvarez, "Triage: a key tool in emergency care," Anales del Sistema Sanitario de Navarra, Gobierno de Navarra, Departamento de Salud, vol. 33, supl.1, pp. 55-68, Pamplona 2010.

A Linear Approach to Improving the Accuracy of City Planning and OpenStreetMap Road Datasets

Alexey Noskov and Yerach Doytsher
Mapping and Geo-Information Engineering
Technion – Israel Institute of Technology
Haifa, Israel
emails: {noskov, doytsher}@technion.ac.il

Abstract—**The developed method allows the user to integrate polygonal or linear datasets. Most existing approaches do not work well in the case of partial equality of polygons or polylines. The suggested method consists of two phases: searching for counterpart boundaries or polylines by a triangulation, and rectifying objects without correspondent polylines by a transformation and a shortest path algorithm. Data covering the Haifa region of Israel have been used for evaluation of the approach. City Planning datasets have been rectified by precise cadastre data. Positional accuracy of the City Planning datasets has been increased significantly. Average distance between segments of the datasets has been decreased in almost five times. Standard deviation has been decreased by thirty-five percent. In addition, more complete road layer of OpenStreetMap covering the city has been rectified by a more precise statutory road layer. Positional accuracy of the rectified layer has been improved significantly. The rectified layer has been utilized to prepare a large-scale map depicting roads with individual widths and statutory buildings. OpenStreetMap rasterization rules have been applied for road widths calculation. The prepared map depicts real-size buildings and roads' widths in scale.**

Keywords-Geometry spatial data integration; triangulation; shortest path; topology; OpenStreetMap; road layers; city planning and cadastral datasets.

I. Introduction

This paper is an extended version of the work published in [1]. In order to confirm the effectiveness of our algorithm, a rectification of an OpenStreetMap road layer by more accurate statutory road data is considered

We live in the information age. Terabytes of spatial information are available today. Hundreds of sources produce thousands of maps and digital layers every day. We encounter serious problems when trying to use different maps together.

Let us list some popular data producers. Survey companies and agencies prepare accurate topographic maps and plans. Aero and satellite images act as a basis for numerous variations of derivative maps (e.g., thematic and topographic maps). A special niche is reserved for crowd sourcing maps, e.g., OpenStreetMap (OSM) [5]. Significant parts of this sort of map contain data derived from users' devices, mainly GPS devices.

It is very difficult to use all these data together. In many cases, the user decides to draw a map from scratch, despite having existing maps with most of the required elements for the user's map. One of the reasons for this situation is a low degree of integration of existing datasets even when we consider maps containing many identical elements. For instance, soil maps need to be based on topographic maps. Today, soil maps could take basic contours from different sources.

In an ideal situation, spatial datasets use the objects (polylines or polygons) from more accurate datasets. In the real world, many maps are produced by measuring/digitizing objects from satellite images. As a result, despite the fact that most of the objects on different maps are identical, they are presented with small positional discrepancies. The problem is compounded by the fact that different objects in a Geographic Information System (GIS) environment could be depicted by the same geometries (e.g., square or circle). Thus, specific tools and algorithms need to be developed. This makes it difficult to detect identical objects on different maps. The obvious advantage of integrated databases is efficiency of data storing. Equal elements from different maps link to the same object in the storage memory. We do not need to take up extra storage on a disk. Additionally, the editing of objects will be reflected on all those maps which contain them.

The benefits of data integration are demonstrated in this paper by using city planning and cadastral datasets. A cadastral map is a comprehensive register of the real estate boundaries of a country. Cadastral data are produced using quality large-scale surveying with TotalStations, Differential Global Positioning System devices or other surveying systems with a centimeters-level precision. Normally, the precision of maps based on non-survey large-scale data (e.g., satellite images) is lower. City planning data contain proposals for developing urban areas. Most city planning maps are developed by digitizing handmade maps, using images from space. Almost all boundaries have small discrepancies in comparison to cadastral maps. We need to integrate these datasets, where the identical elements in the datasets have to be linked to the same geometries. All the non-identical elements have to be coherent with shared geometries.

In addition, our algorithm was tested on road datasets. Data covering Haifa City (Israel) were used. An OpenStreetMap (OSM) road layer was rectified by a statutory (more accurate) road layer provided by Survey of Israel (SOI). Road data provided by SOI do not contain width attribute. Roads' widths could be obtained from the

OSM road layer. In order to integrate an OSM road layer with SOI data (e.g., building and landuse layers), the OSM road layer was rectified using linear approach and SOI road layer.

The approach we suggest enables the user to resolve the described problems. It consists of two main stages: defining correspondent boundaries using triangulation technique, and rectification of the remaining polylines by transformation and the shortest path algorithm. The suggested approach could be applied to polygonal and linear datasets.

This paper is structured as follows: related work is considered in Section II. The initial processing of the source datasets is described in Section III. Section IV focuses on correspondent boundary definition. The problem of resolving line pair conflicts is described in Section V. The shortest path approach for fusion boundaries with and without counterpart is discussed in Section VI. The rectified City Planning data are discussed in Section VII. A review of road datasets is presented in Section VIII. Preprocessing of an OpenStreetMap road dataset is described in Section IX. In Section X, a process of rectifying road layer is presented. Calculating the widths of OpenStreetMap roads is discussed in Section XI. The conclusion is presented in Section XII.

II. Related Work

The main groups of approaches for data matching and data fusion are considered in this section

The wide spread of databases is the reason for developing attribute-based matching methods. Schema-based [18] and Ontology-based types of attribute matching could be selected. In [23], an approach based on both types is presented. Attribute-based matching could be effective when data with sustainable and meaningful structure and content of attribute database is processed.

The map conflation approaches [19] are based on data fusion algorithms; the aim of the process is to prepare a map which is a combination of two or more maps [8]. The merging and fusion of heterogeneous databases has been extensively studied, both spatially [16] and non-spatially [25].

Geometry, size, or area is used in feature-based matching. These allow us to estimate the degree of compatibility of objects. The process is carried out by the structural analysis of a set of objects and analysis of the result, to see whether similar structural analysis of the candidates fits the objects of the other data set [4]. In [22], comparison of objects is based on the analysis of a contour distribution histogram. A polar coordinates approach for calculating the histogram is used. A method based on the Wasserstein distance was published by Schmitzer et al. [20]. A special shape descriptor for defined correspondent objects on raster images was developed by Ma and Longin [13]. Focusing on single shapes does not allow us to apply these algorithms in our task.

In [7], topological and spatial neighborly relations between two datasets, preserved even after running operations such as rotation or scale, were discovered. In relational matching, the comparison of the object is implemented with respect to a neighboring object. We can verify the similarity of two objects by considering neighboring objects. The problem of non-rigid shape recognition is studied by Bronstein et al. [6]; the applicability of diffusion distances within the Gromov-Hausdorff framework and the presence of topological changes have been explored in this paper.

In [2], spatial data integration is considered as a process of unifying layers in a unique database to provide a unified environment for processing, modeling, and visualization. Three main aspects are considered: spatial reference of the data, projection of the data, and format of the data. A geo-spatial data integration method for three-dimensional subsurface stratification is proposed by Kim et al. in [10]. In [26], integration of remotely sensed data is considered. A proposed framework can provide an effective solution for distributed storage, data format conversion and interoperability for satellite remote sensing big data. Foster and Mayfield consider geospatial data integration in the context of defense and security. Integration of global land cover datasets was considered in [24]. Kipf and Kemper extended high-performance main-memory database systems with temporal and geospatial processing capabilities to tackle emerging mobility workloads in [11]. Integration of geospatial data regarding crimes is discussed in [17].

We concluded that the approaches mentioned could not be applied to resolve the considered problem. This derives from the fact that the mentioned approaches have been developed for specific conditions. For instance, feature-based matching is effective for detecting separate outstanding objects; attribute-based matching is effective for definite and well-designed databases. Thus, a new approach should be developed.

III. City Planning Data preparation

Spatial data sets covering a part of Yokne'am (a town in the northern part of Israel) have been used. They are depicted in Figure 1. Land-use city planning and cadastre polygons are displayed as color areas and as black boundaries, correspondingly. As can be seen in the figure, in most cases the boundaries of two datasets are the same. Some boundaries are presented in the first dataset and are not presented in the second. The white background of the cadastre polygons means that this area is not covered by the city planning dataset. It is presented mainly in the upper part of the figure. The case where black cadastre boundaries cross an area with a similar background color means that these boundaries are not presented in the city planning datasets.

The city planning data have sensitive positional irregular discrepancies. Because of the small scale, they cannot be observed in Figure 1; hence, the problem is illustrated in Figure 2. The figure shows that the problem could not be resolved by transformation only, and that a more sophisticated technique is required. The figure leads us to an approach based on defining corresponding objects and further modification of the remaining objects with respect to found pairs.

In the previous approach [15], we defined correspondences between polygons. We encountered two problems. Because whole polygons are processed, it is difficult to precisely define the points connecting polygons with and without counterparts. Considering a polygon as a separate object does not allow us to unambiguously detect polygons' shared nodes. As a result, in some cases, it is difficult to correctly eliminate gaps between objects. Using centroids in the polygon triangulation approach is the reason for the second problem. For non-compact polygons, even small changes in the polygon's boundary lead to significant changes in the centroid position. It could negatively impact the results.

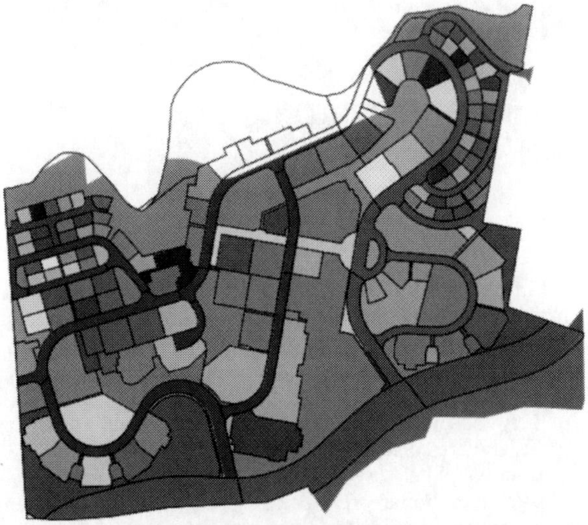

Figure 1. Source data: land-use city planning (colored background) and cadastre (black outline) maps.

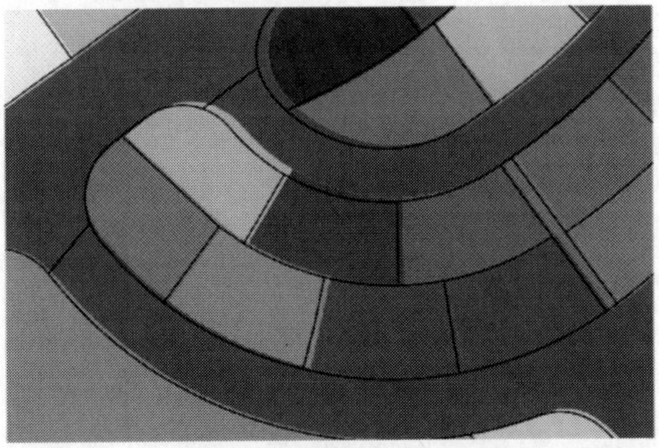

Figure 2. Positional discrepancies of city planning (colored areas) and cadastre (black lines) datasets.

In this paper, we propose a technique which is based on defining line pairs by triangulation. In most cases, spatial data are found in non-topological data format (e.g., ESRI's Shape Files, GeoJSON, MapInfo Tab Files). This means that the boundaries of neighboring objects are repeated for each polygon. This fact leads us to the possibility of modifying the boundary of neighbor polygons independently. In the most cases, it is a source of many difficulties; e.g., small gaps between boundaries or the necessity of repeating the same action for each polygon separately. Because of the problems mentioned we use topological data format provided by GRASS GIS 7 [12]. The source shape files have been converted to this format. A sample part of the city planning dataset found in a topological format is presented in Figure 3. Polygon data comprise 3 types of elements: boundary, node, and centroids. Nodes separate boundary polylines. Each group of closed boundaries could be considered as an area. The polygons' centroids link the polygons to certain rows in an attribute table by category numbers. Each raw in the attribute table starts with a "cat" field, which could be connected to a centroid with a given "cat" value.

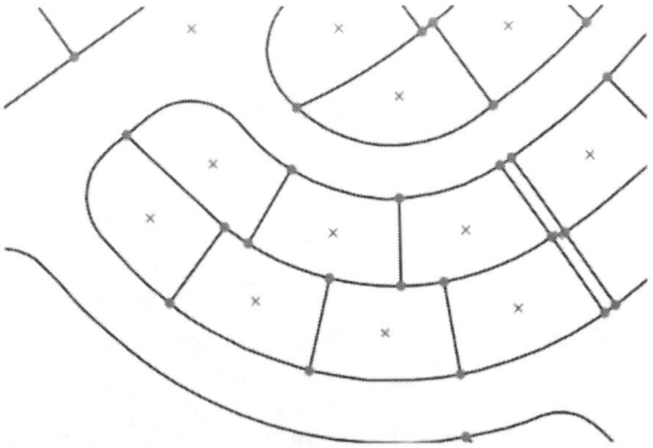

Figure 3. A sample of the city planning dataset residing in GRASS GIS's topologycal format. Nodes – red circles, centroids – blue croses, and boundaries – black lines.

We can conclude from the first two figures, that most of the counterpart polygon boundaries of the datasets are located close to each other and present the same objects. It is efficient to define a measure for detecting the fact that two objects certainly could not be defined as counterparts. In other words, we can use it as a filter. A maximal distance parameter could fulfill this role.

In addition, it is quite popular to use buffers for detecting the fact that two objects certainly could not be defined as counterparts. For instance, in [27] the authors have applied a buffer with a certain buffer size, where all objects outside the buffer could not be considered as counterparts. We have found that a segmentation technique could be more sensitive and flexible in this context. Segmentation means dividing polygon boundaries (or any other sort of polyline) into equidistant segments. Point delimiters are used to calculate distances between the considered datasets. An example of segmentation is depicted in Figure 4.

Maximal distance (D_{max}) is calculated as follows. For each point in the first dataset, a distance to the closest point belonging to the second dataset is assigned. Then we apply a loop from the first to the last percentile (from the percentile with maximal number and minimal distance to that with minimal number and maximal distance) on a list of 100 percentiles of the calculated distances. D_{max} equals percentile i if the standard deviation of distances between percentiles i-

1 and i is more then 1. D_{max} is used mainly to filter considered objects. In our case, the distances between the nearest equidistant points of the cadastre and the city planning data sets' boundaries are in an interval from 0 to 92.7 meters. The boundaries of the percentiles number (i.e., i decrement) 6, 5, 4, and 3 are 2.09, 4.97, 7.88, and 17.75 meters, correspondingly. Standard deviations for distances in intervals between percentiles 6-5, 5-4, and 4-3 are as follows: 0.78, 0.89, 1.46, and 2.77. Hence, D_{max} equals 7.88, because 7.88 belongs to percentile number 4 (the first with a standard deviation of more than 1). Objects residing further than D_{max} are excluded from the processing. For Yokne'am datasets, D_{max} equals 7.9 meters. A 2-meter distance between nearest points has been assigned for our test.

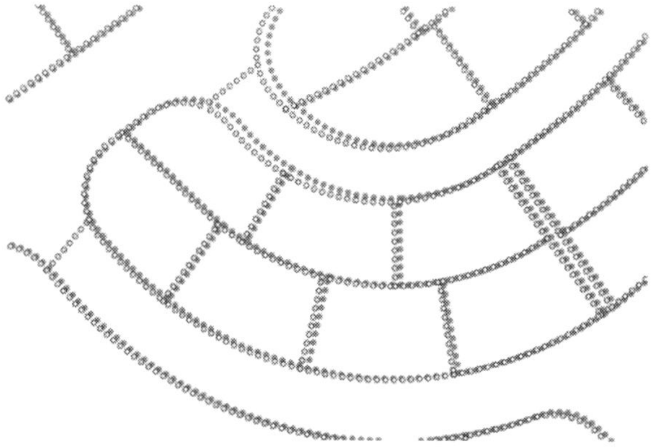

Figure 4. Point delimiter of equidistant segments. City planning – red, cadastre - black points.

IV. DEFINING CORRESPONDING LINES OF DATASETS BY TRIANGULATION

In this section, the main process is described. It is based on identifying correspondent triples of polygon boundaries of the considered datasets. Delaunay triangulation enables us to easily connect points by triangles. We use it to divide boundaries into triples. Figure 5 illustrates the triangulation process. The triangulation is based on the middle points of boundaries' polylines. In the figure, the boundaries' middle points are depicted as gray circles; the boundaries are colored lines; and the triangulation layer is presented as a colored background.

Now, we have grouped middle points into triples boundaries of cadastre and city planning datasets. The next step is searching for correspondent triple candidates, and it is implemented as follows.

First, the lengths of all boundary polylines are calculated. Sorted lengths of correspondent boundaries are stored into "A", "B" and "C" fields of attribute table for each triple. "A" stores the shortest length; "C" stores the longest. Then, we compare all possible pairs of triples.

To reduce the number of comparisons we consider only the nearest triples. These are defined by comparing the coordinates of the start and end nodes of their boundaries. For further consideration, all start and end nodes of the second triple boundaries have to be inside the extent of the first triple's nodes (defined by an enlarged buffer). Buffer size is equal to the square root of the median polygon area. In our case it is 32 meters. The areas of both datasets are sorted into one list to find a median value.

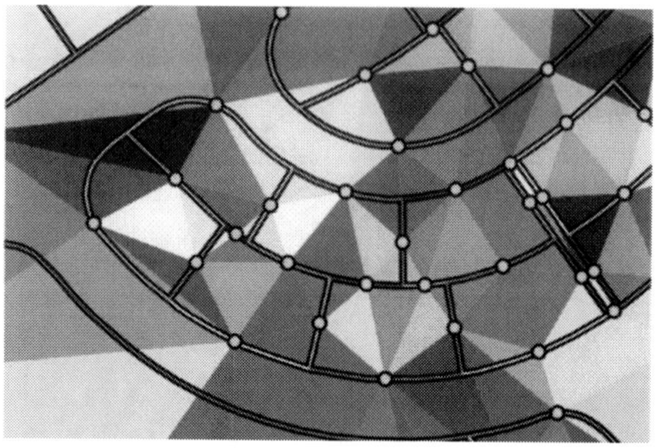

Figure 5. The triangulation of boundaries' middle points of a city planning dataset.

In the next step, we compare boundary lengths. As mentioned above, ordered lengths are stored in an attribute table ("A", "B" and "C" fields). Triple pairs are added into a list for further processing if a correspondent length (A-A, B-B, or C-C) resident in the second triple is within an interval of between 80% to 120% of a length resident in the first triple, and are considered as triple pair candidates. This two-step initial filter by extents and lengths comparison is illustrated in Figure 6. In the figure, blue lines are city planning boundaries; black lines are cadastre boundaries; grey and green triangles are candidate cadastre boundaries obtained by an extent (red rectangle) and by length comparisons, correspondingly. Candidates are defined for a triple of city planning boundaries marked by a red triangle.

At this point, we have a few candidates. In order to define the "winner" candidate, we calculate distances between nodes of the correspondent boundaries. We need to determine pair boundaries belonging to a considered triple candidate. The brute force process is implemented; all possible combinations are considered. The most acceptable combination is one with a minimal sum of distances between correspondent points. The brute force process is not time sensitive, because it is implemented only for a few filtered candidates. A candidate is marked as a triple pair if the maximal distance between correspondent nodes is less than D_{max}, as defined in Section III.

In this section, correspondent boundaries have been defined. The candidate triples have been filtered by extent and lengths comparison, then line pairs have been defined by distances between nodes.

V. RESOLVING LINE PAIRS' CONFLICTS

In this section, we describe the process of searching for wrongly defined boundary pairs and resolving these situations.

First of all, in many cases line pairs are repeated in neighboring triples. The participation of a line in different pairs is marked as a problem. It is quite obvious that a boundary from the first dataset could have only one counterpart boundary in the second dataset. In order to resolve conflicts, we compare the number of times they participate in triples. For instance, we have two line pairs A1-B1 and A1-B2. If A1-B1 pair is encountered in 2 triples and A1-B2 in 1, then the combination A1-B2 is eliminated and A1-B1 remains. If both are encountered simultaneously, both candidates are eliminated.

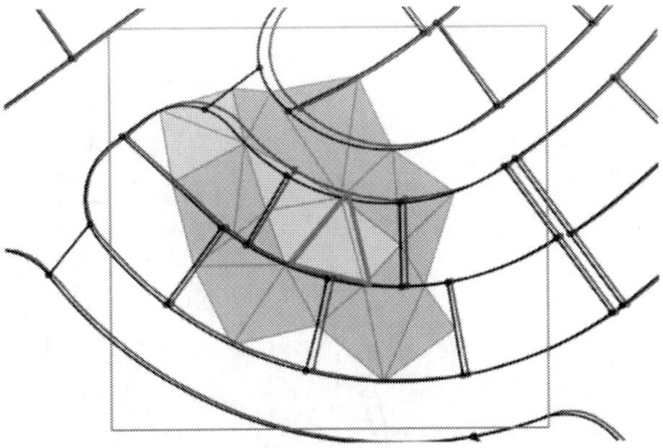

Figure 6. Filtering possible triple pairs.

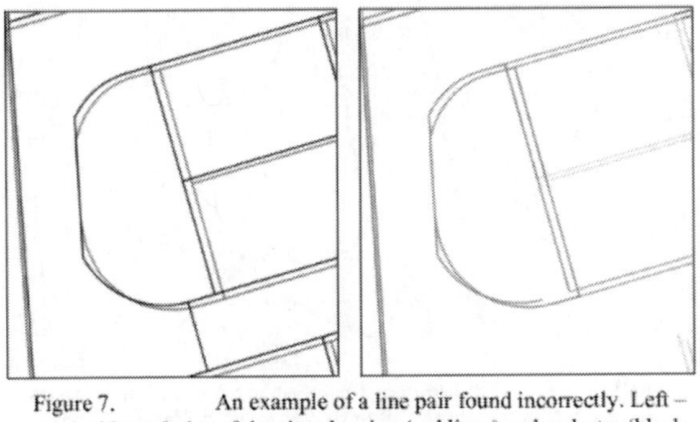

Figure 7. An example of a line pair found incorrectly. Left – original boundaries of the city planning (red lines) and cadastre (black lines) datasets. Right – detected linepairs.

Figure 8. Detecting incorrect pairs. Left – incorrect nodes and line pairs are marked in red. Right – final line pairs.

Additionally, we need to consider the situation illustrated in Figure 7. The curved purple line pair is detected incorrectly. This line is composed of two lines in the cadastre dataset, because of the line, which is connected to the bottom part. The connected line does not exist in the city planning dataset.

These types of errors could be detected by analyzing the line junctions. Each node is identified by a set of ids of lines connected to the node. The required conditions for the remaining line pairs are as follows. First, node values (a set of ids of lines) have to be unique. Second, each node has to have a node of equal value, and vise versa. If one of the conditions is false, all lines connecting with the incorrect node are eliminated on both datasets. The process is illustrated in Figure 8.

VI. A SHORTEST PATH APPROACH FOR BOUNDARIES FUSION

At this point, we have the pairs of corresponding boundaries. As mentioned in Section I, cadastre datasets are produced using quality large-scale data. They are more accurate than city planning datasets. Hence, replacing the city planning boundaries with their cadastre counterparts will significantly improve the accuracy of the resulting map. This was done in the previous step. In this section, we consider how to integrate boundaries without counterparts with pair boundaries. This is implemented in two steps.

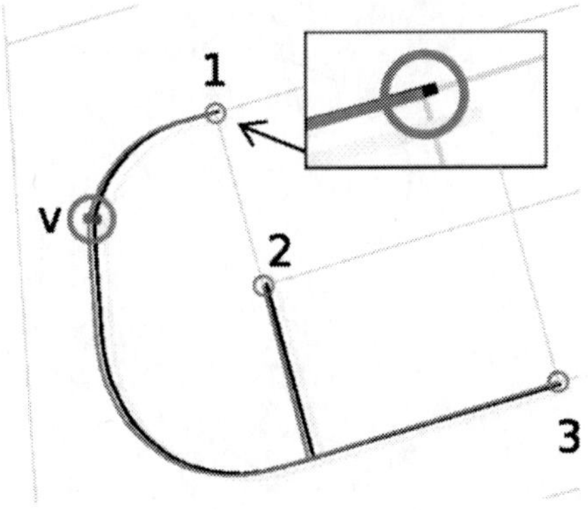

Figure 9. A vertex moved with respect to the shortest paths to bridge nodes.

In the first step we use coordinates of correspondent pair nodes as Ground Control Points for second-order affine transformation. We transform the boundaries without counterpart to make them closer to the cadastre dataset. We shall henceforth call it "transformed boundaries or dataset".

The transformed boundaries still have gaps between them and the remaining boundaries. A shortest path approach has been developed to integrate both types of boundaries.

The idea of the approach is quite simple. Each vertex (including nodes) of the transformed boundaries is processed. We calculate the shortest path from a vertex to each bridge node. Bridge nodes connect a nest (group of lines joined without gaps) of transformed boundaries to boundaries with counterparts. In figure 9, the described elements are presented.

The figure explains the algorithm. Green lines are cadastre counterparts. Black lines are transformed city planning boundaries without pairs. They still have small gaps with cadastre counterparts. Red lines are the result of applying the shortest path approach to each vertex. Vertex v is the considered vertex and 1, 2, and 3 are the bridge nodes. Bridge nodes of a transformed dataset differ from the other nodes by having a counterpart node in the cadastre pair boundaries. Thus, we can precisely say how to move bridge nodes in order to locate them exactly on the node of cadastre boundaries with pairs. It is not correct to only move a bridge node; we need to move other vertices too.

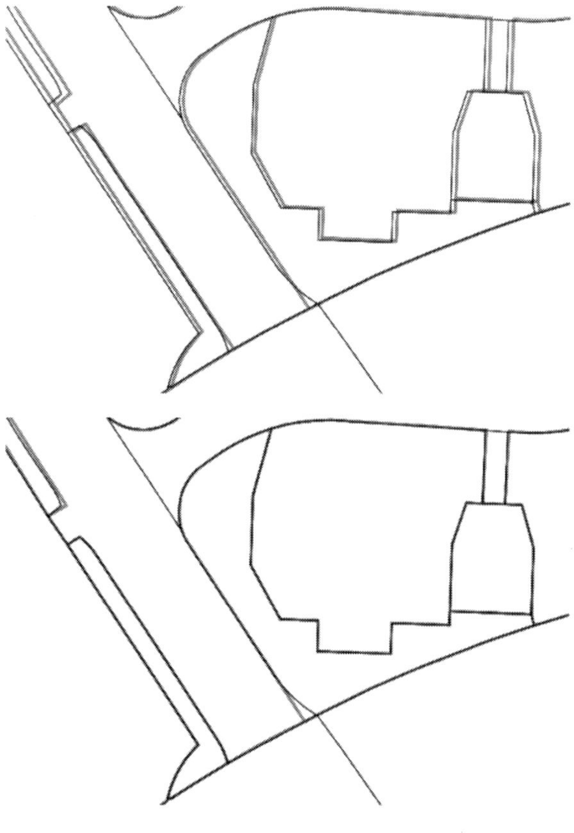

Figure 10. Zoomed-in extent 1. Boundaries of original (upper) and result (lower) datasets: city planning – red, cadastre - black.

To define new coordinates we use shortest paths. Three nodes are impacted for the vertex "v". Thus, three shortest paths are calculated: v-1, v-2, and v-3. v-2 and v-3 are partially overlapped paths. We need to note an important condition. If a path touches more then 1 bridge node, the path is eliminated from further consideration. Only paths intersected by one bridge node are considered. The new coordinates of a vertex are calculated as follows.

$$c_2 = c_1 + \sum_{0}^{n} (c_{oi} - c_{ti}) \cdot (1 - l_i / l_{sum}) \quad (1)$$

In (1), c denotes x or y coordinate; c_1 is the source coordinate; c_2 is the target. n is number of bridge nodes, i is index of the current bridge node. c_o and c_t are x or y coordinates of pair bridge nodes resident in cadastre counterpart and transformed (without pair) city planning boundaries, correspondingly. l_i is the length of the shortest path to be considered as a bridge node. l_{sum} is the sum of lengths of the shortest paths to bridge nodes from the vertex.

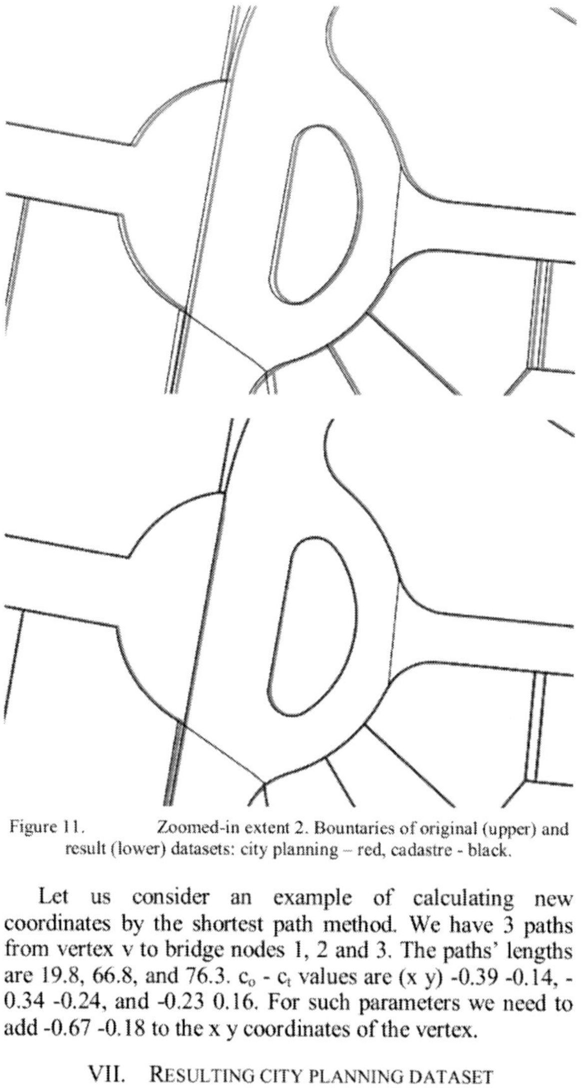

Figure 11. Zoomed-in extent 2. Bountaries of original (upper) and result (lower) datasets: city planning – red, cadastre - black.

Let us consider an example of calculating new coordinates by the shortest path method. We have 3 paths from vertex v to bridge nodes 1, 2 and 3. The paths' lengths are 19.8, 66.8, and 76.3. c_o - c_t values are (x y) -0.39 -0.14, -0.34 -0.24, and -0.23 0.16. For such parameters we need to add -0.67 -0.18 to the x y coordinates of the vertex.

VII. RESULTING CITY PLANNING DATASET

In order to acquire a final result, cadastre pairs of the boundaries are merged with the rectified boundaries without counterparts. Since pair boundaries have the same id and the rectified boundaries of the city planning dataset without cadastre pairs inherit the original ids, the correspondences between original and final polygons could be established by comparing ids of boundaries comprising a polygon. It is derived from the fact that each polygon could be identified by a unique set of ids of boundaries.

TABLE I. AVERAGE DISTANCES AND STANDARD DEVIATIONS

Parameter	Dataset compared with cadastral layer	
	Original city planning	*Result city planning*
Average distance, m	1.15	0.24
Standard deviation, m	0.64	0.41

The result datasets are presented in Figure 10 and Figure 11. We can conclude that most boundaries have been taken from the cadastral dataset; others have been rectified to connect boundaries without corresponding pairs and boundaries with pairs. The result looks satisfactory; the final map is holistic and does not contain significant deficiencies. A review implemented by specialists enables us to state that the results are satisfactory.

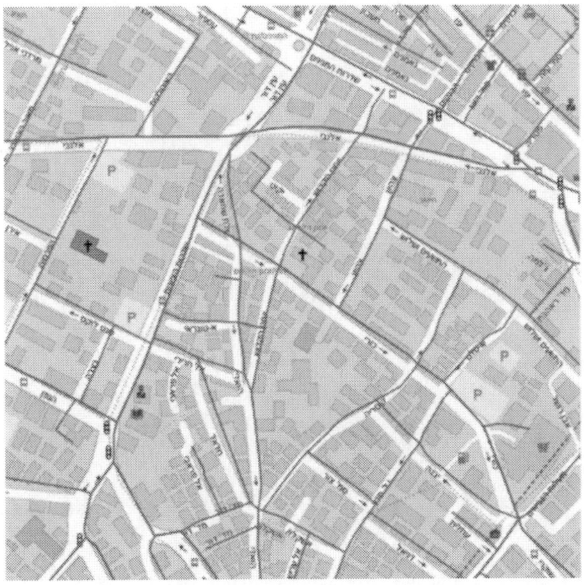

Figure 12. OpenStreetMap (background image) and SOI roads (red lines).

In order to estimate the results quantitatively, we use distances between the closest equidistant points of the cadastral and the city planning data sets' boundaries. The distances have been calculated between original city planning and cadastral datasets, as well as between the result and cadastral datasets. Only distances less than D_{max} have been taken into account. In Table I, average distances and standard deviations are presented.

According to the table, the average distance has been reduced five times over; standard deviation has been reduced by a factor of three. We can conclude from the table that the accuracy of the original dataset has been significantly improved.

Figure 13. Positional discrepancies of OSM (green) and SOI (red) road networks.

VIII. ROAD DATASETS REVIEW

A linear approach was successfully applied to City Planning polygonal data. In order to confirm the quality of our algorithms, another dataset was used. As mentioned at the beginning of this paper, this approach could be applied to linear data as well.

We encountered a significant problem using geodata covering Haifa City area: an absence of widths in roads' attributes. In order to use a road network with known individual widths of roads, OSM road layer was rectified according to statutory SOI road maps. Unfortunately, OSM road layer covering Haifa does not contain width attributes. Road widths were obtained from the rules of road type rasterization.

The source datasets were retrieved from different sources in ESRI shape file format. The data were preprocessed with GDAL/OGR command line tools and converted to GRASS GIS 7 topological geodatabase.

Haifa datasets were provided by Survey of Israel (SOI). The data contain ESRI shape files: contour lines (line layer), roads (line layer), and buildings (polygon layer). These data are proprietary. In addition, the OpenStreetMap (OSM) road data covering Haifa were processed in this work. The data (actual shape files) were downloaded from Geofabrik web site.

SOI roads consist of only two types of roads (main and regular). Attributes allowing us to calculate individual road widths (even approximately) are not provided. Thus, another source of road dataset was found. We decided to use OpenStreetMap (OSM) data. They are freely available and the quality is fairly high. We could use the rules of rasterization vector OSM elements to raster tiles to define the width of individual road types. In Figure 12, OpenStreetMap and SOI roads are depicted.

In Figure 13, two extents of overlaid OSM and SOI maps are depicted. From the figure, we could note irregular positional discrepancies. OSM roads should be rectified. From the figure, one could conclude that, in many cases, OSM roads intersect SOI buildings and it is impossible to correctly set building-quarter correspondences. In this work, we will evaluate the quality of rectified data by intersections with building layers. If buildings are located correctly to the right or to the left of a road, the road is considered to be correctly rectified.

IX. PREPROCESSING OF OSM ROAD DATASET

Figure 14 reflects two significant problems. First, OSM roads contain many more road types (including paths, pedestrian ways, steps, etc.) than SOI. Second, circular intersections (roundabouts) are not presented in the SOI layer. Regular intersections are used instead. The preprocessing stage of data integrations consists of two steps: removing minor road types and eliminating circular intersections.

Excessive OSM roads were removed by the following SQL request: "type NOT IN ('construction', 'cycle way', 'footway', 'path', 'pedestrian', 'platform', 'proposed', 'steps', 'track', 'bridleway', 'rest area') AND type NOT LIKE '%link%' AND tunnel=0". This SQL request eliminated all road lines contained in 'type' string column word 'link', roads with 'tunnel' attributes equaling '1', and minor road types: 'construction', 'cycle way', 'footway', 'path', 'pedestrian', 'platform', 'proposed', 'steps', 'track', 'bridleway', and 'rest area'.

Figure 14. OSM (red) and SOI (green) roads.

Figure 15. Cleaned OSM roads: black – result roads, red – removed.

Next, we need to calculate the compactness of polygons formed by closed road segments using the following equation.

$$compactness = perimeter / (2 \cdot \sqrt{\pi \cdot area}) \tag{2}$$

In the next step, segments constructing polygons with compactness < 1.01 (i.e., circular intersections) are removed. In the final step, surrounding polylines nodes are snapped to the centroids of polygons formed by removed polylines.

Figure 16. Carmel Center, Haifa. Original data – upper, rectified data – lower. Brown – SOI buildings, black – SOI roads, red – OSM roads.

In Figure 15, the OSM cleaning results are presented. Minor roads have been removed. The circular intersections have been replaced by regular intersections.

Now, the OSM roads dataset is more suitable for integration with an SOI road layer. Roads datasets are quite complex for processing (many intersections of polylines, complex topology, different types of roads, dissimilarity of counterpart objects, etc.).

Figure 17. Carmel Center, Haifa. Original data – upper, rectified data – lower. Brown – SOI buildings, black – SOI roads, red – OSM roads.

X. Applying a Linear Approach for OSM Road Dataset and Evaluating Results

In order to improve the positional accuracy of an OSM road network and integrate it with SOI road data, the developed linear fapproach was applied. OSM road data were rectified. Figure 16 and Figure 17 demonstrate the results of the integration.

In order to estimate the quality of a rectified road layer, building and road datasets were converted to raster layers (resolution 1 meter). The pixels touching vector objects got value "1"; the reminded pixels got value "0". The road raster layers were overlaid with building raster layers. In raster algebra terms [21], "AND" or "&&" condition was applied and pixels with value "1" on two overlaid dataset were selected. The following table contains numbers of pixels with value "1" from different raster maps.

TABLE II. STATISTICS OF RECTIFICATION RESULTS ("1"-VALUED PIXEL NUMBER OR SQUARE METERS).

Source data (square meters or number of pixels)			
SOI Buildings	6,367,165	OSM Buildings	6,167,209
SOI Roads	411,189	OSM Roads	639,855
Overlay			
OSM roads && OSM buildings	1,371	OSM roads && SOI buildings	39,589
SOI roads && SOI buildings	291	Rect. OSM roads && SOI buildings	3,067

According to the table, the number of intersections of OSM roads and SOI buildings was significantly reduced, from 39,589 to 3,067. We can conclude from this that the rectification results are satisfactory. The rectified OSM road network can be used in further research.

XI. CALCULATING WIDTHS OF OSM ROADS

Now, we need to calculate the widths of roads. OSM data covering the Haifa area do not have width attributes, but the rasterization rules of OSM vector data allows us to get road widths in pixels. The OSM wiki web page [28] provides an equation for estimating pixel size in meters for any zoom level:

$$Ps_z = \frac{C \cdot \cos y}{2^{z+8}} \quad (3)$$

Where, Ps is pixel size, z is zoom level, C is the (equatorial) circumference of the Earth; y is the latitude of the position. According to the equation, tile pixel size of zoom level 15 and 16 could be defined as follows:

$$Ps_{16} = \frac{40075696 \cos 32.795}{2^{16+8}} \approx 2 \quad (4)$$

$$Ps_{15} = \frac{40075696 \cdot \cos 32.795}{2^{15+8}} \approx 4 \quad (5)$$

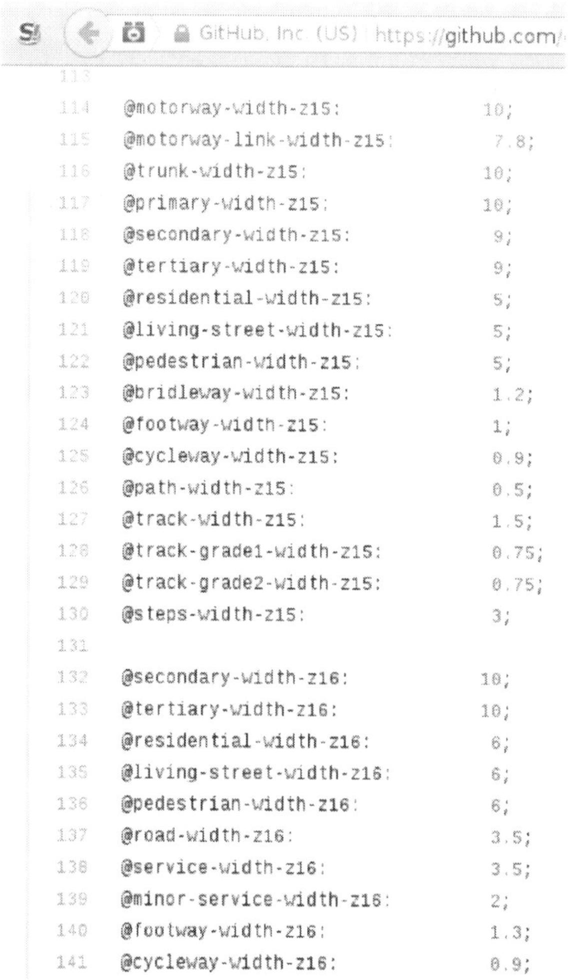

Figure 18. CartoCSS web site, roads.mss files actual lines. Line widths in pixels.

The widths of roads are equal to Ps multiplied by width in pixels. Width in pixels could be derived from CartoCSS open project (road.mss file [29]). The screenshot of the actual lines of the style sheet is presented in Figure 18.

The calculated road types' widths are presented in Table III.

In Figure 19, a map of OSM roads is depicted. The map is colored randomly by road type. Each road has a width according to Table III.

XII. Conclusion and Future Work

An approach for improving linear and polygonal spatial datasets is presented. Land-use city planning dataset locations have been corrected according to the cadastral dataset.

TABLE III. ROAD TYPES' WIDTHS.

Type	Pixels	Zoom level (pixel size)	Width (meters)
Living Street	6	16 (2)	12
Motorway	10	15 (4)	40
Primary	10	15 (4)	40
Residential	6	16 (2)	12
Road	3.5	16 (2)	7
Secondary	10	16 (2)	20
Service	3.5	16 (2)	7
Tertiary	10	16 (2)	20
Unclassified	6	16 (2)	12

The outline of the approach is as follows. The conventional polygon data have been converted to topological data format. Boundaries have been split into equidistant segments to calculate D_{max}. Then, correspondent boundaries have been defined using triangulation technique. Rectification of the remaining polylines by transformation and the shortest path algorithm has been implemented.

The developed algorithm has been tested on a city planning polygonal dataset and an OpenStreetMap road linear layer. In both cases, the resulting datasets are satisfactory. The resulting data quality has been evaluated by two different approaches: the first approach is based on equidistant points' statistics, while the second approach is based on defining intersections of building and road layers.

In the future, we need to test the approach with more datasets and different parameters, to compare it with other approaches. In order to improve the presented approach by also defining correspondences between parts of boundaries (not only whole boundaries), we would like to combine this approach with the segmentation-based algorithm published in [14]. This will allow us to apply the method to other types of datasets.

Acknowledgement

This research was supported by the Survey of Israel as a part of Project 2019317. The authors would like to thank the Survey of Israel for providing the financial support and data for the purpose of this research.

Figure 19. Map of roads with individual widths, randomly colored by road type.

References

[1] A. Noskov and Y. Doytsher, "A Linear Approach for Spatial Data Integration," GEOProcessing 2016, Venice, Italy, 2016, pp. 93-99.

[2] R. Abdalla, "Geospatial Data Integration", Introduction to Geospatial Information and Communication Technology (GeoICT), Springer International Publishing, 2016, pp. 105-124.

[3] A. Arozarena, G. Villa, N. Valcárcel, and B. Pérez, "Integration of Remotely Sensed Data Into Geospatial Reference Information Databases. Un-Ggim National Approach," ISPRS-International Archives of the Photogrammetry, Remote Sensing and Spatial Information Sciences, vol. 721-5, 2016.

[4] S. Belongie, J. Malik, and J. Puzicha, "Shape matching and object recognition using shape contexts," IEEE Trans. on Pattern Analysis and Machine Intelligence, 24(4), 2002, pp. 509—522.

[5] J. Bennett, "OpenStreetMap - Be your own cartographer," ISBN: 978-1-84719-750-4, Packt Publishing, 2011.

[6] A. Bronstein, R. Kimmel, M. Mahmoudi, and G. Sapiro, "A Gromov-Hausdorff framework with diffusion geometry for topologically-robust non-rigid shape matching," International Journal of Computer Vision, vol. 89(2-3), 2010, pp. 266-286.

[7] X. Chen, "Spatial relation between uncertain sets," International archives of Photogrammetry and remote sensing, vol. 31(B3), Vienna, 1996, pp. 105-110.

[8] S. Filin and Y. Doytsher, "The detection of corresponding objects in a linear-based map conflation," Surveying and land information systems, vol. 60(2), 2000, pp. 117-127.

[9] D. Foster and C. Mayfield, "Geospatial Resource Integration in Support of Homeland Defense and Security", International Journal of Applied Geospatial Research (IJAGR), vol. 7(4):53-63, 2016.

[10] H. Kim and C. Chung, "Geo-spatial data integration for subsurface stratification of dam site with outlier analyses," Environmental Earth Sciences, vol. 75(2), 2016

[11] A. Kipf and A. Kemper, "An Integration Platform for Temporal Geospatial Data. Digital Mobility Platforms and Ecosystems," 2016.

[12] M. Landa, "GRASS GIS 7.0: Interoperability improvements," GIS Ostrava, Jan. 2013, pp.21-23.

[13] T. Ma and J. Longin, "From partial shape matching through local deformation to robust global shape similarity for object detection," Computer Vision and Pattern Recognition (CVPR), IEEE Conference on. IEEE, 2011, pp. 1441-1448.

[14] A. Noskov and Y. Doytsher, "A Segmentation-based Approach for Improving the Accuracy of Polygon Data," GEOProcessing 2015, Portugal, 2015, pp. 69-74.

[15] A. Noskov and Y. Doytsher, "Triangulation and Segmentation-based Approach for Improving the Accuracy of Polygon Data," International Journal on Advances in Software, vol. 9 (1-2), 2016.

[16] C. Parent and S. Spaccapietra, "Database integration: the key to data interoperability," Advances in Object-Oriented Data Modeling, M. P. Papazoglou, S. Spaccapietra, Z. Tari (Eds.), The MIT Press, 2000.

[17] K. Piętak, J. Dajda, M. Wysokiński, M. Idzik, and L. Leśniak, "Geospatial Data Integration for Criminal Analysis", Man-Machine Interactions 4, Springer International Publishing, 2016, pp. 461-471.

[18] E. Rahm and P. Bernstein, "A survey of approaches to automatic schema matching," The International Journal on Very Large Data Bases (VLDB), vol. 10(4), 2001, pp. 334–350.

[19] A. Saalfeld, "Conflation-automated map compilation," International Journal of Geographical Information Science (IJGIS), vol. 2 (3), 1988, pp. 217–228.

[20] B. Schmitzer and C. Schnorr, "Object segmentation by shape matching with Wasserstein modes," Energy Minimization Methods in Computer Vision and Pattern Recognition, Springer Berlin Heidelberg, 2013.

[21] M. Shapiro and J. Westervelt, "r. mapcalc: An algebra for GIS and image processing", Construction Engineering Research Lab (ARMY), Champaign IL; 1994.

[22] X. Shu and X. Wu, "A novel contour descriptor for 2D shape matching and its application to image retrieval," Image and vision Computing, vol. 29.4, 2011, pp. 286-294.

[23] P. Shvaiko and J. Euzenat, "A survey of schema-based matching approaches," Journal on Data Semantics IV, Springer Berlin Heidelberg, 2005, pp. 146-171.

[24] N. Tsendbazar, S. Bruin, S. Fritz, and M. Herold, "Spatial Accuracy Assessment and Integration of Global Land Cover Datasets", Remote Sensing, vol. 7(12):15804-21, 2015.

[25] G. Wiederhold, "Mediation to deal with heterogeneous data sources," Interoperating Geographic Information System, 1999, pp. 1–16.

[26] R. Xie, Y. Liu, X. Li, L. Yu, "A Framework of Satellite Observation Data Integration System," International Conference on Mechatronics, Electronic, Industrial and Control Engineering (MEIC 2015), 2015.

[27] S. Zheng and J. Zheng, "Assessing the completeness and positional accuracy of OpenStreetMap in China," Thematic Cartography for the Society, Springer International Publishing, 2014, pp. 171-189

[28] http://wiki.openstreetmap.org/wiki/Zoom_levels [accessed 15.06.2017]

[29] https://github.com/gravitystorm/openstreetmap-carto/blob/master/roads.mss [accessed 15.06.2017]

Comparative Evaluation of Background Subtraction Algorithms for High Performance Embedded Systems

Lorena Guachi, Giuseppe Cocorullo, Pasquale Corsonello, Fabio Frustaci, Stefania Perri
Department of Informatics, Modeling, Electronics and System Engineering
DIMES - University of Calabria
Arcavacata di Rende, Italy
e-mail: loreanggeles@hotmail.com, g.cocorullo@unical.it, p.corsonello@unical.it, ffrustaci@deis.unical.it, perri@dimes.unical.it

Abstract— **Background Subtraction technique is widely used in surveillance systems to identify moving objects. Although color features have been extensively used in several background subtraction algorithms, demonstrating high efficiency and performances, in actual real-time applications the background subtraction performance is still a challenge due to high computational requirements. In this paper, two approaches and their optimized versions are evaluated to implement high-performance background subtraction algorithms for real-time applications. Gaussian Mixture Model and the Multimodal Background Subtraction are characterized by two different color descriptors: Gray scale and H color invariant combined with Gray scale information respectively. Different experimental analysis allows evaluating the efficiency in terms of computational complexity and accuracy for outdoor and indoor environments. Experimental tests demonstrated that the Multimodal Background Subtraction approach with its variants is established as affordable for real-time applications and particularly suitable on hardware platforms with on-board memory and limited computational resources.**

Keywords- Real-Time; Image processing; Background subtraction; Segmentation.

I. Introduction

In recent decades, great interest has been shown for Background Subtraction (BS) technique to achieve a precise pixel classification as background (static) and foreground (dynamic) and then to identify the objects of interest [1] within observed scenes. Since cameras are less expensive than most other sensors and they are already installed on security environments, video sequences are used to build intelligent surveillance systems [2], where many BS algorithms work for specific environments in very controlled situations. Unfortunately, several applications are too slow to be practical as a consequence of their high computational requirements.

The BS algorithms typically use five features as descriptor: color, edge, motion and texture features [3]. Each one is particularly robust to handle critical issues in a different way. For instance, color feature is highly discriminative but depends on the way of representing colors in the image. Therefore, different color representations obtain different accuracies, which are limited in the presence of shadows, illumination changes, and camouflage [1]. On the other hand, edge feature is very discriminative in the presence of ghost and illumination variations. Texture feature works well with shadows and illumination variations, while stereo is robust in order to handle the camouflage issue. Finally, motion feature is useful for detecting articulated objects, but at the expense of increased the computational cost [4].

In order to be more robust in the presence of critical situations, some algorithms combine different features. Therefore, the best solution should reach higher accuracy to classify correctly a pixel as background or foreground. Moreover, it should achieve high speed to incorporate changes from the environment with the ability to run in real-time (RT) without demanding high computational capabilities. In this context, the multi-scale region BS algorithm [5] performs the Gaussian Mixture modeling (GMM) in conjunction with color histograms, texture information, and consecutive division of image regions to efficiently detect edges of the moving objects. Also, in [6], the use of color and edge information is applied to handle slow illumination changes and camera noise, being able to run on standard platform for RT applications.

Although numerous BS algorithms have been introduced with demonstrated efficiency, RT applications, mainly for surveillance systems, remain challenging. One of the reasons is that more robust algorithms usually perform complex operations, thus requiring higher computational capabilities; as a consequence, they are not suitable for RT applications, where portability, low weight, low size, low computational load and low power consumption are required. On the contrary, lower computational loads are usually related to simple background models that lack adaptive background updates and sensitivity to even small background changes.

This paper presents a comparative evaluation of two light and efficient BS algorithms for RT applications oriented to hardware friendly implementations. GMM [7] uses Gray scale and takes advantage of exploiting a color space that does not require complex color transformations. Meanwhile, the Multimodal Background Subtraction (MBSCIG) algorithm [8] exploits two simple background models separately build for the color invariant H and the Gray scale pixels intensities. Experimental tests demonstrate that MBSCIG with its optimized variations can reach higher percentages of correct classified pixels with a reduced computational complexity.

The rest of this paper is organized as follows. Section II describes the most relevant related works. Section III introduces the color descriptors. We briefly explain the

GMM algorithm and its optimized version in Section IV. MBSCIG and its variations are presented in Section V. Section VI presents comparison results, and conclusions are finally drawn in Section VII.

II. Related Works

In the last years, many different BS algorithms have been introduced, and nearly each of them can provide improvements over the basic algorithms and among each other. They can range from very simple algorithms, usually providing poor performance, to more robust algorithms, which commonly are unsuitable for RT applications due to their high computational complexity. For instance, the Running Gaussian Average [9] uses three color channels for background modeling and models each pixel of each color channel with single Gaussian distribution. The GMM method is exploited in several state-of-the-art algorithms, such as [10-15], to achieve more robustness against frequent and small illumination changes. These algorithms model the history of each pixel over the time by the mean and variance values of a fix number of Gaussian distributions.

The Kernel Density Estimation (KDE) [16] was originally presented by Elgammal like a non-parametric approach to cope with the drawbacks of manually tuning. After that some enhancements have been proposed to decrease the computational complexity using techniques such as histogram approximation and recursive density estimation [17]. The algorithm presented in [18] quantizes each background pixel into codebooks, which represent a compressed form of background model for a long image sequence and are composed of one or more codewords. This allows capturing structural background variation due to periodic motion over a long period of time under limited memory and can handle scenes with moving background, shadows and highlights.

The K-mean algorithms proposed in [19-21] model each pixel of the generic input frame by a group of clusters that are sorted in order of the likelihood to deal with lighting variations and dynamic background. Incoming pixels are analyzed against the corresponding cluster group and are classified according to whether or not the analysis cluster is considered as a part of the background. A fuzzy inference for thresholding is proposed in [22] and [23] in order to improve the thresholding technique avoiding the empirical selection of threshold values by trial and error approach.

In [24], a neural network architecture is proposed to model background images for object segmentation based on an unsupervised Bayesian classifier. The approach proposed in [25] is based on self-organizing through artificial neural networks. It can handle the bootstrapping problem, dynamic scenes containing moving backgrounds, gradual illumination variations and camouflage, which can be included into the background model shadows that cast by moving objects, thus achieving robust detection for different types of videos taken with stationary cameras.

In order to present the aids and constraints of methods based on spatial correlation, density estimates, parametric and non-parametric models, comprehensive reviews are reported in [14], [26] and [27], where the algorithms are evaluated in terms of precision, speed and memory requirements (critical features for RT applications). Concentrated in mathematical models and the solution for critical situations, the author in [3] provides a classification of the traditional and recent works.

To improve stability, accuracy and efficiency, and to support RT applications, a dynamic multi-level feature grouping [2] can be exploited. It introduces the BS and corner cue to detect and handle various sizes of moving objects. To cope the presence of shadows and shading, a basic statistical background modeling at pixel-level is presented in [28] and [29]. However, a dynamic background cannot be handled efficiently with a single-model, especially at the beginning, where the slow learning does not allow differentiating the moving objects from the moving shadows. To solve these limitations, adaptive BS methods are proposed in [30-32]. The latter can efficiently handle quick illumination changes, moving backgrounds and shadow removal.

Additionally, several original methods have been established. As an online estimation of the background in a linear regression, the model demonstrated in [33] achieves high efficiency, while categorizes the foreground as outliers and considers that the background pixels are based on low rank subspace. Parallel analysis at pixel level, presented in [34], holds for each pixel historical and occurrence background values, thus being suitable for both software and hardware implementations. The spatial probability is used in [35], where the eigen background builds the background reference image from a training set of background frames. Based on local texture patterns, the SILTP descriptor is enhanced in [36] to segment the image sequences across of the spatial and temporal analysis of neighborhood. PBAS algorithm [37] relies on the local decision thresholds to segment the foreground, modeling the background with an array of historical frames and choose randomly the observed background pixel to be replaced with the current value.

The most popular algorithms model the temporal video sequences as a parametric form across the Mixture of Gaussians. Such probabilistic technique is shown in [11], where a learning training is required ahead to detect the motion and the interaction between multiple moving objects in the presence of slow light variations and suddenly background changes. A classification of the methods that use the Mixture of Gaussians for foreground detection has been presented in [38], discussing challenges, issues to reduce the computational load, improvements and critical situations that they claim to handle. Based on the remarkable GMM results, in [7] a hardware implementation was proposed for the OpenCV version of the GMM algorithm, and tunings to minimize the word length of the signals able to run on RT applications was performed.

Reached performance by BS algorithms existing in literature also depends on the exploited colors representation [3], [9], [10], [12], [14], [39], [41]. In fact, the color model can significantly influence the achieved quality. In [42] and [43], it is shown that the usage of YCbCr and HSV color spaces can improve the pixels classification. Whereas [44] demonstrates that using the normalized RGB color components leads to higher overall quality and speed performance than those reachable with the c1c2c3 color representation. In [45], color invariant (CI) expressions have been derived that allow the effects of a large set of disturbing factors, such as illumination, viewing direction, surface orientation and highlights, to be significantly reduced in Computer Vision applications. A way to efficiently exploit CIs in BS algorithms has been investigated in [9], where the background model is built referring to N previous frames; each frame is described by the color invariants H, Wx and Wy, and each pixel is modeled with a single Gaussian distribution. An alternative approach was presented in [10], where mixtures of Gaussians are calculated on both the Gray scale pixels intensity and the color invariant Hx. The two channels are then combined to reduce the number of pixel misclassifications in the presence of shadows, noises and illumination changes. In this context, the useful experimental study introduced in [1] provided a point-of-view to choose the best color combination considering accuracy and channel numbers which can be applied for BS. The results demonstrate that the combination of the CI H with Gray scale achieves higher performance for foreground segmentation for both indoor and outdoor video sequences. Then, to make hardware implementation friendlier, the Author exploited in [8] an approximated formulation for CI H transformation from RGB.

Apart of the color representation adopted by BS algorithms, RT oriented algorithms demand a relatively low computational load and must be highly efficient to detect moving objects in diverse environments at common video sequences rates. Therefore, with the aim of establishing the efficiency of the GMM modifications [7] and the MBSCIG [8] algorithm, which are focused on high-performance for RT segmentation, several experimental analysis have been performed using purpose-written C++ routines, which exploit the OpenCV libraries.

In order to reduce efficiently the computational cost of the MBSCIG algorithm, two alternative updating processes are proposed and described in the following. It is notably that, while original techniques provide high robustness, herein, experimental tests show that good performances can be achieved also with the proposed pixel-by-pixel computational scheme through quite tunings. Additionally, performances reached in terms of accuracy, percentage of correct classification, and computational load are comparable with the GMM algorithm presented in [7].

III. Color Descriptor

Most of the work presented in the literature have demonstrated how the color features interfere with the achieved accuracy, typical descriptors are based on specific spectral information (RGB, HSV, HIS, Gray scale, among others). On the other hand, the CIs are derived from a physical model and can take into account color spectral information and color spatial structure. Therefore, in order to build a robust descriptor, handling the issues of pixel-level analysis, an experimental study was presented in [1], which evaluated the color spaces with properties independent of illumination intensity, reflectance property, viewing direction, and object

TABLE I. Set of Color Invariants

CI	*Definition*
H	$E\lambda / E\lambda\lambda$
N	$(E\lambda\chi \times E - E\lambda \times E\chi) / (E \times E)$
C	$E\lambda / E$
W	$E\chi / E$

surface orientation, which are defined as the color invariants [46], in conjunction with Gray scale color model.

A. *Color invariant (CI)*

Any method for describing CI model relies on assumptions about the physical variables involved on photometric configuration [44]. Photometric CIs are characterized as functions of surface reflectance, illumination spectrum and the sensing device, which consider the spatial configuration of color, and also the color spectral energy distribution coding color information [9].

Color invariant properties [46] characterize the image color configuration discounting highlights, shadows, noise and shading. As an example, the Gaussian color model with spectral and spatial parameters is exploited in [9] to define a framework for the robust measurement of colored object reflectance.

The CIs are derived from a physical reflectance model based on the Kubelka-Munk theory for colorant layers [45], where illumination and geometrical invariant properties depend on the use of reflectance model. The invariants are useful for materials as dyed paper and textiles, paint films, opaque plastics, dental silicate cements and up to enamel. The CIs derived from Kubelka-Munk theory are listed in Table I. The latter shows how computing the CIs named H, N, C, and W, with E, $E\lambda$ and $E\lambda\lambda$ being the spectral differential quotients based on the scale-space theory [47]. The CIs defined in Table I can be combined incrementally to achieve an alternative to invariant features extraction [44].

B. *Gray scale*

The Gray color space model is based on the brightness information and uses the measurement of amount of light (intensity). It is applied for object tracking often on a blob or a specific region [48]. However, taking into account that the color furnishes more information on the objects in a scene, it would be expected that this model can be used in conjunction with other models to achieve more robust solutions and higher accuracy in comparison with the basic separated models. For this reason, the Gray color space computed by (1) is included in the proposed evaluation to take the advantage of using a color space that does not require complex color transformations.

$$GS = 0.299R + 0.58G + 0.114B \quad (1)$$

IV. Gaussian Mixture Model

The statistical Background Modeling presented in [12] uses the Gaussian Mixture Model (GMM) to handle efficiently dynamic background. The reported GMM algorithm heads the effectiveness in RT applications, with a good deal between constraints of low computational load and memory requirement, robustness and the ability to cope critical situations, like illumination variation and introduced or removed objects. The improvements of this approach included in the OpenCV library are shown in the following. Some optimizations have been introduced in [7] to obtain efficient hardware implementations. They are cited in the text as "GMM optimized".

A. *GMM implemented in OpenCV*

The GMM algorithm operates on the probability of observing one process more than one time over a video sequence [10], [12], and assumes that the set of background pixels is visible more frequently than any set of foreground pixels. Based on [12], the algorithm implemented in OpenCV considers that each pixel of each input frame in the video sequence is modeled using *K* mixture of Gaussian distributions in terms of the mean (μ), weight (w), variance (σ^2), and matchsum (counter introduced in OpenCV). Additionally, Fitness (F) is used as a sorting parameter to arrange in decreasing order the *K* distributions, and α_w is the learning rate.

To update the background model, each new pixel value (x_t) is checked with respect to *K* Gaussian distributions, calculating the difference between them. If at least one mean difference is less or equal than 2.5σ ($|x_t - \mu_{k,t}| \leq 2.5\sigma$), then the distribution is updated as given in the following equations:

$$\alpha_{k,t} = \alpha_w / w_{k,t} \quad (2a)$$

$$\mu_{k,t+1} = \mu_{k,t} + \alpha_{k,t}(x_t - \mu_{k,t}) \quad (2b)$$

$$\sigma^2_{k,t+1} = \sigma^2_{k,t} + \alpha_{k,t}[(x_t - \mu_{k,t})^2 - \sigma^2_{k,t}] \quad (2c)$$

$$w_{k,t+1} = w_{k,t} - \alpha_w . w_{k,t} + \alpha_w \quad (2d)$$

$$matchsum_{k,t+1} = matchsum_{k,t} + 1 \quad (2e)$$

Otherwise, the distribution with the lowest Fitness value is replaced with a new one, for which the mean is set to the current pixel value, whereas the variance and the weight are set to predetermined high variance (*highV*) and low weight (*lowW*), respectively, as shown in the equations below.

$$\mu_{k,t+1} = x_t \quad (3a)$$

$$\sigma^2_{k,t+1} = high\ v \quad (3b)$$

$$w_{k,t+1} = low\ w \quad (3c)$$

$$matchsum_{k,t+1} = 1 \quad (3d)$$

After the updating step, the weights are normalized so that their summation becomes 1. For each acquired frame at time t, the *K* distributions are sorted in decreasing order of *F* defined in (4).

$$F_{k,t} = w_{k,t} / \sigma_{k,t} \quad (4)$$

To establish whether x_t is part of the background, the first n sorted distributions that satisfy equation (5) are selected as background components, and a pixel that matches one of these components is classified as background pixel. In the opposite case, x_t is classified as foreground. The Threshold (*T*) is a fixed value, ranging between 0 and 1, which determines the portion of the distribution weights that defines the background model. Preliminary tests demonstrated that, for the video sequences selected as the benchmarks, *T*=0.75 is the best value.

$$B = arg_n \min \left(\sum_{k=1}^{n} w_{k,t} > T\right) \quad (5)$$

B. *GMM Optimized (GMM v1)*

The GMM algorithm implemented in Open CV is able to work with one or three channels, and its execution involves floating point operations, thus becoming a complex statistical model that provides good accuracy at the expense of a high computational cost, which compromises its use in RT applications. Therefore, in order to reduce the computational cost, the authors proposed in [7] some optimizations based on the following characteristics:

- Handle the algorithm processing with video frames in Gray scale.
- Use fixed-point values for mean (μ) and variance (σ) instead of floating-point values, thus reducing the computational complexity. In fact, floating-point operations use more internal circuitry and require at least 32-bit data paths to manage two parts: the 24-bit integer value (base of the real number) and the 8-bit exponent.
- Establish the word length for each parameter, to reduce the error rate due to the diminution of number of bits.
- Set the number of mixture of Gaussian distributions to *K*=3 as suggested in [34].
- Quantize the learning rates α_w and $\alpha_{k,t}$ as power of two.

$$\alpha_w = 2^{n_w} \quad \alpha_{k,t} = 2^{n_{k,t}} \quad (6)$$

- Use the parameter $IF_{k,t}$, defined in (7) as the square of the inverse of $F_{k,t}$, to sort the Gaussian distributions.

$$IF_{k,t} = (1/F_{k,t})^2 \quad (7)$$

In terms of learning rates, $IF_{k,t}$ is defined as follows:

$$IF_{k,t} = \sigma^2_{k,t} . 2^{2(n_{k,t} - n_w)} \quad (8)$$

where $n_{k,t} = log_2(\alpha_{k,t})$ and $n_w = log_2(\alpha_w)$.

V. Multimodal Background Subtraction MBSCIG

A multimodal BS algorithm has been recently proposed for high performance embedded system MBSCIG [8], with the aim of achieving low computational complexity and high efficiency for RT applications, exploiting the advantage of use a reduced number of channels and historical frames. Only two separate color channels are used to model the Background: one of them is characterized by Gray scale information (G), and another one corresponds to Color Invariant (CI) H. A short detail of the algorithm MBSCIG and its modifications to improve performances are described in the following.

A. MBSCIG

MBSCIG gives an effective and quite method using only a modeled frame *mF*, and a small set *hF* of history observations. This approach firstly processes the captured RGB frame to get the Gray scale and H information as describes [8], then it processes the first N+1 acquired frames. The algorithm starts to measure for each pixel of each *hF* the percentage variation *DD* with respect to the current frame I_t. When *DD* is lower that a given Threshold *T*, the counter λ is increased by one. Whether λ counts at least two and the percentage variation *DD* between *mF* and I_t is lower than *T*, the pixel is classified as a background pixel. Otherwise, it is recognized as belonging to the foreground. This analysis is executed for both the channels H and G, computing λh and λg, respectively. As the next step, *mF* is updated as given in equations (9) and (10), depending on the current pixel has been classified as background or foreground. Finally, the oldest frame in *hF* is replaced by I_t .

$$BG_{t+1} = (1-\propto)\ I_t + \propto\ BG_{t+1} \tag{9}$$

$$FG_{t+1} = \beta\ I_t + (1-\beta)\ FG_{t+1} \tag{10}$$

B. MBSCIG Optimized

We analyze two alternative ways to perform the updating step of the algorithm MBSCIG. In the original algorithm the background and the foreground are updated as shown in Figure 1a. With the target of limiting the number of operations and reducing the computational load, in order to incorporate gradual changes quickly in the background model, the first alternative approach, reported in Figure 1b, updates the foreground pixels with the value of the current pixel, when the percentage variation is higher than *T*. The second proposed approach, shown in Figure 1c, does not perform any updating operation when a pixel belongs to the set of moving objects.

VI. Experimental Results

Since the learning rate (α) has a fundamental impact on the overall classification in algorithms based on GMM, establishing an appropriate value of α is crucial to achieve high performance with the lowest overall error. Therefore, values in the range [0.01 ÷ 0.05] are evaluated in [49]. In order to select the ideal learning rate value for all tested video sequences, providing good classification, in this work performances achieved are measured not only for α in the range [0.01 ÷ 0.05], but for α equal to 0.1 and 0.005, as suggested in [49] and [50]. The F1 metric is computed for five benchmark video sequences. The F1, introduced in [51] and defined in (11), combines Recall and Precision metrics, defined in (12) and (13), to measure an overall quality of the BS based on True and False Positive and Negative (TP, TN, FP and FN) classifications. The results summarized in Figure 2 show that, when $\alpha = 0.05$, F1 differs from the average of only ±3.3.

```
capture the current frame
For each pixel It(x,y) in the frame
  ...
    if (DD<T and λ>=2)
      IsFg=0 //a background pixel is detected
      BG_{t+1} = (1−∝) . I_t +∝. BG_{t+1}
    else
      IsFg=1 //a foreground pixel is detected
      FG_{t+1} = β. I_t + (1 − β). FG_{t+1}
  ...
End for
```

a)

```
capture the current frame
For each pixel It(x,y) in the frame
  ...
    if (DD<T and λ>=2)
      IsFg=0 //a background pixel is detected
      BG_{t+1} = (1−∝) . I_t +∝. BG_{t+1}
    else
      IsFg=1 //a foreground pixel is detected
      if ( DD > T)
        FG_{t+1} = I_t
  ...
End for
```

b)

```
capture the current frame
For each pixel It(x,y) in the frame
  ...
    if (DD<T and λ>=2)
      IsFg=0 //a background pixel is detected
      BG_{t+1} = (1−∝) . I_t +∝. BG_{t+1}
    else
      IsFg=1 //a foreground pixel is detected
  ...
End for
```

c)

Figure 1. The updating process of the MBSCIG: a) original version; b) MBSCIG v1; c) MBSCIG v2

$$F1 = (2 \times P \times R)/(P + R) \tag{11}$$

$$Recall\ (R) = TP/(TP + FN) \tag{12}$$

$$Precision\ (P) = TP/(TP + FP) \tag{13}$$

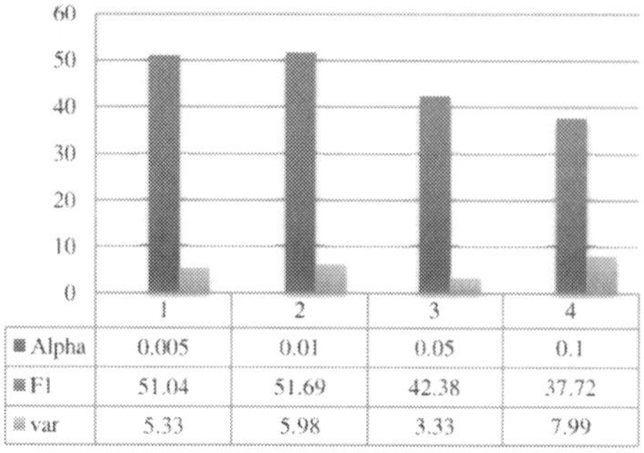

Figure 2. Learning rate performance in GMM

This suggests that using $\alpha = 0.05$, as proposed in [13], is well suited for all tested sequences and can be applied in both indoor and outdoor environments to achieve good object identification.

The versions of GMM and MBSCIG presented in this paper were tested on I2R [52], Wallflower [53], 2012 and 2014 dataset [54]. Lobby is part of I2R dataset, which is defined by illumination changes and complex background, and contains twenty ground-truth images for evaluation target. Wallflowers Dataset includes video sequences with dynamic motions and movement of background objects, such as Waving Trees, which we used in tests considering its ground-truth provided. 2012 and 2014 Datasets contain outdoor and indoor environments, respectively, where Bootstrapping is evaluated based on its one ground-truth, while Office and Highway video sequence have been tested comparing the segmented results with respect to ten ground-truth given.

TABLE II. AVERAGE OF FALSE POSITIVE AND FALSE NEGATIVE RATE

Algorithm	Looby		Waving Tree		Bootstrap		Highway		Office	
	FPR	FNR	FPR	FNR	FPR	FNR	FPR	FNR	FPR	FNR
GMM [12]	**0,64**	**1,02**	**0,28**	18,14	**2,08**	14,33	**0,32**	5,47	**0,26**	7,06
GMM v1 [7]	0,71	1,07	10,98	25,17	4,80	14,37	1,45	5,87	2,80	4,71
MBSIG [8]	0,87	1,23	33,18	9,69	7,15	8,46	1,48	4,39	1,16	6,90
MBSIG v1	1,07	1,19	32,88	**7,85**	6,54	6,70	2,16	**3,16**	2,42	3,16
MBSIG v2	7,73	1,21	23,62	8,02	18,97	**4,88**	2,46	3,37	2,73	**1,50**

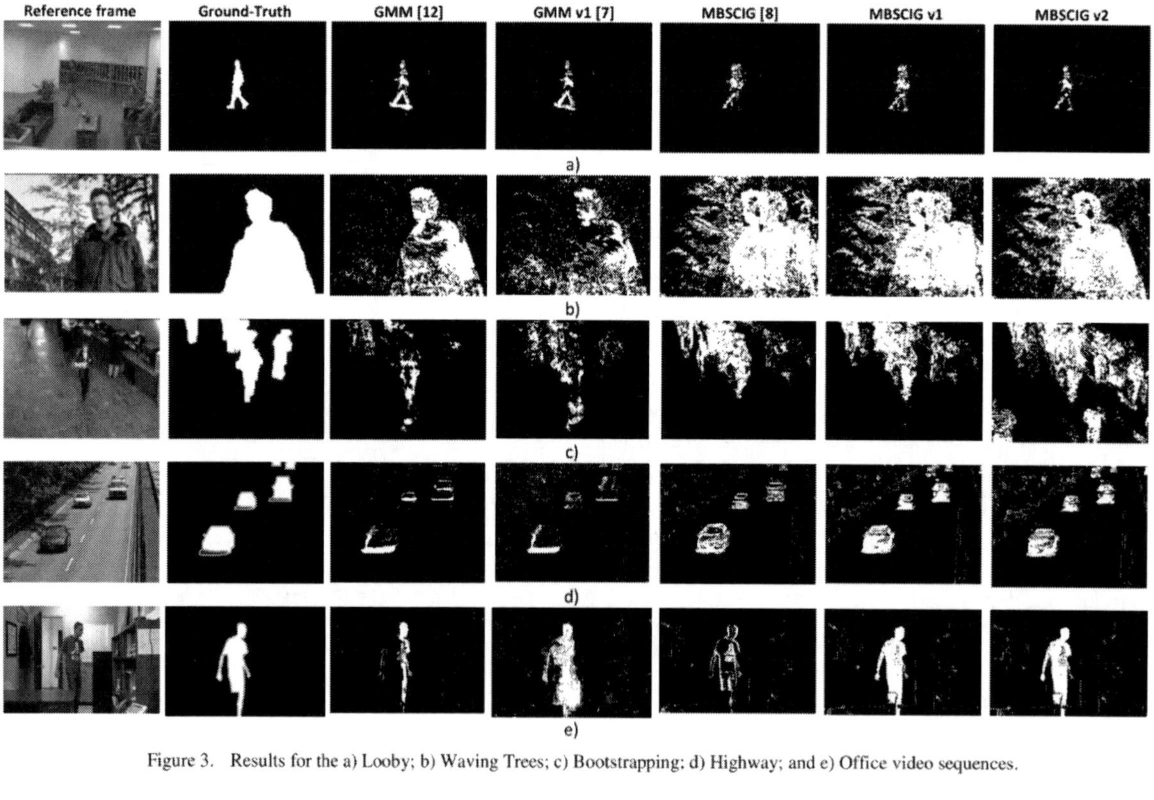

Figure 3. Results for the a) Looby; b) Waving Trees; c) Bootstrapping; d) Highway; and e) Office video sequences.

TABLE III. QUANTITATIVE ACCURACIES.

Algorithm	Lobby		Waving Tree		Bootstrap		Highway		Office	
	F1	PCC	F1	PCC	F1	PCC	F1	PCC	F1	PCC
GMM [12]	**47,62**	**98,37**	67,40	**82,54**	30,71	86,08	38,96	94,67	31,27	93,32
GMM v1 [7]	43,57	98,25	51,22	74,92	27,30	83,74	28,91	93,27	49,21	93,10
MBSCIG [8]	33,58	97,93	61,66	70,27	54,93	86,77	48,46	94,60	30,49	92,63
MBSCIG v1	34,17	97,78	64,06	71,74	**62,99**	**88,78**	**58,74**	**95,09**	**77,68**	**96,41**
MBSCIG v2	20,18	91,21	**69,55**	78,05	52,31	79,78	55,66	94,63	75,03	96,00

TABLE IV. COMPUTATIONAL LOAD

	Color Model	# Channels	Size	Background Model	Foreground Segmentation	Total
GMM [12]	Gray Scale	1	K=3	(27AS+21MD) x Np	2AS x Np	(29AS + 21MD) x Np
GMM v1 [7]	Gray Scale	1	K=3	(30AS+33MD) x Np	2AS x Np	(32AS + 33MD) x Np
MBSCIG [8]	Gray Scale+H (CI)	2	N=4	(8AS+8MD) x Np	(18AS + 20MD) x Np	(26AS + 28MD) x Np
MBSCIG v1	Gray Scale+H (CI)	2	N=4	(4AS+4MD) x Np	(18AS + 20MD) x Np	(22AS + 24MD) x Np
MBSCIG v2	Gray Scale+H (CI)	2	N=4	(4AS+4MD) x Np	(18AS + 20MD) x Np	(22AS + 24MD) x Np

C++ software routines using OpenCV library have been implemented to evaluate the algorithms. In order to evaluate the performance reachable, for each analyzed algorithm the average of the numerical results achieved processing the selected video sequences has been computed for the evaluated metrics. Table II presents the percentage of False Positive (FPR: Percentage of misclassified pixels detected as foreground) and False negative Rate (FNR: Percentage of misclassified pixels detected as background) defined in (14) and (15). It can be seen that the GMM algorithm obtains the lowest FPR for all the examined video sequences, since it processes only the Gray scale features, which leads to less classification errors. It can also be observed that the FNR takes advantage of the appropriate tuning of the updating process in the MBSCIG algorithm. This is the effect of the modified updating process applied to the foreground pixels, in order handle the sensitivity to small and fast background changes. In fact, the FNR is significantly reduced in Waving Tree, Bootstrap and Highway sequences.

$$FPR = FP/(FP + TN) \quad (14)$$

$$FNR = FN/(TN + FP) \quad (15)$$

Figure 3 illustrates qualitative results for reviewed and optimized BS algorithms. From Figure 3b, we can see that the original version of GMM works better than other algorithms in dynamics backgrounds with small movements. However, the use of only three Gaussian Mixtures in both versions, diminishes the overall accuracy in all experiments. On the other hand, the variants of the MBSCIG algorithm perform much better than original MBSCIG, but all of them are still weak against the dynamic backgrounds.

To present the quantitative accuracy of the tested methods, our experiments compare F1 and Percentage of correct classification (PCC) using equations (11) and (16).

$$PCC = TP + TN/(TP + TN + FP + FN) \quad (16)$$

The results reported in Table III confirm that the variants of the MBSCIG algorithm are robustly capable of detecting moving objects. While, the original GMM algorithm [12] implemented in OpenCV is robust when operating in environments with illumination changes and quick small movements introduced in the background.

Figure 4 plots the F1 average and the percentage of variation of PCC with respect to original version of GMM, and demonstrates that the change in updating process of MBSCIG gives the highest overall accuracy (F1=59.53) with the lowest variation in PCC (only 1.04%).

The computational load of the evaluated algorithms is presented in Table IV separately for the segmentation and the modeling steps in terms of Additions-Subtractions (AS) and Multiplications-Divisions (MD). Also, the number of pixels Np within each Frame is taken into account with the number of channels, and the number of distributions (K) or of historical frames (N). Figure 5a shows that the higher computational load of GMM does not ensure the higher accuracy scores in terms of F1 and PCC metrics. On the contrary, Figure 5b shows that the tuning of the MBSCIG algorithm maintains low values of both FPR and FNR reducing the computational load. From the accuracy and the computational complexity analysis, we can observe that the conjunction between H and Gray scale provides a soft and efficient method with a low computational load.

The variants here proposed for the MBSCIG algorithm have been hardware implemented referring to the system architecture proposed in [8]. The 85K Logic Cells xc7z020 FPGA chip, used to process RGB QQVGA (128×160 pixels per frame) video sequences, allows a 154Mhz running frequency to be reached. Resources requirements are summarized in Table V. It can be seen that the proposed variants occupies less LUTs due to the simplified updating process. Table V also shows that, at a parity of the frame resolution, the hardware designs exhibit computational times reached more than 132 times lower than the pure software executions when performed by one of the Cortex A9 cores running at 800 MHz clock frequency available within the chosen device.

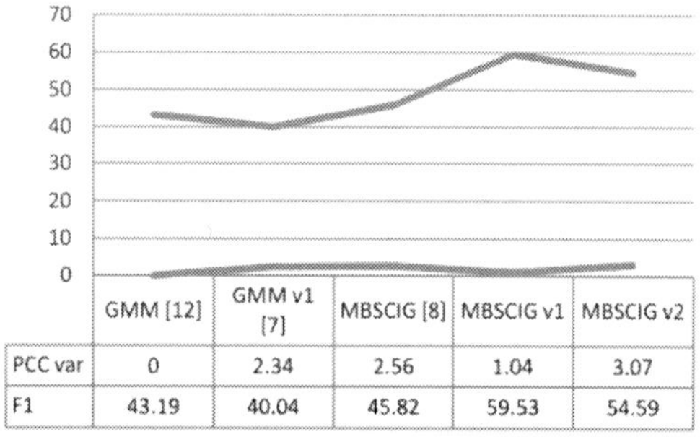

Figure 4. Average and percentage variations of F1 and PCC.

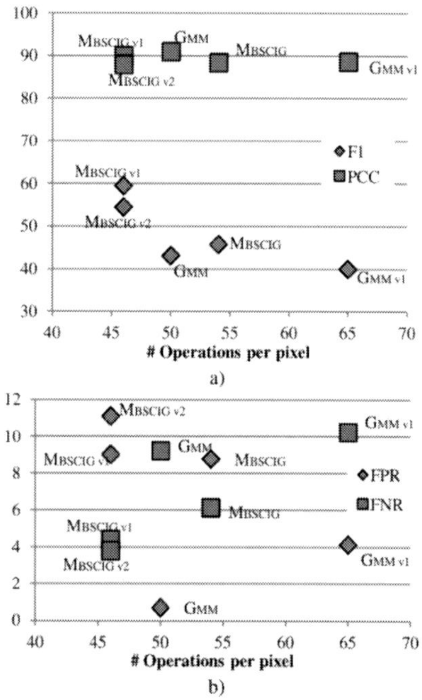

Figure 5. Accuracy vs complexity

TABLE V. HARDWARE DESIGNS VS PURE SOFTWARE EXECUTIONS

	Hardware designs		Software Design
	Resources	Time	Time
MBSCIG [8]	75 BRAM 1868 LUTs 1376 FFs	~0.13ms	~17ms
MBSCIG v1	75 BRAM 1523 LUTs 1376 FFs	~0.107ms	~14ms
MBSCIG v2	75 BRAM 1408 LUTs 1376 FFs	~0.107ms	~14ms

VII. CONCLUSIONS

We have tested two efficient real-time approaches for BS. Based on accuracy metrics we can see that the efficiency in terms of FPR, FNR and F1 are very closer between GMM implemented in OpenCV and MBSCIG with their variations. However, considering the high robustness as the convergence between a good effectiveness with a low computational cost, we can see that MBSCIG and their variations are affordable for real-time applications, and particularly suitable on hardware platforms with on-board memory and limited computational resources and FPGA-based hardware accelerators. As another advantage, the parameters used by the MBSCIG algorithms can be properly chosen, during the design phase, based on preliminary tests performed on video sequences that are typical of the actual scene where the embedded system should work. The adaptability of the algorithms, as well as their performance scalability with video frames of different resolution, will be investigated in future works.

REFERENCES

[1] L. Guachi, G. Cocorullo, P. Corsonello, F. Frustaci, and S. Perri, "Color Invariant Study for Background Subtraction," in *CENICS 2016 : The Ninth International Conference on Advances in Circuits, Electronics and Micro-electronics*, pp.1-5, 2016.

[2] Z. Kim, "Real Time Object Tracking based on Dynamic Feature Grouping with Background Subtraction," 2008.

[3] T. Bouwmans, "Traditional and Recent Approaches in Background Modeling for Foreground Detection : An Overview," *Comput. Sci. Rev.*, pp. 31–66, 2014.

[4] D. Park, C. L. Zitnick, D. Ramanan, and P. Dollar, "Exploring weak stabilization for motion feature extraction," *Proc. IEEE Comput. Soc. Conf. Comput. Vis. Pattern Recognit.*, vol. 1, no. c, pp. 2882–2889, 2013.

[5] P. Darvish, Z. Varcheie, M. Sills-lavoie, and G. Bilodeau, "A Multiscale Region-Based Motion Detection and Background Subtraction Algorithm," *Sensors, 2010*, pp. 1041–1061, 2010.

[6] S. Jabri, Z. Duric, and H. Wechsler, "Detection and Location of People in Video Images Using Adaptive Fusion of Color and Edge Information."

[7] M. Genovese and E. Napoli, "ASIC and FPGA implementation of the gaussian mixture model algorithm for real-time segmentation of high definition video," *IEEE Trans. Very Large Scale Integr. Syst.*, vol. 22, no. 3, pp. 537–547, 2014.

[8] P. Corsonello, G. Cocorullo, F. Frustaci, L. Guachi, and S. Perri, "Multimodal Background Subtraction for high performance embedded systems," *J. Real-Time Image Process.*, 2016.

[9] H. Zhou, Y. Chen, and R. Feng, "A novel background subtraction method based on color invariants," *Comput. Vis. Image Underst.*, vol. 117, no. 11, pp. 1589–1597, 2013.

[10] L. Guachi, G. Cocorullo, P. Corsonello, F. Frustaci, and S. Perri, "A novel background subtraction method based on color invariants," in *Security Technology (ICCST), 2014 International Carnahan Conference on. IEEE*, 2014, pp. 1–5.

[11] C. Stauffer and W.E.L. Grimson, "Learning patterns of activity using real-time tracking," *IEEE Trans. Pattern Anal. Mach. Intell.*, n°8 vol. 22, pp. 747–757, 2000.

[12] C. Stauffer and W. E. L. Grimson, "Adaptive background mixture models for real-time tracking," *Proc. 1999 IEEE Comput. Soc. Conf. Comput. Vis. Pattern Recognit. Cat No PR00149*, vol. 2, no. c, pp. 246–252, 1999.

[13] J. Sep and S. A. Velast, "F1 Score Assesment of Gaussian Mixture Background Subtraction Algorithms Using the MuHAVi Dataset,"

Imaging Crime Prev. Detect. (ICDP-15), 6th Int. Conf. on. IET, pp. 1–6, 2015.

[14] A. Sobral and A. Vacavant, "A comprehensive review of background subtraction algorithms evaluated with synthetic and real videos," *Comput. Vis. Image Underst.*, vol. 122, pp. 4–21, 2014.

[15] V. J. Butler, Darren and Sridharan, Sridha and Bove, "Real-time adaptive background segmentation," *Acoust. Speech, Signal Process. 2003. Proceedings.(ICASSP'03). 2003 IEEE Int. Conf.*, vol. 3, pp. III–349–52, 2003.

[16] A. Elgammal, R. Duraiswami, D. Harwood, and L. S. Davis, "Background and foreground modeling using nonparametric kernel density estimation for visual surveillance," *Proc. IEEE*, vol. 90, no. 7, pp. 1151–1162, 2002.

[17] J. Lee and M. Park, "An Adaptive Background Subtraction Method Based on Kernel Density Estimation," *Sensors*, vol. 12, pp. 12279–12300, 2012.

[18] K. Kim, T. H. T. H. Chalidabhongse, D. Hanuood, L. Davis, and D. Harwood, "Background modeling and subtraction by codebook construction," *Int. Conf. Image Process. ICIP '04.*, vol. 5, pp. 3061–3064, 2004.

[19] D. E. Butler and V. M. B. Jr, "Real-time adaptive foreground / background segmentation," *EURASIP J. Appl. Signal Processing*, vol. 2005, no. 14, pp. 2292–2304, 2005.

[20] T.-H. Nguyen, Van-Toi and Vu, Hai and Tran, "An Efficient Combination of RGB and Depth for Background Subtraction," *Springer*, vol. 341, no. January, pp. 49–63, 2015.

[21] P. Parmar, G. Sunilkumar, and P. Jain, "Performance Analysis and Augmentation of K-means Clustering , based approach for Human Detection in Videos," vol. 3, no. 2, pp. 1029–1035, 2015.

[22] X. Lijun, "Moving object segmentation based on background subtraction and fuzzy inference," *2011 Int. Conf. Mechatron. Sci. Electr. Eng. Comput.*, pp. 434–437, 2011.

[23] S. S. Dhar Joydip, Kurele Ritika, Arora Surbhi, "Background Subtraction in Surveillance systems- A Neural Fuzzy Approach," *Int. J. Imaging Robot.*, no. April, 2015.

[24] D. Culibrk, O. Marques, D. Socek, H. Kalva, and B. Furht, "Neural network approach to background modeling for video object segmentation," *Neural Networks, IEEE Trans.*, vol. 18, no. 6, pp. 1614–1627, 2007.

[25] L. Maddalena and A. Petrosino, "A Self-Organizing Approach to Background Subtraction for Visual Surveillance Applications," vol. 17, no. 7, pp. 1168–1177, 2008.

[26] S. Y. Elhabian, K. M. El-Sayed, and S. H. Ahmed, "Moving Object Detection in Spatial Domain using Background Removal Techniques - State-of-Art," *Recent Patents Comput. Sci.*, vol. 1, no. 1, pp. 32–54, 2010.

[27] M. Piccardi, "Background subtraction techniques : a review *," pp. 3099–3104, 2004.

[28] M. Sankari and C. Meena, "Estimation of Dynamic Background and Object Detection in Noisy Visual Surveillance," *Int. J. Adv. Comput. Sci. Appl.*, vol. 2, no. 6, pp. 77–83, 2011.

[29] E. Hayman and J. Eklundh, "Statistical Background Subtraction for a Mobile Observer," no. Iccv, 2003.

[30] P. Kaewtrakulpong and R. Bowden, "An Improved Adaptive Background Mixture Model for Real- time Tracking with Shadow Detection 2 Background Modelling," pp. 1–5, 2001.

[31] Y. Tian, M. Lu, and A. Hampapur, "Robust and Efficient Foreground Analysis for Real-time Video Surveillance," in *Computer Vision and Pattern Recognition, 2005. CVPR 2005. IEEE Computer Society Conference*, 2005, pp. 1182–1187.

[32] S. Huwer, "Adaptive Change Detection for Real-Time Surveillance Applications," no. July, pp. 37–45, 2000.

[33] E. Signal and P. Conference, "An Online Background Subtraction Algorithm Using A Contiguously Weighted Linear Regression Model", University of Kent , UK Pontificia Universidad Católica del Perú , Peru," vol. 1, no. d, pp. 1890–1894, 2015.

[34] B. Wang and P. Dudek, "A Fast Self - tuning Background Subtraction Algorithm," pp. 4321–4324.

[35] L. Vosters, S. Caifeng, and G. Tommaso, "Real-time robust background subtraction under rapidly changing illumination conditions." Image and Vision Computing 30.12 (2012): 1004-1015.

[36] H. Wu, N. Liu, X. Luo, and J. Su, "Real-time background subtraction-based video surveillance of people by integrating local texture patterns," pp. 665–676, 2014.

[37] M. Hofmann, P. Tiefenbacher, and G. Rigoll, "Background Segmentation with Feedback : The Pixel-Based Adaptive Segmenter."

[38] T. Bouwmans, F. El Baf, B. Vachon, T. Bouwmans, F. El Baf, B. Vachon, B. Modeling, T. Bouwmans, F. El Baf, and B. Vachon, "Background Modeling using Mixture of Gaussians for Foreground Detection - A Survey To cite this version : Background Modeling using Mixture of Gaussians for Foreground Detection - A Survey," 2008.

[39] J. M. Guo, Y. F. Liu, C. H. Hsia, M. H. Shih, and C. S. Hsu, "Hierarchical method for foreground detection using codebook model," *IEEE Trans. Circuits Syst. Video Technol.*, vol. 21, no. 6, pp. 804–815, 2011.

[40] V. Reddy, C. Sanderson, and B. C. Lovell, "Improved foreground detection via block-based classifier cascade with probabilistic decision integration," *IEEE Trans. Circuits Syst. Video Technol.*, vol. 23, no. 1, pp. 83–93, 2013.

[41] O. Barnich and M. Van Droogenbroeck, "ViBe : A universal background subtraction algorithm for video sequences," *Image Process. IEEE Trans.*, vol. 20, no. June, pp. 1709–1724, 2011.

[42] S. R. Sivanantham S, Nitin Paul, "Object Tracking Algorithm Implementation for Security Applications," *Far East J. Electron. Commun.*, vol. 16, no. 1, p. 17654, 2016.

[43] R. H. Luke, S. Member, D. Anderson, S. Member, and J. M. Keller, "Human Segmentation from Video in Indoor Environments Using Fused Color and Texture Features." Technical Report, University of Missouri. 2007.

[44] B. Shoushtarian and H. E. Bez, "A practical adaptive approach for dynamic background subtraction using an invariant colour model and object tracking," vol. 26, pp. 5–26, 2005.

[45] J. Geusebroek, R. Van Den Boomgaard, I. C. Society, A. W. M. Smeulders, S. Member, and H. Geerts, "Color Invariance," vol. 23, no. 12, pp. 1338–1350, 2001.

[46] T. Gevers and A. W. M. Smeulders, "Color-based object recognition," *Pattern Recognit.*, vol. 32, no. 3, pp. 453–464, 1999.

[47] M. A. Florack, Luc MJ and ter Haar Romeny, Bart M and Koenderink, Jan J and Viergever, "Scale and the differential structure of images," *Image Vis. Comput.*, vol. 10, pp. 376–388, 1992.

[48] P. Sebastian, Y. V. Voon, and R. Comley, "Colour Space Effect on Tracking in Video Surveillance," vol. 2, no. 4, pp. 298–312, 2010.

[49] S. S. Mohamed, N. Tahir, and R. Adnan, "Background modelling and background subtraction performance for object detection Background Modelling and Background Subtraction Performance for Object Detection," in *Signal Processing and Its Applications Conference*, 2010.

[50] A. Bouzerdoum and S. L. Phung, "On the analysis of background subtraction techniques using Gaussian mixture models," pp. 4042–4045, 2010.

[51] P. Goyette, Nil and Jodoin, Pierre-Marc and Porikli, Fatih and Konrad, Janusz and Ishwar, "Changedetection . net : A New Change Detection Benchmark Dataset," *IEEE Comput. Soc. Conf. Comput. Vis. Pattern Recognit. Work.*, pp. 1–8, 2012.

[52] "Statistical Modeling of Complex Background for Foreground Object Detection." [Online]. Available: http://perception.i2r.a-star.edu.sg/bk_model/bk_index.html. [Accessed: 23-Sep-2016].

[53] B. M. Kentaro Toyama, John Krumm, Barry Brumitt, "Test Images for Wallflower Paper," 1999. [Online]. Available: http://research.microsoft.com/en-

us/um/people/jckrumm/wallflower/testimages.htm. [Accessed: 23-Sep-2016].

[54] "ChangeDetection.Net (CDNET) A video database for testing change detection algorithms." [Online]. Available: http://www.changedetection.net/. [Accessed: 23-Sep-2016].

Improving FPGA-Placement with a Self-Organizing Map Accelerated by GPU-Computing

Timm Bostelmann, Philipp Kewisch, Lennart Bublies and Sergei Sawitzki

FH Wedel (University of Applied Sciences)
Wedel, Germany
Email: bos@fh-wedel.de, publications@kewis.ch, edu@bublies-it.de, saw@fh-wedel.de

***Abstract*—Programmable circuits and, nowadays, especially field-programmable gate arrays (FPGAs) are widely applied in computationally demanding signal processing applications. Considering modern, agile hardware/software codesign approaches, an electronic design automation (EDA) process not only needs to deliver high quality results. It also has to be swift because software compilation is already distinctly faster. Slow EDA tools can in fact act as a kind of show-stopper for an agile development process. One of the mayor problems in EDA is the placement of the technology-mapped netlist to the target architecture. In this work a method to improve the results of the netlist placement for FPGAs with a self-organizing map is presented. The admittedly high computational effort of this approach is covered by the exploitation of its inherent parallelism. Different approaches of parallelization are introduced and evaluated. A concept to accelerate the self-organizing map by using the single instruction multiple data (SIMD) capabilities of the central processing unit (CPU) and the graphics processing unit (GPU) for low-level vector operations is presented. This work is based on our previous publications, which are joined, updated and extended. Specifically, a new metric to generate training vectors for the self-organizing map – that has been introduced by Amagasaki et al. – was integrated into our work. It is shown that – in case of our application – the original vectorization metric creates higher quality results, even though the new metric is unmistakably faster. Addressing this issue, in addition to the previous low-level parallelization, a new high-level parallelization approach is introduced and detailed benchmark results are presented.**

Keywords–FPGA; netlist placement; OpenCL; GPU-computing; parallelization; SIMD.

I. INTRODUCTION

The ever-growing complexity of FPGAs has a high impact on the performance of EDA tools. A complete compilation from a hardware description language to a bitstream can take several hours. One step highly affected by the vast size of netlists is the NP-complete placement process. It consists of selecting a resource cell (position) on the FPGA for every cell of the applications netlist. In this work, our previous publications regarding the optimization of the placement process [1], [2] are joined, updated and extended. Explicitly, a new GPU-accelerated implementation is presented and benchmarked. Furthermore, an additional method for the generation of training vectors is evaluated.

Due to the complexity of the netlist placement problem, many current algorithms work in an iterative manner. A well known example is simulated annealing [3], which starts with a random initial placement and swaps blocks stepwise. The result of every step is evaluated by a cost function. A step is always accepted, if it reduces the cost. If it increases the cost, it is accepted with a probability that declines by time (cooling down). An annealing schedule determines the gradual decrease of the temperature, where a low temperature means a low acceptance rate and a high temperature means a high acceptance rate. Generally, the temperature is described by an exponentially falling function like

$$T_n = \alpha^n \cdot T_0 \tag{1}$$

where typically $0.7 \leq \alpha \leq 0.95$. However, there has been a lot of research on the optimization of the annealing schedule like in [4], [5], [6]. As a result, there are many variations available for any related problem.

It has been shown by Banerjee et al. [7] that the speed and result of an iterative placement algorithm can be improved by the use of an initial placement created in a constructive manner out of the structural information of the netlist. For this purpose, the netlist was recursively bisectioned, resulting in an one-dimensional mapping. This mapping was spread to a two-dimensional plane with space-filling curves to create an initial placement for the simulated annealing algorithm. In comparison to the classical random initialization the computation time was reduced by about 44.5 percent without having a significant impact on the quality.

Self-organizing maps [8] – also known as Kohonen maps after their inventor Teuvo Kohonen – are used to classify multidimensional datasets. They belong to the group of unsupervised learning algorithms. Therefore, neither the input data nor the resulting classes have to be known beforehand. The input data is grouped by similarity and mapped to an usually two-dimensional plane.

In this work, it is shown how a self-organizing map can be adapted to map a netlist to a two-dimensional plane and how a valid placement for the netlist can be derived. Additionally, different approaches to utilize the inherent parallelism of this modified self-organizing map are introduced and evaluated. These approaches are based on using the SIMD capabilities of the CPU and the GPU.

In Section II, the problem of netlist placement for FPGAs is introduced and the functional principle of a self-organizing map is described. Furthermore, the basics and challenges of GPU-computing are introduced. In Section III, the proposed algorithm is described including details on how the training algorithm of the self-organizing map has been modified to assure that only valid placements are produced. Furthermore, different metrics for the mapping of the structural netlist-information to so called training vectors are introduced and evaluated. In Section IV, the results of a prototypic software implementation of the proposed algorithm are presented. A reasonable usage of the structural information is proven by placing synthetic, homogeneous netlists. As representation for real world applications a selection of Microelectronics Center of North Carolina (MCNC) benchmarks [9] is introduced. A modified version of the Versatile Place and Route (VPR) [10] tool for FPGAs is used to show the gain of using an initial placement for simulated annealing, which has been created using a self-organizing map. In Section V, the levels of parallelism inherent to the self-organizing map (i.e., vector-level and map-level) are analyzed and different approaches to exploit them are introduced. Specifically, a low-level and a high-level parallelization approach on CPU and GPU are described and benchmarked in detail. Finally, in Section VI, this work is summarized and a prospect to further work is given.

II. Background

In the following subsections the problem of netlist placement for FPGAs is introduced and the functional principle of a self-organizing map is described. Furthermore, the basics and challenges of GPU-computing are introduced.

A. Netlist placement for FPGAs

The problem of netlist placement for FPGAs can be roughly described as selecting a resource cell (a position) on the target FPGA for every cell of the given netlist. In Figure 1, an exemplary graph of a netlist is defined. An exemplary placement for this netlist is presented in Figure 2. The positions must be chosen in a way that:

1) Every cell of the netlist is assigned to a resource cell of the fitting type (e.g., IO, CLB or DSP).
2) No resource cell is occupied by more than one cell of the netlist.
3) The cells are arranged in a way that allows the best possible routing.

The first two rules are necessary constraints. A placement that is failing at least one of them is illegal and therefore unusable. The third rule is a quality constraint, which is typically described by a cost function. The goal of a placement algorithm is to optimize the placement regarding this function without violating one of the necessary constraints. Usually, the length of the critical path and the routability are covered by the cost function.

B. Principle of self-organizing maps

A self-organizing map is a special kind of artificial neuronal network. Figure 3 shows the general structure of a two dimensional self-organizing map. It consists of two layers, the competition layer $K_{i,j}$ with $i \in \{1, 2, \ldots, n\}$ and $j \in \{1, 2, \ldots, m\}$ and the input layer E_k with $k \in \{1, 2, \ldots, l\}$. The neurons of the competition layer are placed in a two dimensional grid. They are horizontally and vertically adjacent. Furthermore, every neuron of the competition layer is connected to every neuron of the input layer by a weight $W_{i,j,k}$. The input layer corresponds to a vector with l elements and is able to classify l-dimensional input data.

In Figure 4, the training-cycle of a self-organizing map is shown as a flowchart. The self-organizing map is trained

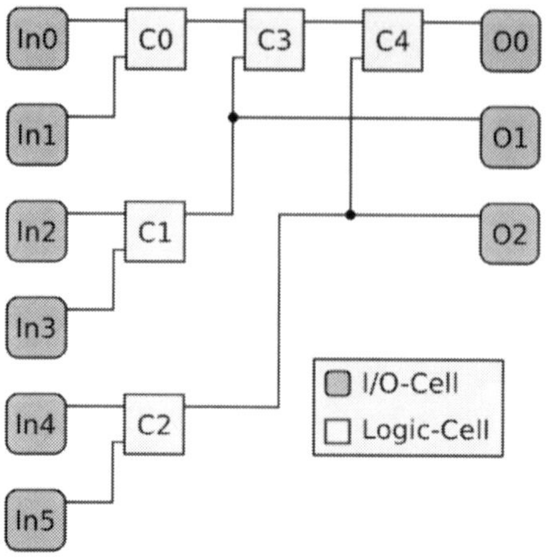

Figure 1. An exemplary graph of a netlist consisting of input-, output-, and logic-cells

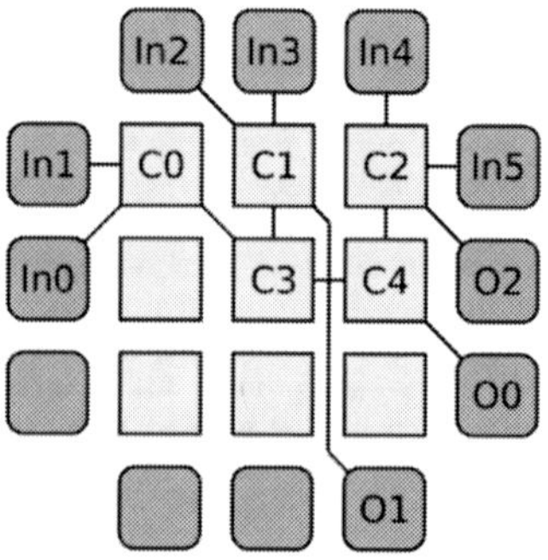

Figure 2. A valid placement for the graph in Figure 1 on a simple island-style FPGA architecture

by repeated stimulation of the input layer with the input data (training vectors) in a random order. In every step – thus for every stimulation – a winning neuron is determined by the distance of its weight vector to the current stimulation of the input layer, so that the neuron with the smallest Euclidean distance to the training vector wins. After this step the weights of the winning neuron and its neighbors are pulled towards the current stimulation by the function

$$W'_{ijk} = W_{ijk} + (E_k - W_{ijk}) \cdot \beta_{ij} \tag{2}$$

where $0 \leq \beta_{ij} \leq 1$ is the influence. The influence is depending on the distance to the winning neuron on the competition layer by the function

$$\beta_{ij} = e^{-\left(\frac{|I-i| + |J-j|}{r}\right)} \tag{3}$$

where (I, J) is the position of the winning neuron, so that $|I-i|+|J-j|$ is the rectilinear distance between the influenced and the winning neuron, and r is the radius of the function. Hence, the influence on the winning neuron itself is the highest and decreases by distance. Consequentially, similar training vectors stimulate mainly adjacent neurons, so that a clustering by similarity is developed.

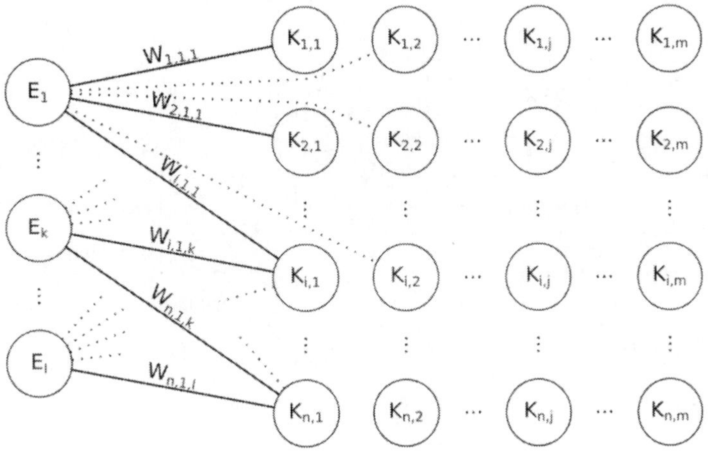

Figure 3. General structure of a self-organizing map

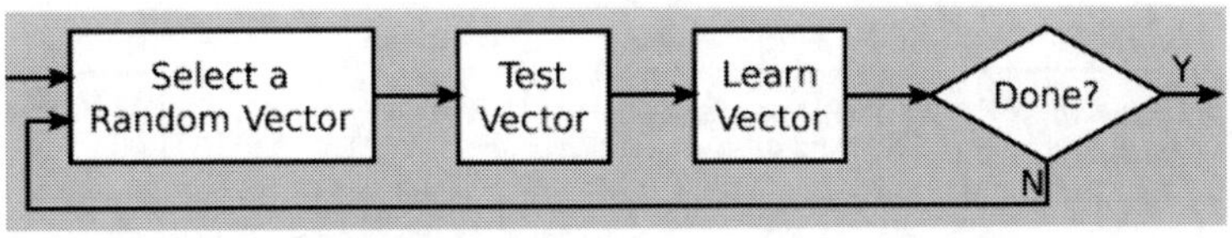

Figure 4. Flowchart of the training-cycle of a self-organizing map

C. GPU-computing with OpenCL

OpenCL is an universal interface for parallel SIMD-computing. It supports various kinds of target hardware. These are multicore CPUs and their streaming extensions as well as GPUs and even special hardware like FPGAs. Especially GPUs are – due to their structure – able to execute large amounts of uniform tasks in parallel. For example, the *AMD® RADEON™ RX 480* GPU is specified with a peak performance of up to 5.8 teraflops, utilizing 2304 stream processors and a memory bandwidth of 224 gigabytes per second. This computation power is usually used for the calculation of pixel-colors in a three-dimensional scene, namely computer games. Even so, thanks to interfaces like OpenCL it is also available for general purpose computing. However, due to the special hardware architecture of GPUs, several specifics must be taken into account when using OpenCL. Besides the obvious need for parallelization, the differences regarding the memory model convey the highest impact to the programmer. Instead of a global memory model with transparent caches, which is used in CPUs, an explicit multi level model is used. In Figure 5, the memory model of OpenCL is shown. It can be mapped to any recent GPUs memory structure. The work-items of the GPU are grouped to workgroups. Each workgroup shares a fast local memory. Work-items can be efficiently synchronized within a workgroup. An exchange of data over the boundaries of workgroups is only possible by using the global memory.

Assuming the GPU implements dedicated memory – as every GPU with considerable computing power does – the transfer between host memory and global memory is comparably slow and has to be reduced to the minimum. Even though the global memory of the GPU is noticeably faster than the host memory of the host-device, it has to feed all the work-items. Thus, the global memory should be used as sparsely as possible. Instead, the workgroup's local memory should be used, if applicable. Copying data from the global memory to the local memory should be done sequentially to exploit the burst capabilities of the dynamic random access memory (RAM).

Finally, it has to be noted that all parameters like the size of the workgroups and the speed and the size of the memories are varying significantly between different devices, let alone different device-classes. Therefore, an implementation performing well on one GPU might lack performance on another model.

III. Proposed Method

In the following subsections the proposed algorithm is described including details on how the training algorithm of the self-organizing map has been modified to assure that only valid placements are produced. Furthermore, different metrics for the mapping of the structural netlist-information to so called training vectors are introduced and evaluated.

A. Principle of netlist placement with a self-organizing map

To generate a netlist placement with a self-organizing map, in addition to the training process described above two general steps are necessary (Figure 6). Those are the generation of training vectors (preparation) and the extraction of placement information from the self-organizing map after the training (interpretation).

For every cell of the netlist, which has to be placed, a training vector is generated in a way that highly connected cells are represented by similar vectors. Since the self-organizing map will cluster these vectors by similarity, the vectors of highly connected cells will cluster together on the competition

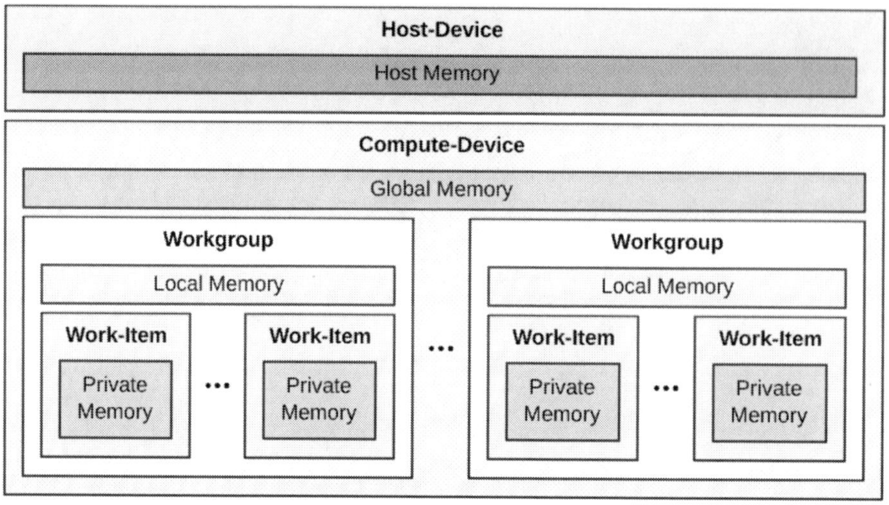

Figure 5. The OpenCL memory- and computation-model

Figure 6. Flowchart of the placement algorithm based on a self-organizing map (SOM)

layer. A favorable placement of the cells can therefore be determined by the positions of the corresponding training vectors on the competition layer. To allow a distinct interpretation the neurons of the competition layer are arranged in a one-to-one mapping with the FPGA resources. This means every neuron is corresponding to a resource cell and the neighborhood relationships between the neurons are corresponding to the interconnections of the FPGA architecture.

To support different cell types (e.g., logic bocks and input/output blocks) every neuron is tagged with the type of the corresponding FPGA resource cell and every training vector is tagged with the type of the corresponding cell of the netlist. During the determination of the winning neuron only neurons of the same type as the training vector are analyzed, so that only a fitting neuron (position) can win. The training – namely the manipulation of the weights around the winning neuron – happens independently of the type to assure a global clustering. On the level of the neuronal model this means that there is one input layer for every cell type. The neurons of the competition layer are connected only to those input neurons that are of the same type as their corresponding resource cell. Consequentially, the training vectors are stimulating only the input neurons that are of the same type as their corresponding cell of the netlist.

B. Mapping of the structural information into training vectors

As shown before the training data has to be available in form of homogeneous sized vectors – one for every cell of the netlist – to be processed by the self-organizing map. Five metrics for the generation of these vectors, depending on the structural information of the netlist, have been evaluated.

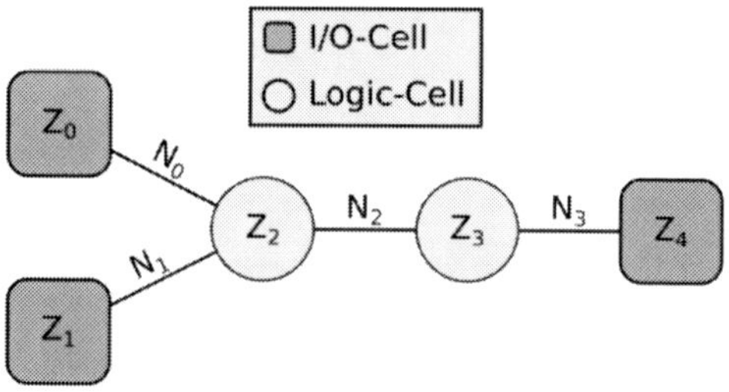

Figure 7. Graph of an exemplary netlist

TABLE I. Training vectors for the graph shown in Figure 7 generated by the vectorization method "net membership"

Cell	Vector
Z_0	$(1, 0, 0, 0)$
Z_1	$(0, 1, 0, 0)$
Z_2	$(1, 1, 1, 0)$
Z_3	$(0, 0, 1, 1)$
Z_4	$(0, 0, 0, 1)$

Metric 1 Net membership: In the first metric the vectors are generated depending on the membership of cells in nets. The dimension of the vectors is equal to the number of nets in the netlist. Thereby, every element of a vector is mapped to a net of the netlist. An element is 1, if the cell corresponding to the vector is connected to the respective net, otherwise it is 0. The vector generation using this approach is very fast because the vectors are generated directly from the netlist. Figure 7 shows a graph of a simple netlist, where Z_i for $i \in \{0, 1, \ldots, 4\}$ are cells and N_j for $j \in \{0, 1, \ldots, 3\}$ are nets of the netlist. The vectors generated for this graph are shown in Table I.

Metric 2 Hyperbolic distance: In the second metric the vectors are generated depending on the pairwise distance between cells. The dimension of the vectors is equal to the number of cells in the netlist. Thereby, every element of a vector is mapped to a cell of the netlist. Let V_i be the vector

TABLE II. Training vectors for the graph shown in Figure 7 generated by the vectorization method "hyperbolic distance"

Cell	Vector
Z_0	$\left(\frac{1}{1}, \frac{1}{3}, \frac{1}{2}, \frac{1}{3}, \frac{1}{4}\right)$
Z_1	$\left(\frac{1}{3}, \frac{1}{1}, \frac{1}{2}, \frac{1}{3}, \frac{1}{4}\right)$
Z_2	$\left(\frac{1}{2}, \frac{1}{2}, \frac{1}{1}, \frac{1}{2}, \frac{1}{3}\right)$
Z_3	$\left(\frac{1}{3}, \frac{1}{3}, \frac{1}{2}, \frac{1}{1}, \frac{1}{2}\right)$
Z_4	$\left(\frac{1}{4}, \frac{1}{4}, \frac{1}{3}, \frac{1}{2}, \frac{1}{1}\right)$

TABLE III. Training vectors for the graph shown in Figure 7 generated by the vectorization method "linear distance"

Cell	Vector
Z_0	$\left(\frac{4}{4}, \frac{2}{4}, \frac{3}{4}, \frac{2}{4}, \frac{1}{4}\right)$
Z_1	$\left(\frac{2}{4}, \frac{4}{4}, \frac{3}{4}, \frac{2}{4}, \frac{1}{4}\right)$
Z_2	$\left(\frac{3}{4}, \frac{3}{4}, \frac{4}{4}, \frac{3}{4}, \frac{2}{4}\right)$
Z_3	$\left(\frac{2}{4}, \frac{2}{4}, \frac{3}{4}, \frac{4}{4}, \frac{3}{4}\right)$
Z_4	$\left(\frac{1}{4}, \frac{1}{4}, \frac{2}{4}, \frac{3}{4}, \frac{4}{4}\right)$

corresponding to the cell Z_i and let d_{ij} be the minimal distance between the cells Z_i and Z_j. The hyperbolic equation

$$v_{ij} = \frac{1}{1 + d_{ij}} \tag{4}$$

describes the generation of the training vectors. Table II shows the vectors generated for the graph (Figure 7) used in the previous example.

Metric 3 Linear distance: The third metric – like the second one – depends on the pairwise distance between cells. Therefore, the structure of the vectors is the same. In addition to the former definition let d_{max} be the greatest distance occurring in the netlist. The linear equation

$$v_{ij} = 1 - \frac{d_{ij}}{d_{max} + 1} \tag{5}$$

describes the generation of the training vectors. Table III shows the vectors generated for the graph (Figure 7) used in the previous examples.

Metric 4 Distance to I/O-cells: This metric has to the best of our knowledge been introduced by Amagasaki et al. in [11]. Instead of the pairwise distances between all cells, only the distances to the input- and output-cells (I/O-cells) are used. The dimension of the vectors is equal to the number of the I/O-cells in the netlist. Table IV shows the vectors generated for the graph (Figure 7) used in the previous examples.

Metric 5 Hyperbolic distance to I/O-cells: The fifth metric is equal to the fourth metric, with the difference that the distances are normalized by the hyperbolic equation (4) like the third metric. Table V shows the vectors generated for the graph (Figure 7) used in the previous examples.

TABLE IV. Training vectors for the graph shown in Figure 7 generated by the vectorization method "I/O-distance"

Cell	Vector
Z_0	$(0, 2, 3)$
Z_1	$(2, 0, 3)$
Z_2	$(1, 1, 2)$
Z_3	$(2, 2, 1)$
Z_4	$(3, 3, 0)$

TABLE V. Training vectors for the graph shown in Figure 7 generated by the vectorization method "hyperbolic I/O-distance"

Cell	Vector
Z_0	$\left(\frac{1}{1}, \frac{1}{3}, \frac{1}{4}\right)$
Z_1	$\left(\frac{1}{3}, \frac{1}{1}, \frac{1}{4}\right)$
Z_2	$\left(\frac{1}{2}, \frac{1}{2}, \frac{1}{3}\right)$
Z_3	$\left(\frac{1}{3}, \frac{1}{3}, \frac{1}{2}\right)$
Z_4	$\left(\frac{1}{4}, \frac{1}{4}, \frac{1}{1}\right)$

A disadvantage of the the second and third metric is that the pairwise distance between all cells has to be determined before the training vectors can be generated. Thanks to heuristics like the one introduced by Edmond Chow [12] this is not as time consuming as it might seem. An advantage of the fourth and fifth metric is the comparatively small vector size.

C. Assuring a valid placement

A problem of all proposed metrics is that very similar vectors will not activate two adjacent neurons as desired, but exactly the same neuron. This leads to the generation of an invalid placement because the cells must be placed distinctly and are not allowed to overlap. The placement could be legalized in an additional step, but this would clearly increase the computational effort. An approach of making the vectors distinguishable by the addition of orthogonal data, which causes repulsion between them, also drastically increases the computational effort for the self-organizing map. Therefore, both approaches were rejected.

Instead, the self-organizing map was modified in a way that the activation of the same neuron by different vectors is already prevented during the training and thereby only valid placements are generated. Therefore, first of all the training of the self-organizing map was divided into training-cycles, where each training-cycle means the stimulation with all training vectors in a random succession. Furthermore, neurons that have already won during a training-cycle are blocked until the end of this cycle, so that they cannot win again. On the level of the neuronal model this means the connection between the winning neuron on the competition layer and the input layer is temporarily muted until the end of the training-cycle. Thereby, it cannot be activated again by a similar vector corresponding

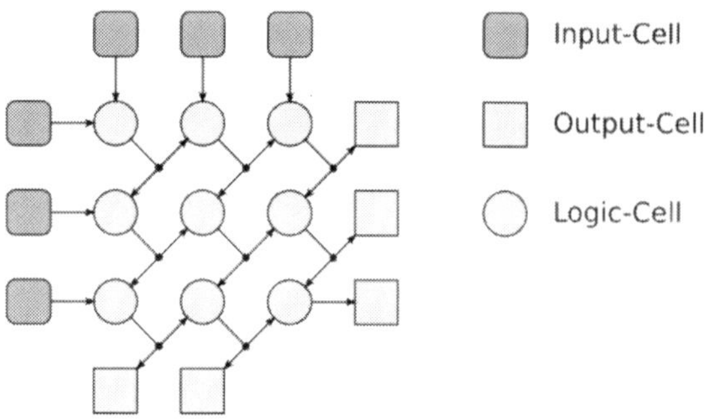

Figure 8. Synthetic, homogeneous graph of the size three

TABLE VI. Results for a synthetic, homogeneous 8 × 8 graph similar to Figure 8

Nr.	Metric	Channels	Path length
1	VPR	8	10.9 ns
2	membership	10	12.8 ns
3	linear distance	8	10.9 ns
4	hyperbolic distance	6	10.4 ns
5	I/O-distance	8	10.6 ns
6	hyperbolic I/O-distance	8	10.7 ns
7	hyperbolic distance	8	9.0 ns

to another cell. Instead, because the neighborhood influence between the neurons on the competition layer remains active, a similar vector will probably activate a neuron adjacent to the blocked one. All the blocked neurons are released at the beginning of every cycle. The mandatory competition between the vectors about the neurons on the competition layer is not suppressed by the blocking because of two reasons. First, because in every cycle the vectors are used in a random succession, a different vector has the chance to be the first one in each cycle. Second, because neurons that have been blocked are still influenced by their neighbors for the rest of a cycle, neurons may "attract" totally or marginally different vectors in the next cycle, depending on how much they have been influenced.

With this approach not only the generation of a valid placement is assured, but also the computational effort of the determination of the winning neuron is reduced. This is because there is no need to evaluate the distances between the input vector and the weight vectors of the blocked neurons, which cannot win anyway.

IV. Results

For a first analysis the proposed method was implemented prototypically in Python. The focus of this implementation lies in adaptivity and interchangeability of the different modules instead of a high computational performance. The software has been used to evaluate the five metrics for vector generation proposed in Section III. Therefore, synthetic, homogeneous netlists were placed by the self-organizing map and routed by VPR. Figure 8 shows a graph of the used netlist of the size three meaning 3×3 logic blocks plus input and output blocks.

Table VI shows the results for a similar graph of the size eight. The first line contains the results of VPR and should be considered as the reference. The lines two to six show the results of the different vectorization metrics for the self-organizing map. The result achieved with vectorization by net membership is worse than the reference solution of VPR both in terms of the channel width and the length of the critical path. The result achieved by linear distance is similar to the reference. The vectorization by hyperbolic distance produces a smaller minimal channel width than the reference (see line four). This placement is one of the ideal solutions for the given problem. To allow a fair comparison of the critical path's length the placement was routed again with the channel width achieved by VPR. The result is shown in line seven. The results for the I/O-distance based vector generation – with and without normalization – are shown in line six and seven. Both generate slightly better results than VPR, but the difference is in the margin of error. As can be seen the critical path of the reference placement generated by simulated annealing is about 21 percent longer than the one generated by the self-organizing map with vectorization by hyperbolic distance.

TABLE VII. Results for a synthetic, homogeneous 16 × 16 graph similar to Figure 8

Nr.	Metric	Channels	Path length
1	VPR	8	21.1 ns
2	membership	12	33.9 ns
3	linear distance	8	25.5 ns
4	hyperbolic distance	8	18.6 ns
5	I/O-distance	10	26.1 ns
6	hyperbolic I/O-distance	8	25.9 ns

TABLE VIII. Characteristics of the selected MCNC benchmarks

Nr.	Name	CLBs	Nets	Inputs	Outputs
1	e64	273	338	65	64
2	ex5p	1 064	1 072	8	63
3	apex4	1 261	1 270	9	18
4	misex3	1 397	1 411	14	14
5	alu4	1 522	1 536	14	8
6	seq	1 750	1 791	41	35
7	apex2	1 878	1 916	38	3
8	ex1010	4 598	4 608	10	10

Table VII shows the results for a graph of the size 16. These results and further tests with synthetic benchmarks have shown that the vectorization by hyperbolic distance creates the best results, often even ideal ones. It has to be mentioned that the large vector-size of this method has a high impact on the the computation time of the self-organizing map. If this poses a problem, then a vectorization method based on the I/O-distance should be considered. However, this work concentrates on the quality of the placement by selecting the hyperbolic distance method. The computational effort is handled by parallelization and utilizing the GPU.

To test the suitability of the self-organizing map for real world netlists a selection of MCNC benchmarks was used. Netlists with a global routing flag – often used for the clock signal – were not supported by the first prototypic implementation and therefore were not examined. Table VIII shows the selected benchmarks and their characteristics, namely the number of logic blocks (CLBs), nets, input and output pins.

In a first approach the MCNC benchmark netlists were placed by the self-organizing map and routed by VPR like

TABLE IX. Placement results for MCNC benchmarks generated by the self-organizing map (SOM) in comparison to the classical annealing with random initialization (VPR)

Nr.	Name	Critical Path		Min. Channels	
		VPR	SOM	VPR	SOM
1	e64	7.4 ns	10.5 ns	14	10
2	ex5p	10.4 ns	16.4 ns	20	36
3	apex4	10.1 ns	14.7 ns	22	42
4	misex3	8.8 ns	11.6 ns	18	48
5	alu4	11.0 ns	16.0 ns	16	48
6	seq	8.7 ns	15.5 ns	18	46
7	apex2	10.4 ns	22.6 ns	20	46
8	ex1010	17.1 ns	31.8 ns	18	72

TABLE X. Detailed placement results for the MCNC benchmark *e64* generated by the self-organizing map in comparison to the classical annealing with random initialization (VPR)

Nr.	Metric	Channels	Path length
1	VPR	14	7.4 ns
2	Membership	10	11.9 ns
3	Membership	14	11.7 ns
4	linear distance	10	9.5 ns
5	linear distance	14	9.5 ns
6	hyperbolic distance	10	10.5 ns
7	hyperbolic distance	14	10.2 ns

the synthetic benchmarks before. The results are shown in Table IX. It is obvious that the self-organizing map is not able to compete with the reference by any measure. The MCNC benchmarks (like real world applications) are not as structured as the previous synthetic examples. Because the self-organizing map only uses the structural information of the netlist and neither the critical path's length, nor the channel width is optimized directly, the sobering results concerning these two indicators are not surprising.

The only exception is how well the self-organizing map handles the *e64* netlist regarding the minimal channel width (see line one of Table IX). Because of this property, the detailed results of this particular netlist were analyzed and are shown in Table X. Even though the vectorization by liner distance surpasses the vectorization by hyperbolic distance in this special case, the latter method is kept up. The different results of the *e64* netlist are ascribed to its special structure and characteristics. The *e64* netlist has an unusually high I/O to CLB ratio, which leads to a full occupation of the surrounding I/O-cells, whereas the CLB-cells are used sparsely. In this special case the self-organizing map tends to scatter the logic over the whole plane (Figure 9), thereby optimizing the routability and channel width. The simulated annealing in contrast groups the logic in one part of the plane (Figure 10) because it primarily optimizes the length of the critical path.

Because of the formerly stated drawbacks in using the self-organizing map directly for the generation of the final placement, its suitability as an initial placement for the iterative algorithm simulated annealing was examined. The initial temperature of the simulated annealing process was reduced, so that only approximately the final 20 percent of the usual swapping steps are executed. By this it is assured that the generated initial placement is not "melted down" completely,

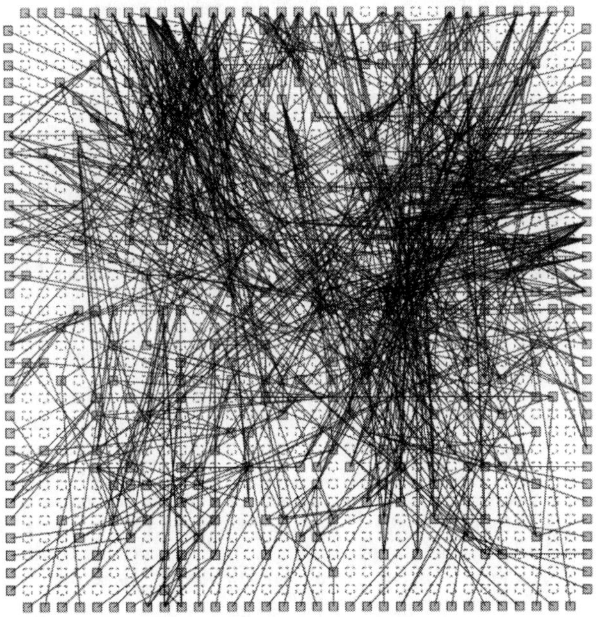

Figure 9. A placement generated with a self-organizing map for the *e64* netlist on a 33 × 33 CLB island-style architecture. Visualization by VPR

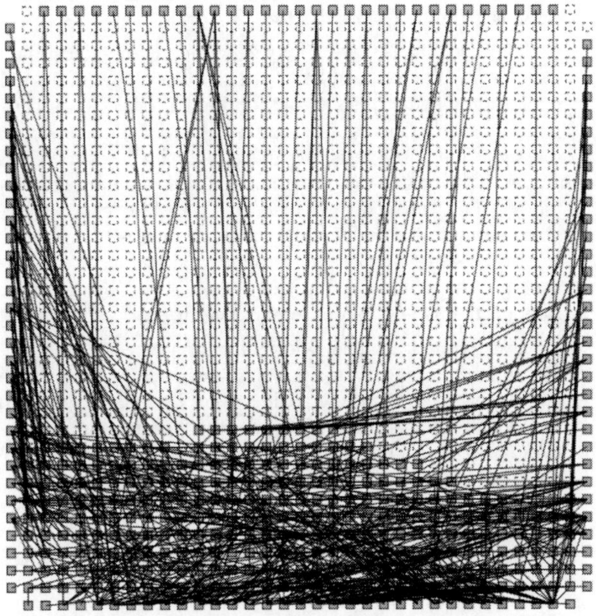

Figure 10. A placement generated with simulated annealing for the *e64* netlist on a 33 × 33 CLB island-style architecture. Visualization and placement by VPR

which would result in the loss of the structural information gained through the self-organizing map. Instead, it is optimized locally to improve the length of the critical path and the minimal channel width. For this series of measurements VPR was modified to allow the loading of an initial placement and used with a custom annealing schedule.

TABLE XI. Placement results for MCNC benchmarks generated by the self-organizing map (SOM) with additional low temperature annealing in comparison to the classical annealing with random initialization

Nr.	Name	Size	Channels	Critical Path Random	Critical Path SOM	Critical Path Relative	Min. Channels Random	Min. Channels SOM	Min. Channels Relative
1	e64	33 × 33	14	7.4 ns	5.9 ns	0.80	14	12	0.86
2	ex5p	33 × 33	22	10.4 ns	8.9 ns	0.86	20	22	1.10
3	apex4	36 × 36	22	10.1 ns	8.8 ns	0.87	22	20	0.91
4	misex3	38 × 38	18	8.8 ns	9.6 ns	1.09	18	16	0.89
5	alu4	40 × 40	16	11.0 ns	10.7 ns	0.97	16	16	1.00
6	seq	42 × 42	20	8.7 ns	8.2 ns	0.94	18	20	1.11
7	apex2	44 × 44	20	10.4 ns	10.4 ns	1.00	20	20	1.00
8	ex1010	68 × 68	18	17.1 ns	16.9 ns	0.99	18	16	0.89
Average						0,94			0,97

Table XI shows the results of placements for the formerly introduced MCNC benchmarks. Column two shows the name of the tested netlist, column three the size of the target architecture. The length of the critical path obtained by simulated annealing with random initialization – the reference – is shown in column five, the length of the critical path for simulated annealing with initialization by the self-organizing map in column six. Because the two approaches sometimes reach different minimal channel widths – as shown in column eight and nine – the larger channel width is used to determine the critical path's length, which is shown in column four. Column seven shows the length of the critical path produced by the initialization with the self-organizing map in relation to the reference (random initialization).

The benchmarks are arranged by ascending size. Statistically the results for the relative critical path's length for smaller netlists are better than those for bigger ones. This can be partially ascribed to the fact that in this series of measurements the same amount of training cycles was used for all netlists. The results for the *misex3* netlist are of special interest. Even though the proposed method needs a smaller channel width than the reference for the routing of this netlist, it is the only netlist for which the length of the critical path gets worse. On average, the critical path's length is reduced by six percent through the use of the self-organizing map.

The minimal channel width is also affected by the use of the self-organizing map. In four cases it is reduced by two and in three other cases it is increased by two. Note that the architecture demands an even channel width, so a change by two is in fact only one step. The relative results are shown only for the sake of completeness. On average, the minimal channel width is reduced by three percent through the use of the self-organizing map. Due to the small sample size and the formerly described distribution of the results the significance of this value is precarious.

V. PARALLELIZATION

The previous tests have shown that the sequential implementation of the self-organizing map is very slow, compared to simulated annealing. For this reason, the algorithm has been profiled to analyze the options to speedup its execution. In Table XII the profiling results of the unoptimized implementation of the self-organizing map for different sized netlists from the MCNC benchmark-set introduced above are summarized. It shows the relative computation times of the steps introduced above. Especially for larger netlists, the test and learning functions together consume almost all of the computation time. In this part of the work, the focus is on the test process because (with 73 percent on average) it consumes the highest amount of time. In the test process, the Euclidean distance between the stimulating vector and every neuron is determined. The neuron with the lowest distance is selected as winning neuron. The subfunction for the calculation of the distance consumes more than 99 percent of the test process (e.g., 368 seconds out of 369 seconds for the ex5p netlist). Based on these numbers, two levels of parallelism that could be exploited have been identified:

TABLE XII. Profiling results of the unoptimzed self-organizing map implementation

Netlist Name	Netlist Size	FPGA Size	Relative Computation Time Test	Learning	Others
net16	256	16 × 16	69.0 %	29.0 %	2.0 %
ex5p	1 064	33 × 33	73.9 %	25.8 %	0.3 %
ex1010	4 598	68 × 68	75.4 %	24.6 %	0.0 %
Average			72.8 %	26.5 %	0.7 %

1) **Vector-level:** The vector operation to determine the distance d between the stimulating vector $\vec{v}$ and a neuron's weight $\vec{w}$ as described in (6), assuming $\vec{v}$ and $\vec{w}$ have N elements.
2) **Map-level:** The calculation of all the distances and the selection of the lowest distance.

$$d = \sum_{i=0}^{N} (\vec{v}_i - \vec{w}_i)^2 \tag{6}$$

Implementations to exploit both these levels of parallelism have been developed and benchmarked. The corresponding results are presented in the following subsections.

A. Vector-level parallelization

In a first attempt, the parallelism of the vector operations was exploited to speedup the implementation of the self-organizing map. Therefore, two alternative, parallel implementations of the distance function used heavily in the test loop were created. One implementation is using the processor's *Streaming SIMD Extensions (SSE)* for vector operations, the other is delegating the vector operations to the GPU using OpenCL.

TABLE XIII. Time consumption of the parallel implementations of the distance function (6) for different vector sizes

	CPU	CPU SSE		GPU OpenCL	
Vector Size	Time	Time	Speedup	Time	Speedup
100 cells	27 µs	64 µs	0.4	170 µs	0.2
1 000 cells	200 µs	74 µs	2.7	300 µs	0.7
10 000 cells	2 000 µs	112 µs	17.9	400 µs	5.0
100 000 cells	23 ms	458 µs	50.2	454 µs	50.7
1 000 000 cells	238 ms	7 000 µs	34.0	669 µs	355.8

TABLE XIV. Configuration of the "desktop class" test-system

CPU	GPU
Intel® Core™2 Duo E8400	NVIDIA® GeForce® GTX 950
2 Cores	768 CUDA Cores
3 GHz Core Clock	1024 MHz Core Clock
6 MB Level 2 Cache	105.6 GB/s Memory Bandwidth
4 GB DDR2 RAM	2048 MB GDDR5 RAM

Table XIII shows the results of the parallel implementations for different vector sizes. The speedups are given as the ratios between the reference and the corresponding new approach as follows:

$$Speedup = \frac{Reference\ Time}{Benchmarked\ Time} \quad (7)$$

In this case these are the ratios between the calculation time of a sequential implementation on a CPU (reference time) and the parallel implementations on a CPU and GPU mentioned above (benchmarked times). For this benchmark a desktop computer with an "Intel® Core™2 Duo E8400" processor and a "NVIDIA® GeForce® GTX 950" GPU was used. The detailed configuration of the test-system is shown in Table XIV. In comparison to the unoptimized implementation, the SSE implementation breaks even between vector sizes of 100 and 1000 cells, whereas the GPU implementation breaks even between 1000 and 10000 cells. The SSE implementation and the GPU implementation break even at a vector size of 100000 cells. Even tough there are commercial FPGAs available with more than a million CLBs today, the netlists are typically partitioned to a smaller size before the placement and need much faster placement algorithms anyway. Further analysis has shown that the main problem of the tested OpenCL implementation lies in the low complexity of a single distance calculation. This causes a relatively large overhead for the memory transfer between host and GPU memory.

Based on these findings, an improved version of the prototypic, sequential implementation of the self-organizing map was created. It uses the CPUs SSE extensions for all vector operations. Table XV shows the computation times of both implementations of the self-organizing map for a subset of the netlists used in our previous work. The time is given for one training cycle, meaning the training of every vector. The overall speed of the training process was increased by a factor of up to 20. Especially the larger netlists benefit from the parallelization because the wider vectors give a better utilization of the SIMD-hardware. However, the simulated annealing algorithm of VPR is still about one hundred times faster than the proposed SSE implementation.

TABLE XV. Comparison of the computation times for one training cycle of the original implementation of the self-organizing map (SOM) and an improved version using SSE-accelerated vector operations

Netlist		FPGA	Computation Time		
Name	Size	Size	SOM CPU	SOM SSE	Speedup
net16	256	16 × 16	5 s	2 s	2.5
e64	273	33 × 33	23 s	7 s	3.3
ex5p	1 064	33 × 33	350 s	31 s	11.3
seq	1 750	42 × 42	1 476 s	95 s	15.5
ex1010	4 598	68 × 68	27 211 s	1 259 s	21.6

B. Map-level parallelization

To bridge this gap, the exploitation of map-level parallelism with OpenCL on a GPU is evaluated. The goal is to create bigger chunks of computational work and minimize the overhead for memory transfer between host and GPU. Ideally, the complete training loop takes place on the GPU, so that a memory transfer is only necessary after the vector generation and for the placement export. In Figure 11, a flowchart of the proposed implementation is presented. The management of the training data and the random selection of training vectors is still executed on the host CPU, but the rest of the training-cycle is executed on the GPU. Especially the comparatively large datastructure of the self-organizing map is kept in the GPU's memory over the complete training. The set of training vectors is kept in the GPU's memory as well, eliminating the need to copy the data from host- to device-memory for every training loop. This is achieved by transferring only the individual starting address of the vector to the kernel. Another approach could be to address the vectors by transferring an index. The computation on the GPU is done by three OpenCL kernels, which are described in the following:

1) Calculate Distances: The *Calculate Distances* kernel receives the map of weight vectors, the training vector and a map marking the already occupied positions by reference. The kernel is calculating the distance between every weight and the given training vector, storing the results in a two-dimensional map. It is rolled out in three dimensions, calculating each distance (6) in a workgroup (if large enough). Thereby, a fast workgrop-local buffer can be used to build the sum. If the vector size is larger than the workgroup-size, the partial sums of each workgroup are stored temporarily and summed up after synchronization. If the corresponding position of the kernel is marked as already occupied the distance is set to "MAXFLOAT", so that it will be ignored in the following reduction.

2) Find Lowest Distance: The *Find Lowest Distance* kernel receives the two-dimensional map of distances created by the *Calculate Distances* kernel by reference. It searches the map for the lowest distance and returns the corresponding position, as well as the distance. Again the reduction is done in workgroups, utilizing the fast local memory.

3) Learn Vector: The *Learn Vector* kernel – like the *Calculate Distances* kernel – receives the map of weight vectors, the training vector and a map marking the already occupied positions by reference. Additionally, it receives the position of the previously determined minimal distance weight (the winning position). The kernel modifies the weights in the map according to their distance to the winning position and marks

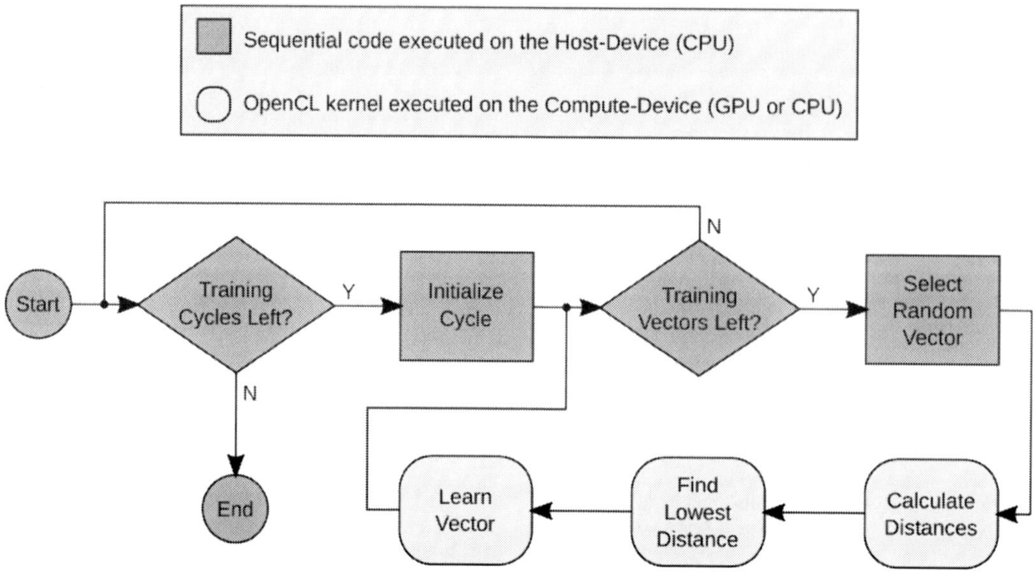

Figure 11. Flowchart of a training-cycle of the self-organizing map using OpenCL

the winning position itself as occupied in the corresponding map. There is no explicit grouping into workgroups and no local memory is used because all operations happen independently of each other and the results have to be stored in the global memory.

To benchmark this implementation two test-systems have been used. The first system is the "desktop class" computer that has already been used to benchmark the vector-level parallelization approach (see Table XIV). The second system is a "workstation class" system. Its detailed configuration is shown in Table XVI.

The benchmark results of the "desktop class" computer are presented in Table XVII. They compare the computation times of the high-level parallelization approach (GPU OpenCL) with the low-level approach (CPU SSE) introduced above. The durations are given for a complete placement-generation from reading the netlist over ten full training-cycles to writing the generated placement into a file. The speedup is given as the ratio between the two approaches (7). It is shown that even the placement of small netlists can be accelerated even further compared to the already improved SSE implementation. Netlists are placed up to 34 times faster on the GPU than on the CPU's SIMD-hardware. Generally, the speedup is higher for larger netlists. The only exception is the largest netlist in the benchmark (ex1010), which is experiencing the worst gain of all. This is because its vector size supersedes the maximal workgroup-size of the GPU and therefore a partially sequential reduction scheme is used. Compared to the original, sequential implementation the speedup is about 200 on average. For the seq netlist the speedup is even 310.

The benchmark results of the "workstation class" computer are presented in Table XVIII, it contains two additional (even larger) netlists. Furthermore, the ability of OpenCL to target not only GPUs, but also multicore CPUs has been evaluated. Obviously the modern workstation CPU is considerably faster than the comparatively older desktop CPU. However, the work-

TABLE XVI. Configuration of the "workstation class" test-system

CPU	GPU
Intel® Xeon® E3-1245 v5	AMD® RADEON™ RX 480
4 Cores	36 Compute Units
8 Threads	2304 Stream Processors
3.5 GHz Core Clock	1120 MHz Core Clock
8 MB SmartCache	224 GB/s Memory Bandwidth
64 GB DDR4 RAM	8 GB GDDR5 RAM

TABLE XVII. Benchmark results of the high-level parallelization using OpenCL on a "desktop class" system described in Table XIV

Netlist Name	FPGA Size	CPU SSE Time	GPU OpenCL Time	GPU OpenCL Speedup
e64	33 × 33	84 s	5 s	16
ex5p	34 × 34	341 s	23 s	15
apex4	36 × 36	449 s	28 s	16
misex3	38 × 38	570 s	33 s	17
alu4	40 × 40	820 s	38 s	22
seq	43 × 43	958 s	47 s	20
apex2	44 × 44	1 777 s	52 s	34
ex1010	68 × 68	9 100 s	993 s	9

station GPUs performance is comparably weak on average, especially considering that its rated peak performance is more than three times higher than the peek performance of the desktop GPU (5.8 TFLOPS versus 1.7 TFLOPS). Additional tests with other algorithms have underpinned the assumption that the GPU is not unfolding its full potential in the workstation. It has to be evaluated if this is due to driver- or compatibility-problems. Also, the performance of the OpenCL code executed on the CPU is underwhelming. Even though it uses all eight cores of the CPU to full capacity, it is more than thirty times slower than the single threaded SSE implementation on the same hardware.

TABLE XVIII. Benchmark results of the high-level parallelization using OpenCL on a "workstation class" system described in Table XVI

Netlist	FPGA	CPU SSE	GPU OpenCL		CPU OpenCL	
Name	Size	Time	Time	Speedup	Time	Speedup
e64	33 × 33	25 s	6 s	4.0	387 s	0.063
ex5p	34 × 34	121 s	27 s	4.5	4 208 s	0.029
apex4	36 × 36	150 s	32 s	4.7	5 160 s	0.029
misex3	38 × 38	193 s	54 s	3.6	6 895 s	0.028
alu4	40 × 40	297 s	58 s	5.1	7 662 s	0.039
seq	43 × 43	322 s	48 s	6.7	10 159 s	0.032
apex2	44 × 44	364 s	50 s	7.3	11 206 s	0.032
ex1010	68 × 68	3 269 s	313 s	10.4	251 654 s	0.013
s38417	81 × 81	8 086 s	554 s	14.6	513 873 s	0.016
clma	93 × 93	17 004 s	1 486 s	11.4	2 068 893 s	0.008

VI. Conclusion and Future Work

In this work, an approach to improve the results of netlist placement for FPGAs with a self-organizing map has been presented. Different methods to generate the training vectors have been compared based on synthetic benchmarks. For a set of 8 MCNC benchmarks it has been shown that the length of the critical path can be reduced by 6 percent on average. The cost is a high computational effort for the training of the self-organizing map.

To accelerate the self-organizing map, two parallelization approaches have been introduced and benchmarked. A low-level approach – exploiting the SSE units of the CPU – was shown to accelerate the self-organizing map up to twentyfold. It has been shown that the low-level approach is not suited to be executed on a GPU because the chunks of work are too small, resulting in a high overhead for memory transfer. For this reason a high-level parallelization approach – conveying the complete training loop to the GPU – has been introduced. It has been shown that it again accelerates the execution up to more than thirtyfold. On average, the OpenCL implementation on the GPU is about 200 times faster than the original sequential implementation. The results of OpenCL on a CPU are not satisfying.

In future work the speed of the accelerated self-organizing map should be compared directly to established placement tools. At this point it is expected that the self-organizing map is still perceptibly slower than for example VPR. If this poses a problem, the vector size can be reduced by using the I/O-distance metric for the vector generation. As has been covered by Amagasaki et al. [11], this should improve the speed while slightly reducing the quality.

References

[1] T. Bostelmann and S. Sawitzki, "Improving the performance of a SOM-based FPGA-placement-algorithm using SIMD-hardware," in The Ninth International Conference on Advances in Circuits, Electronics and Micro-electronics (CENICS), July 2016, pp. 13–15.

[2] T. Bostelmann and S. Sawitzki, "Improving FPGA placement with a self-organizing map," in International Conference on Reconfigurable Computing and FPGAs (ReConFig), Dec 2013, pp. 1–6.

[3] S. Kirkpatrick, C. D. Gelatt, and M. P. Vecchi, "Optimization by simulated annealing," Science, vol. 220, no. 4598, May 1983, pp. 671–680.

[4] L. Ingber, "Adaptive simulated annealing (ASA): Lessons learned," Control and Cybernetics, vol. 25, no. 1, 1996, pp. 33–54.

[5] M. M. Atiqullah, "An efficient simple cooling schedule for simulated annealing," in International Conference on Computational Science and Its Applications (ICCSA). Springer, 2004, pp. 396–404.

[6] J. Lam and J.-M. Delosme, "Performance of a new annealing schedule," in Design Automation Conference (DAC), 1988, pp. 306–311.

[7] P. Banerjee, S. Bhattacharjee, S. Sur-Kolay, S. Das, and S. C. Nandy, "Fast FPGA placement using space-filling curve," in International Conference on Field Programmable Logic and Applications (FPL). IEEE, 2005, pp. 415–420.

[8] T. Kohonen, Self-Organizing Maps. Springer, 1995.

[9] S. Yang, "Logic synthesis and optimization benchmarks user guide version 3.0," Microelectronics Center of North Carolina, Tech. Rep., 1991.

[10] V. Betz and J. Rose, "VPR: A new packing, placement and routing tool for FPGA research," in International Conference on Field Programmable Logic and Applications (FPL). Springer, 1997, pp. 213–222.

[11] M. Amagasaki, M. Iida, M. Kuga, and T. Sueyoshi, "FPGA placement based on self-organizing maps," International Journal of Innovative Computing, Information and Control, vol. 11, no. 6, 2015, pp. 2001–2012.

[12] E. Chow, "A graph search heuristic for shortest distance paths," Lawrence Livermore National Laboratory, Tech. Rep., 2005.

International Journal on Advances in Systems and Measurements, vol 10 no 1 & 2, year 2017, http://www.iariajournals.org/systems_and_measurements/

PLD as a new technology for the fabrication of pH glass based planar electrochemical sensors

Kristina Ahlborn, Frank Gerlach, Winfried Vonau
Kurt-Schwabe-Institut für Mess- und Sensortechnik e.V. Meinsberg (KSI)
Waldheim, Germany
info@ksi-meinsberg.de

Abstract—**Traditionally sensitive silicate membranes for pH electrodes are fabricated by glassblowers. Recently, because of a more effective fabrication in certain cases, also so-called blowing machines are in use. In this way neither miniaturization nor a planar arrangement of the sensors can be realized. Pulsed laser deposition (PLD) could provide ideal conditions to reduce the above-mentioned drawbacks. In this contribution, the first results of using this technology for the fabrication of planar glass based electrochemical pH sensors are demonstrated, whereby the characterization of the amorphous silicate glass before and after the PLD process is in the focus of this article.**

***Keywords-** electrochemical sensor; pulsed laser deposition; planarity; sensor miniaturization; thin film; pH measurement; SEM; XPS; µ-RFA; EIS.*

I. INTRODUCTION

Sensitive membranes are essential functional components of potentiometric chemo sensors. In this respect, according to Figure 1, a distinction is made between solid-based and liquid membranes.

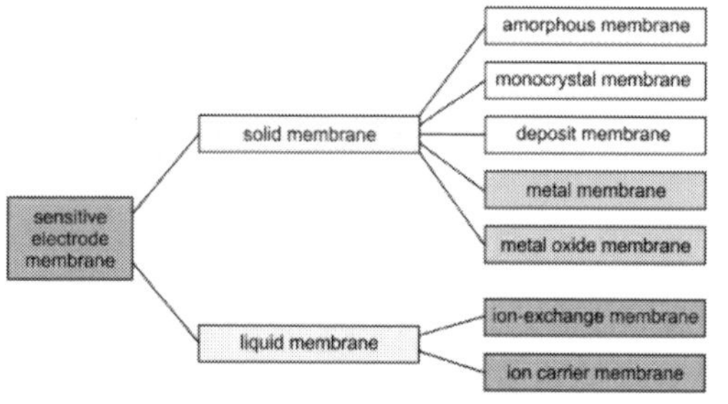

Figure 1. Classification of membrane materials for electrochemical sensors

Amorphous glass materials, which can be realized in different ways [1, 2], play a significant role for the fabrication of solid membranes. The reason is that especially the pH determination, which is one of the analyses performed most frequently worldwide, is carried out with electrochemical electrodes based on such membranes according to standards [3]. The membrane materials used here are silicate glasses with high ionic conductivity, which are mainly achieved by using alkaline as well as alkaline earth metal oxides, changing the silicate glass network [4] like it is shown in Figure 2.

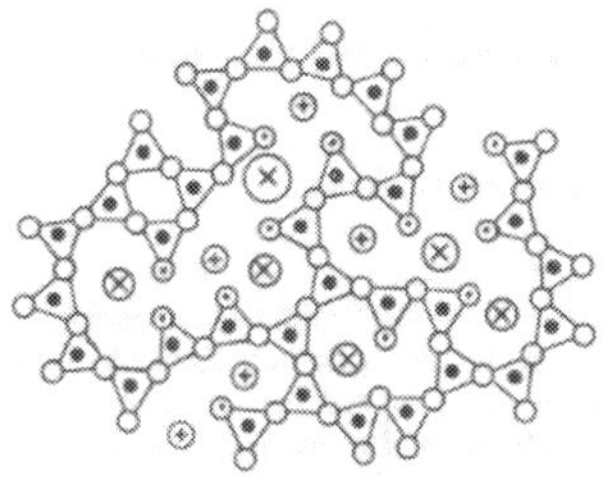

Figure 2. Two-dimensional structure of a silicate glass with network changing components
• Si, o oxygen bridge, ⊖ separate oxygen, ⊗ network changing component, ⊕ cation

Silica based electrode glasses, as a rule, are generated by melting their basic materials in covered platinum crucibles for several hours at temperatures > 1300 °C. For the further processing by the glassblower it is useful to outpour the liquid glass material, e.g., in a graphite flume. In this way, rods of the special glass are obtained. From these, glassblowers for the most parts produce basket or dome-shaped conventional pH electrodes in quantities of several million pieces per year. They contain a buffer solution and an electrochemical reference system (as a rule an electrode of 2nd kind) in its interiors. Modifying the glass composition makes it possible to realize similarly constructed silicate glass based electrodes with sensitivities for a number of other cations, mainly of metals of the first group of the periodic table [5].

Beside the above mentioned sensors, whose functionality is based on ionic conductivity, there are also probes with electron conducting amorphous glass membrane materials. These include redox glass [6] and chalcogenide glass electrodes [7]. For both types of electrodes the selection of an optimal internal reference system is relatively simple. As a result of the predominant electron conductivity of the sensitive membrane materials a direct contact of the special glasses with a (noble) metal is appropriate.

Therefore, liquid system components are not applicable for chemo sensors based on such materials. From constructional point of view, on the one hand, it is possible to fabricate compact electrodes by sticking a wire directly on the surface of the functional amorphous body, e.g., using a conductive varnish (see Figure 3); on the other hand, it is also possible to form a thin metal coating directly on the electron conducting glass by electro-plating (see Figure 4).

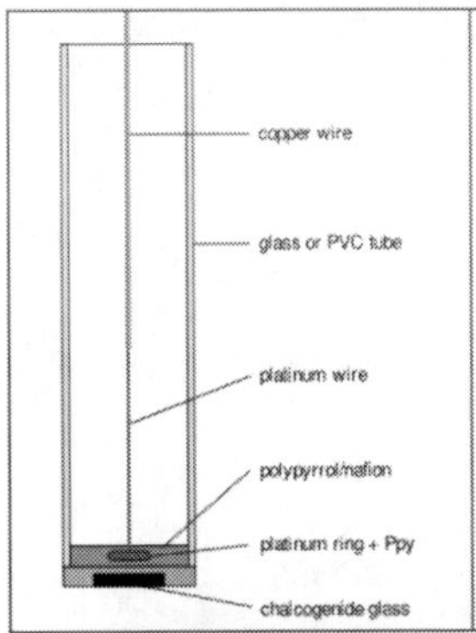

Figure 3. Schematic drawing of a chalcogenide glass electrode [8]

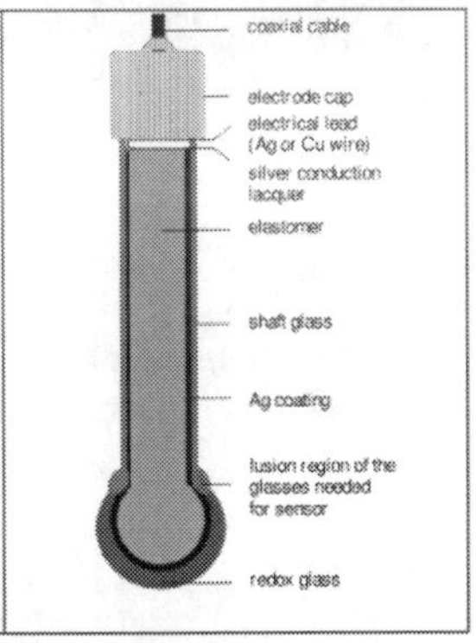

Figure 4. Schematic drawing of a redox glass electrode [9]

Also, for silicate glass based cation selective electrodes it is an interesting task to replace the common liquid system components by solids due to the purpose of their application. The functionality causing ionic conductivity of siliceous pH- but also pLi-, pNa or pK-glasses [10] requires an interlayer with mixed electrical properties on the reverse side of the sensitive membrane. A transition from an ionic conducting material to an electronic conductor (e.g., metal) may lead to a so-called blocked interface and consequently to an unfavorable measurement behavior [11].

In the past, several suggestions were made to realize such interlayers. In the context of the investigations presented here, the possibility to form thin layers of zinc oxide or titanium oxide between sensitive glass and a noble metal should be mentioned [12]. Previous work on all solid state glass electrodes was concerned with sensors fabricated with precision manufacturing techniques and screen printing (see Figure 5). Here, a clear stabilization of the half-cell potentials over the time could be obtained compared to a direct metal contacting [13, 14, 15].

PLD as a preparation method for sensors used in electrolyte containing liquids has still not become widespread. Today the PLD technology is particularly used for the deposition of diamond-like carbon layers (DSL) in order to improve the surface properties of highly stressed tools and components [16]. For the application in optoelectronics and chemical sensors, chalcogenide films were prepared by pulse laser deposition [17, 18, 19]. In the following it is reported on investigations using PLD as fabrication technology to realize planar all solid state pH glass electrodes according to a layer design described above. Beside the realization of an adherent metallic basic electrode on a substrate, special attention will be focused on the stoichiometric deposition of the functional sensor material from a prefabricated glass target by laser ablation. There should be no material loss during the PLD process as described in literature, e.g., for the synthesis of bio glass thin films [20].

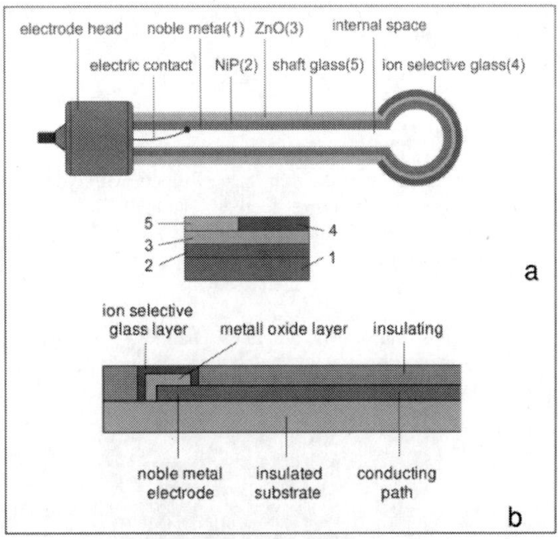

Figure 5. All solid state pH glass electrodes based on ZnO as interlayer
a fabricated in fine and glass mechanics according to [14]
b fabricated in thick film technology according to [15]

In Section II, the fabrication of the glass targets, the PLD process for the glass layer deposition and the characterization of these layers are described. Results of scanning electron microscope investigations, micro-X-ray fluorescence analysis, X-ray photoelectron spectroscopy and electrochemical measurements are presented in Section III.

II. EXPERIMENTAL

A. *Fabrication of the glass targets*

The targets of the sensitive pH glasses for the PLD process are obtained by pouring the molten glass in a preheated graphite mold according to Figure 6a. This manufacturing method delivers homogeneous and also amorphous target materials with defined geometries. According to Figure 6b, the glass cylinders were fabricated and singularized in discs with a thickness of 5 mm by means of a precision saw (Accutom-50, Fa. Struers GmbH, Willich, Germany). To improve the mechanical stability the glass rods were embedded in an epoxy resin and fixed on the target holder for the PLD process (Figure 6c).

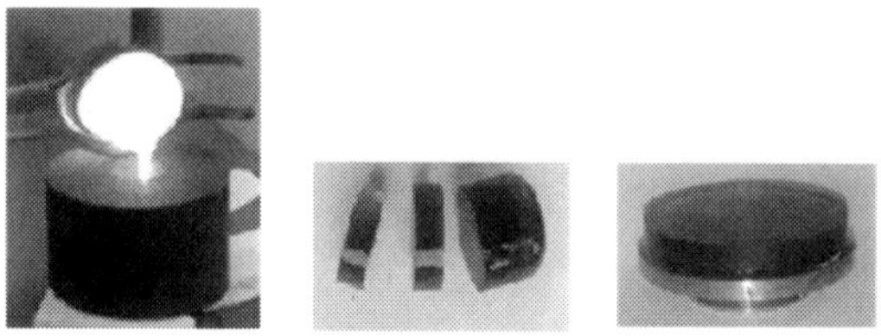

a) Pouring of molten glass in a graphite mold | b) Targets of pH glass | c) pH glass target fixed on target holder

Figure 6. Fabrication of the glass targets

B. PLD process

The preparation of the thin sensory functional layers was carried out by sputtering methods and PLD. For this purpose, a combined coating system CREAMET 500 PLD S2 (Creavac Vacuum Coating Technology GmbH, Dresden, Germany) was used, which provides both deposition processes (see Figures 7 and 8). Furthermore, a simultaneous substrate and mask handling is possible without an interruption of the vacuum during the coating process.

Figure 7. Combined coating system with PLD (1) and sputter (2) chamber

With integrated substrate handler and mask change system, two sputter targets, six PLD targets and altogether five changeable masks can be used and combined for the process.

As substrates pre-cleaned glass plates consisting of soda-lime glass with a size of 50 mm x 15 mm and a thickness of 1 mm were used. They were pretreated with the initial plasma process at a chamber pressure of 3.0×10^{-2} mbar under an argon atmosphere. As chamber pressure for the following sputtering processes of the adhesive layer (Ti) and the electrical conducting noble metal electrode (Au or Pt) a value of 7.0×10^{-3} mbar was used.

Figure 8a. Transfer device with mask and substrate handler

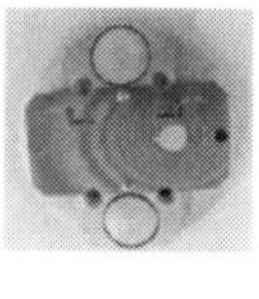

Figure 8b. Substrate holder with changeable mask

After finishing the sputtering processes the coated substrates were removed and the masks were changed in a so-called „Load-Lock-Box". Prepared in this way, the substrates were transferred into the PLD coating chamber using a carrier and the PLD process was started.

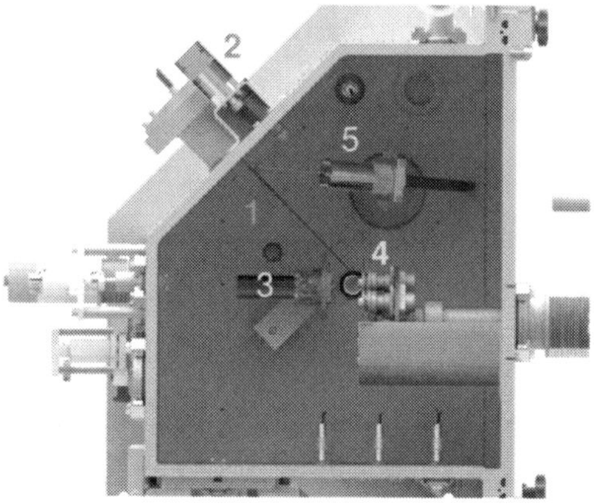

Figure 9. Construction of the PLD chamber

1 laser beam (KrF 248 nm) 2 laser power meter
3 substrate holder 4 target holder
5 ion source

The deposition of the thin pH glass films was conducted by a KrF excimer laser source (ComPexPro 110, Coherent LaserSystems GmbH & Co. KG., Göttingen, Germany) using a wave length of 248 nm, a fluence of 5.6 J/cm^2 at pulse lengths of 20 ns and a pulse frequency of 10 Hz. The determination of the laser power before and after the coating process in connection with a periodical cleaning of the entry window ensured long-term stable and reproducible basic conditions. The PLD process was carried out at a chamber pressure of 3.1×10^{-7} mbar in a N_2 atmosphere. The substrate was kept at room temperature. As ablation time of the sensitive layers a period from 10 to 30 minutes was selected. The substrates were positioned perpendicular to the plasma (On-Axis-PLD) (Figure 9).

C. *Characterization*

Physical Characterization

The energy dispersive micro-X-ray fluorescence analysis (µ-RFA) system M4 Tornado (Bruker Nano GmbH, Berlin, Germany) was used for the position-sensitive chemical elemental analysis. It allows the analysis of large and inhomogeneous samples as well as smallest particles fast and at low vacuum under environmental conditions.

In order to obtain information on the morphology, the surfaces of the prepared *pH glass thin films* were examined using the scanning electron microscope Helios 660 (FEI, Eindhoven, Netherlands).

X-ray photoelectron spectroscopic (XPS) data were acquired with the system SAGE HR 100 Compact High Resolution (company SPECS Surface Nano Analyses GmbH, Berlin, Germany) using non-monochromatised $Mg_{K\alpha}$ radiation (hv=1253.6 eV) with 12.5 kV and 250 W beam settings at a pressure of $2x10^{-8}$ hPa in the analysis chamber. With XPS it is possible to determine the chemical composition of the uppermost atomic layer of a material surface, because low beam energy (12.5 kV) is applied. Other radiographically methods (e.g., like µ-RFA) require beam energies up to 50 kV; elements from the volume will also be detected.

In addition to the described usage of µ-RFA and XPS, which allow statements about bulk properties of the target materials and adsorptive contaminations as well as surface effects, it is also possible to use energy dispersive X-ray analysis (EDX) and x-ray diffraction (XRD) as further radiographically research methods. Their application by means of the systems QUANTAX 400 D on FEI Helios 660 with two XFlash® 6 detectors (Bruker Nano GmbH, Berlin, Germany) (EDX) and D8 Discover High-Resolution Diffractometer (Bruker AXS GmbH, Karlsruhe, Germany) (XRD) show that amorphous sensor glass membranes can be realized using PLD as thin film production method.

Electrochemical Characterization

Electrochemical impedance spectroscopy (EIS) is an approved method for the characterization of resistance changes of systems with ion-sensitive glass membranes even for high-impedance and easily polarizable systems, which are present in pH glass electrodes.

In [21], EIS investigations on glass-metal transitions were carried out. Vonau et al. [22] used this method in combination with concentration analysis studies to describe the change in the pH properties of traditionally produced pH glass electrodes as a function of the duration of the application and the temperature and to elucidate their causes. Impedance spectroscopic methods were used to demonstrate the successful deposition of a glass layer by means of PLD technology on a sensor structure.

On the basis of the determined impedance values (frequency-dependent alternating-current resistors), the electrical conductivities of the PLD thin films could be estimated.

The impedance spectra were recorded using a measurement system Gamry Interface 1000 (Gamry Instruments Inc., Warminster, USA) in different buffer solutions according to the suggestions of the National Bureau of Standards (NBS) and of Thiel, Schulz and Coch (TSC). Potentiometric measurements were carried out using the PC Laboratory Multi-Parameter System LM 2000 (Sensortechnik Meinsberg GmbH, Waldheim, Germany) to evaluate the electrochemical behavior depending on the pH value.

III. RESULTS

A. *Micro-X-ray fluorescence analysis (µ-RFA)*

The results of µ-RFA demonstrate that the pH glass targets used for PLD possess a good homogeneity (see Figure 10).

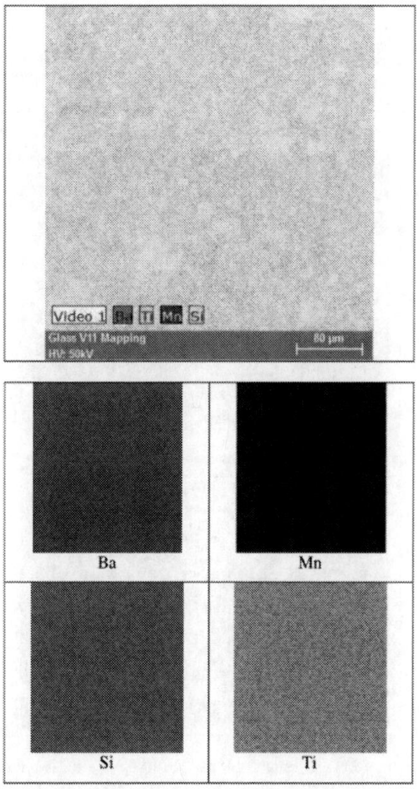

Figure 10. Element mapping of a PLD-based pH glass thin film

Element mappings exhibit a uniform distribution of the elements over the entire analyzed surface; no pronounced defects or areas with an accumulation of an element were detected. This ensures - compared to conventional glass electrodes made by a glassblower - identical conditions of the sensor membrane concerning the interface between measuring solution and electrode surface.

Subject of the investigations was the layering structure of the new pH thin film sensor according to Figure 11, consisting of a substrate (laboratory glass or alumina) with a sputtered gold basic electrode and a sensitive pH glass layer deposited by PLD. Finally, an isolation epoxy layer was applied.

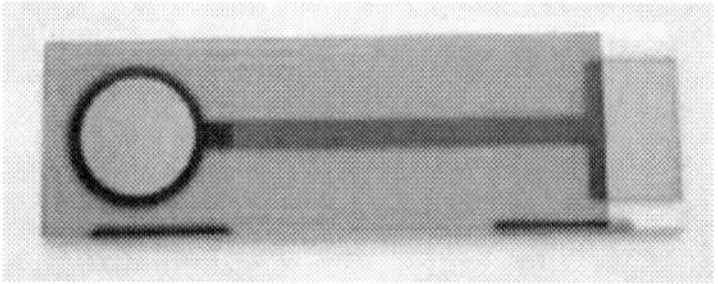

Figure 11: pH thin film electrode

Consequently, the possible presence of gold on the sensor surface will be an indicator for a defect in the PLD based pH glass thin film.

B. Scanning electron microscopy (SEM)

Figures 12 and 13 show SEM images of two different pH glass membranes, which were deposited by PLD process on glass substrates with a sputtered gold basic electrode on it.

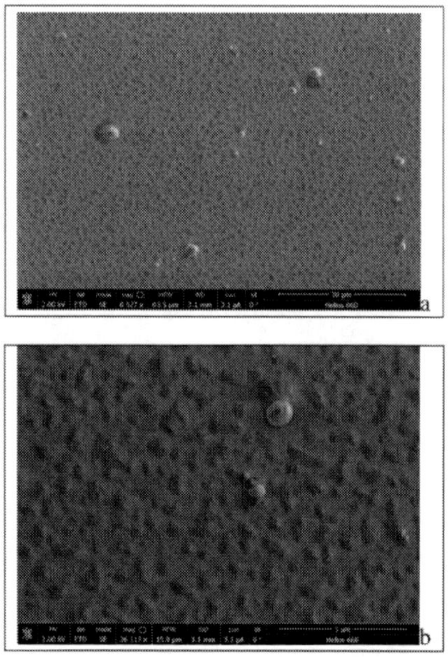

Figure 12. SEM images of Li-pH glass membrane manufactured by PLD Magnification. 6527x (a) and 26113x (b)

As it is to be seen, there are no holes and cracks and only a few droplets on the surface of the thin film.

Small anomalies are to be found specifically in Figure 15 for a Li-containing pH glass. The results of up to date XRD measurements - not presented in this article - suggest that there are no crystallites or areas of segregation.

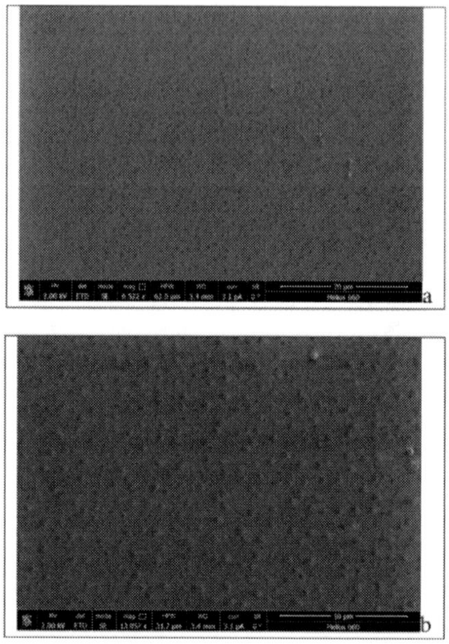

Figure 13. SEM images of a high-temperature pH glass membrane manufactured by PLD - Magnification. 6522x (a) and 13057x (b)

C. X-ray photoelectron spectroscopy (XPS)

Both - the used glass targets and the fabricated PLD based pH glass thin films - were investigated by means of XPS.

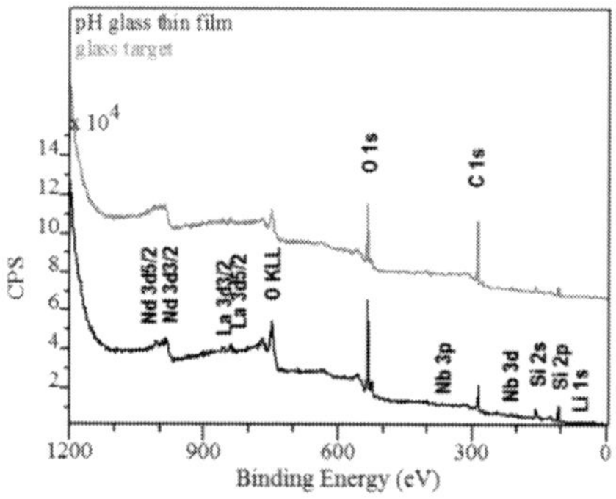

Figure 14. Comparative presentation of XPS spectra from a glass target and a pH glass thin film obtained from this target by PLD

Overview spectra and spectra of the single elements in regions of their highest sensitivity were recorded.

In an exemplary manner, Figure 14 demonstrates a comparative presentation of the overview spectrum from a glass target and of a glass thin film deposited from this source by PLD. These spectra showed no differences in the chemical composition. In addition, a determination of the gold content on the surface of the pH thin film sensors was carried out (see Figure 15). There are no peaks at the typical positions for binding energies of gold to be found in the spectra that would indicate a presence of gold on the surface. This suggests that there are no holes in the thin pH sensitive glass and that this layer is tight.

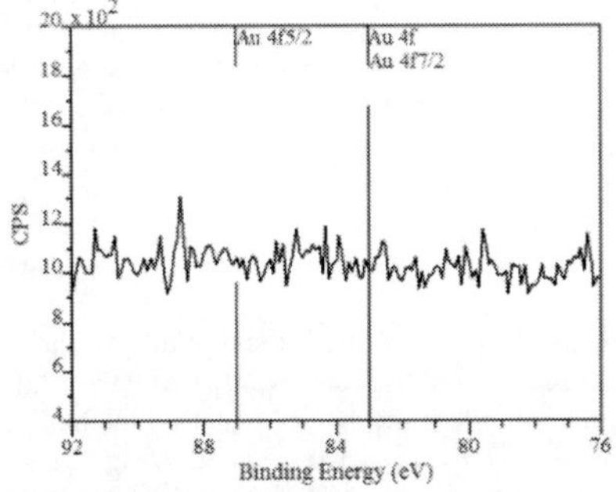

Figure 15. XPS spectrum recorded on a PLD based glass thin film, region of the highest sensitivity for gold

D. XRD

The recording of diffractograms by means of two-dimensional X-Ray diffraction (XRD)[2] is an appropriate tool for the characterization of glass based thin films. Using a High-Resolution Diffractometer with a general area detection diffraction system (GADDS), the detection limit of crystalline amounts can be reduced into a sub-percentage range. The X-Ray diffraction patterns of the PLD films in Figure 16 show significant first sharp diffraction peak, even in sub-µm thicknesses.

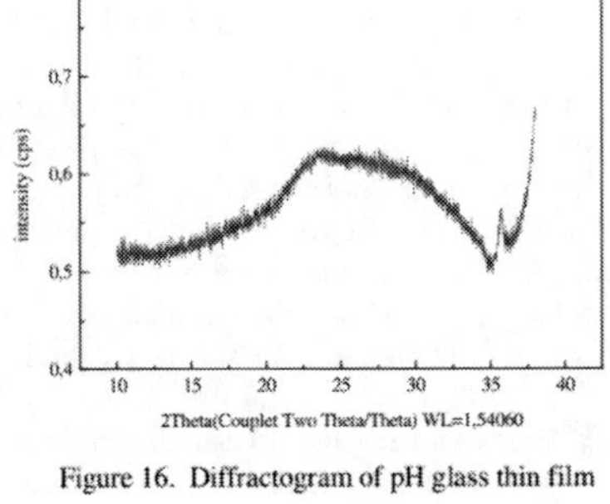

Figure 16. Diffractogram of pH glass thin film

E. Electrochemical Characterization

The investigations concerning the electrochemical behavior were carried out in NBS and TSC pH-buffer solutions at 25 °C [23].

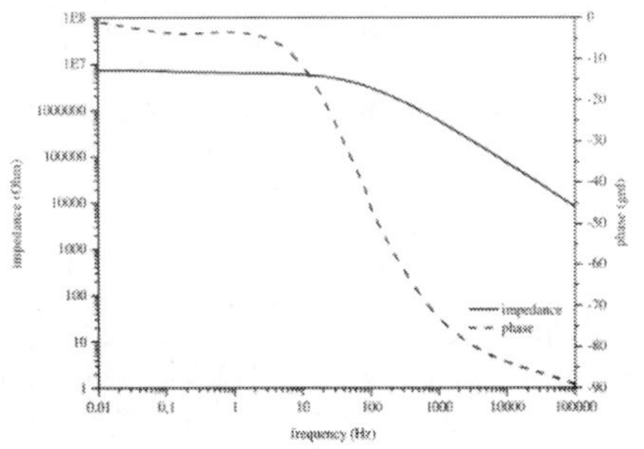

a) pH glass electrode (conventional)

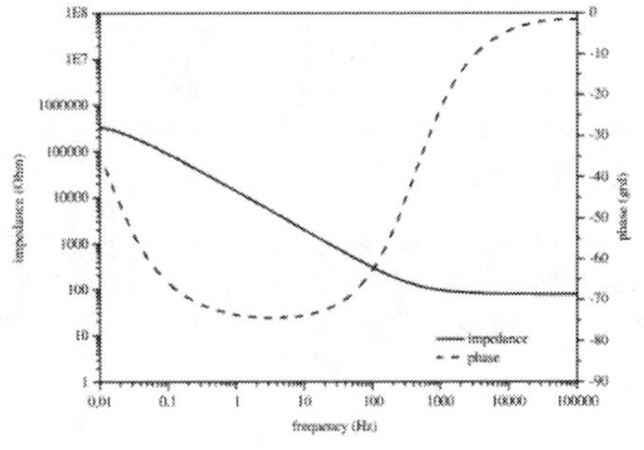

b) gold electrode

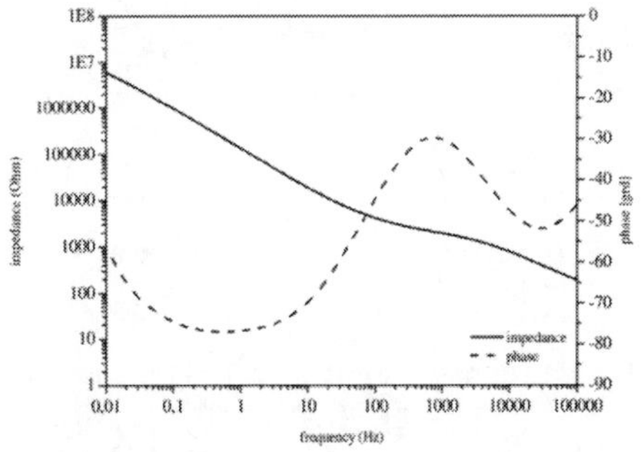

c) PLD based glass membrane

Figure 17. Impedance spectra in a NBS-buffer solution (pH=6.86)

EIS measurements

For EIS measurements in NBS-buffer pH=6.86 (Figure 17) a three electrode arrangement was used, consisting of a working electrode (a traditional glass electrode, a PLD glass membrane electrode with the same glass composition or a gold basic electrode), a KCl-saturated silver chloride reference electrode and a platinum sheet as counter electrode.

The resulting Bode-Plots in the diagrams look quite different. As expected, the impedance of the traditional glass electrode (Figure 17a) is significantly higher than that of the gold electrode (Figure 17b) due to the high glass resistance.

The impedance of the PLD glass membrane is lower than that of the conventional glass electrode – because of the lower thickness – but even higher than that of the gold electrode. This gives an indication, that the PLD glass membrane was deposited tightly and without holes. Nevertheless, the phase characteristic in Figure 15c is not fully understood yet.

pH measurement

Previous studies, as already mentioned above, were mainly carried out to adapt PLD technology for coating planar metallized glass substrates with ion conducting selective glass films. Only a few electrodes were tested for pH-measurements until now.

Figure 18 shows the pH dependence of one of the first PLD electrodes in TSC buffer solutions, measured at 25 °C versus an $Ag/AgCl//KCl_{sat.}$-electrode as a reference electrode.

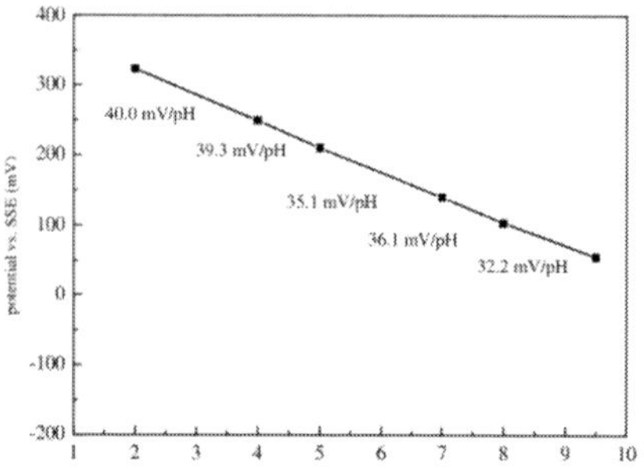

Figure 18. Potential measurement with thin-film pH glass electrode in TSC-buffer solutions

Actually, the PLD glass electrodes do not demonstrate the electrochemical sensitivity of the conventional glass electrodes filled with electrolytic solutions. Here, it could already be shown that PLD based pH glass layers in direct metal contact deliver sensor sensitivities of approximately - 32 mV/pH to 40 mV/pH at 25 °C.

Currently, it is not ensured that a stoichiometric deposition of the functional pH glass takes place in the PLD process. Results of element determination in the deposited thin films by inductively coupled plasma optical emission spectrometry (ICP-OES) and flame photometry suggest that there are losses especially in the case of the alkaline content. If this will be confirmed by further investigations, an adjustment of the glass compositions is absolutely necessary, because changes in the glass composition cause a reduction of pH sensitivity.

Drift behavior and long-term stability have to be optimized for the reasons outlined above by forthcoming integration of interlayers. In case of a positive outcome of the development with respect to resolution, repeatability and accuracy, a realization of miniaturized planar all solid state glass electrodes with properties comparable to at the moment widely used sensor types can be expected. Electrodes with layers prepared by PLD technology should deliver measurement signals with a higher repeatability. This is due to the fact that this manufacturing process provides a better reproducibility of the thicknesses of the deposits.

For the fabrication of corresponding pH glass electrodes with constant stable electrode potentials and electrode functions following the Nernst equation the realization of an additional semi- or mixed conducting interlayer (for example zinc oxide [13]) by the same technology is necessary [24]. This will be the subject of future projects.

IV. CONCLUSIONS AND OUTLOOK

In the present contribution, PLD technology is introduced as a new method for the deposition of sensitive glass membranes with high variability in the choice of the glass composition. Analyzing results and first electrochemical applications of the glass thin film electrodes are described.

Homogeneity and leak-tightness of thin glass films fabricated in such way could be demonstrated by µ-RFA and XPS analyses. Due to the low thickness of the glass membrane planar PLD based pH sensors possess clearly smaller electrode resistances compared to those obtained by glass blowing and screen printing. This fact, as well as the possibility to deposit the sensitive membranes on different sensor substrate materials (glass, ceramics) offer a variety of applications, e.g., in the area of cell research. Here and in a lot of biomedical and biotechnological applications, the transparency of glass is an important progress.

It should be also mentioned that the previously established thin film method for the fabrication of chemo sensors (CHEMFETs) is mainly based on CMOS technology. This requires high investment and running costs and can be introduced economically only if products with identical composition and design are needed in large quantities. The described sensor fabrication by means of PLD allows, amongst others, to abstain completely from using photolithographic processes and additional encapsulation steps with simultaneous cost-efficiency also for small and medium quantities. The sensors described in this contribution work according to the potentiometric principle contrary to CHEMFETs. Thus, future appliers can still use their measurement devices for conventional sensors.

Furthermore, in the future it should be possible to fabricate glass based multi sensors by means of the described method. This could be the case for planar probes to determine other monovalent cations than H^+. For this purpose, it will be necessary to place several targets in the vacuum chamber and to vary the deposition conditions. Under such circumstances, it will be also possible to realize potentiometric multi sensors with several selective membranes consisting not only of glasses. Realizable seems a combination of electrode glasses with defined metal oxide layers with analytical electrode function in solutions, such as vanadium oxide [25, 26].

ACKNOWLEDGMENT

This scientific work was partly funded by the German Federal Ministry of Economics and Energy through the AiF with the scope of the „Industrial Co-operative Research (IGF)“ promotion program (IGF research project 15705 BG of the Research Association „Technik und Glas e.V.).

REFERENCES

[1] W. Vonau, F. Gerlach, K. Ahlborn," PLD as Possible Tool for the Fabrication of Chemosensors Based on Amorphous Membranes," Proceedings of SENSORDEVICES 2016, 7th International Confrerence on Sensor Device Technologies and Applications, July 24-28, Nice, France, ISBN: 978-1-61208-494-7.

[2] R. E. Belford, R. G. Kelly, A. E. Owen, " Thick film devices In Chemical sensors," E. Edmonds, Ed.; Blackie and Sons: London, pp. 236-255, 1988.

[3] DIN EN ISO 10523:2012-04.

[4] K. Schwabe, pH measurement, Dresden: Theodor Steinkopff, pp. 120-186, 1976.

[5] G. Eisenman,"Glass electrodes for hydrogen and other cations," New York: Marcel Dekker, 1967.

[6] B. P. A. Beljustin, S. Bolkhontseva,V. Dolidze, L.Dolmazova, J. Karachentseva, B. Nikolsky, A. Pisarevsky, M Shults, V. Tarasova," Electron-conductive glass," Patent US 3 773 642, 1973.

[7] V. G. Vlasov," New solid-state ion-selective electrodes-Sensors for chemical analysis of solutions," Fresenius Z. Anal. Chem., vol. 335, pp. 92-99, 1989.

[8] S. Pollrich," Chalcogenide glasses as ion-sensitive membranes for potentiometric sensors," Diploma Thesis, Hochschule Mittweida, 2004.

[9] M. M Schults," Glass electrode," Patent DE 2645623, 1978.

[10] H. Galster, pH measurement, Weinheim: VCH, pp. 115-123, 1990.

[11] F. Oehme, Ion-selective electrodes, Heidelberg: Dr. Alfred Hüthig, pp. 1-2, 1986.

[12] T. Bachmann, J. Spindler, F. Gerlach, and W. Vonau," Glass electrode with metal contact for electrochemical applications," Scientific Reports, J. Univ. of Appl. Sci. Mittweida, vol. 6, pp. 3-7, 2006.

[13] W. Vonau, F. Gerlach, U. Enseleit, J. Spindler, and T. Bachmann, "New solid-state glass electrodes by using zinc oxide thin films as interface layer," J. Solid State Electrochem., vol.13, pp. 91-98, 2009.

[14] T. Bachmann, J. Spindler, F. Gerlach, and W. Vonau, "Glass electrode and procedure for its fabrication," Patent DE 10 2005 059 680 A1.

[15] W. Vonau, F. Gerlach, U. Enseleit, J. Spindler, and T. Bachmann," Chemical indicator electrode and procedure for its fabrication," Patent DE 10 2007 016 197 A1.

[16] S.Weißmantel, G. Reiße, D. Rost," Erzeugung von superharten amorphen Kohlenstoffschichten mit niedrigen inneren Spannungen durch sukzessives Laserpulsabscheiden und – Tempern," Galvanotechnik vol. 4, pp. 948-958, 2006.

[17] M. Frumar, B. Frumarova, P. Nemec, T. Wagber, J. Jedelsky, M. Hrdlicka," Thin chalcogenide films prepared by pulsed laser deposition – new amorphues materials applicable in optoelectronics and chemical sensors," Journal of Non-Crystalline Solids, vol. 352, pp. 544-561, 2006.

[18] J.P. Klook, L. Moreno, A. Bratov, S. Huachupoma, J. Xu, T. Wagner, T. Yoshinobu, Y. Ermolenko, Y.G. Vlasov, M.J.Schöning," PLD-prepared cadmium sensors based on chalcogenide glasses – ISFET, LAPS and μISE semiconductor structures," Sensors and Actuators B, vol. 118, pp. 149-155, 2006.

[19] O.G. Pompilian, G. Dascalu, J. Mihaila, S. Gurlui, M. Olivier, P. Nemec, V. Nazabal, N. Cimpoesu, C. Focsa,"Pulsed laser deposition of rare-earth-doped gallium lanthanum sulphide chalcogenide glass thin films," Appl. Phys. A, vol. 117, pp. 197-205, 2014, doi: 10.1007/s00339-014-8359-6.

[20] L. Florian, B. Savu, F. Sima, I.N. Mihailescu, D. Tanaskovic, D. Janackovic,"Synthesisi and characterization of bioglass thin films," Digest Journal of Nanomaterials and Biostructures, vol. 2, No. 3, pp. 285-291, September 2007.

[21] R. E. Belford, A. E. Owen," Temperature Dependent AC Impedance Studies Of Glass To Metal Contacts In Solid State Glass pH Sensors," J. Non Cryst. Sol.,vol. 92, pp.73-88, 1987.

[22] W. Vonau, F. Berthold, U. Guth," Impedance investigations on heat-stressed pH-sensitive glass membranes," J Solid State Electrochem, vol. 15, pp. 95-98, January 2011.

[23] K. Schwabe, Fortschritte der pH-Messtechnik, 2nd ed, Berlin: VEB Verlag Technik, pp. 247-249, 1958.

[24] W. Vonau, and U. Guth," pH Monitoring: a review," J Solid State Electrochem, vol. 10, pp. 746-752, September 2006.

[25] W. Habermann, P. John, H. Matschiner, and H. Spähn, "Partially selective semiconductor redox electrodes", Fresenius J. Anal. Chem., vol. 356, 1996, pp. 182-186, ISSN: 0937-0633.

[26] W. Vonau, M. Decker, J. Zosel, K. Ahlborn, F. Gerlach, S. Weißmantel," Alternative Processes for Manufacturing of Metal Oxide-based Potentiometric Chemosensors," Sensors & Transducers, vol. 193, Issue 10, Oct. 2015, pp. 93-99, ISSN: 2306-8515, e-ISSN 1726-5479

High-Speed Video Analysis of Ballistic Trials to Investigate Simulation Methods for Fiber-Reinforced Plastics Under Impact Loading

Using the Example of Ultra-High Molecular Weight Polyethylene

Arash Ramezani and Hendrik Rothe
Chair of Measurement and Information Technology
University of the Federal Armed Forces
Hamburg, Germany
Email: ramezani@hsu-hh.de, rothe@hsu-hh.de

Abstract—**In the security sector, the partly insufficient safety of people and equipment due to failure of industrial components are ongoing problems that cause great concern. Since computers and software have spread into all fields of industry, extensive efforts are currently made in order to improve the safety by applying certain numerical solutions. This work presents a set of numerical simulations of ballistic tests which analyze the effects of composite armor plates. The focus lies on high-speed videos and modern investigation methods. The goal is to improve fiber-reinforced plastics in order to be able to cope with current challenges. Of course, the maximization of security is the primary goal, but keeping down the costs is becoming increasingly important. This is why numerical simulations are more frequently applied than experimental tests which are thus being replaced gradually.**

Keywords-solver technologies; simulation models; fiber-reinforced plastics; optimization; armor systems; ballistic trials.

I. INTRODUCTION

This work will focus on composite armor structures consisting of several layers of ultra-high molecular weight polyethylene (UHMW-PE), a promising ballistic armor material due to its high specific strength and stiffness. The goal is to evaluate the ballistic efficiency of UHMW-PE composite with numerical simulations, promoting an effective development process. First approaches are discussed in detail in [1].

Due to the fact that all engineering simulation is based on geometry to represent the design, the target and all its components are simulated as CAD models. The work will also provide a brief overview of ballistic tests to offer some basic knowledge of the subject, serving as a basis for the comparison of the simulation results. Details of ballistic trials on composite armor systems are presented. Instead of running expensive trials, numerical simulations should identify vulnerabilities of structures. Contrary to the experimental result, numerical methods allow easy and comprehensive studying of all mechanical parameters. Modeling will also help to understand how the fiber-reinforced plastic armor schemes behave during impact and how the failure processes can be controlled to our advantage. By progressively changing the composition of several layers and the material thickness, the composite armor will be optimized. There is every reason to expect possible weight savings and a significant increase in protection, through the use of numerical techniques combined with a small number of physical experiments.

After a brief introduction and description of the different methods of space discretization in Section III, there is a short section on ballistic trials where the experimental set-up is depicted, followed by Section V describing the analysis with numerical simulations. The paper ends with a concluding paragraph in Section VI.

II. STATE-OF-THE-ART

The numerical modeling of composite materials under impact can be performed at a constituent level (i.e., explicit modeling of fibre and matrix elements, e.g., [2]), a meso-mechanical level (i.e., consolidated plies or fibre bundles, e.g., [3]), or macromechanically in which the composite laminate is represented as a continuum.

In [4–7] a non-linear orthotropic continuum material model was developed and implemented in a commercial hydrocode (i.e., ANSYS® AUTODYN®) for application with aramid and carbon fibre composites under hypervelocity impact. The non-linear orthotropic material model includes orthotropic coupling of the material volumetric and deviatoric responses, a non-linear equation of state (EoS), orthotropic hardening, combined stress failure criteria and orthotropic energy-based softening. For more detail refer to [8].

Lässig et al. [9] conducted extensive experimental characterization of Dyneema® HB26 UHMW-PE composite for application in the continuum non-linear orthotropic material model, and validated the derived material parameters through simulation of spherical projectile impacts at hypervelocity. The target geometry is homogenized. The projectile is an aluminum ball in simplified terms. However, homogenized target geometries with orthotropic material models are not able to reproduce different modes of failure. The results are valid for aluminum spherical-shaped projectiles in hypervelocity range only.

Nguyen et al. [10] evaluated and refined the modeling approach and material model parameter set developed in [9] for the simulation of impact events from 400 m/s to 6600 m/s. Across this velocity range the sensitivity of the numerical output is driven by different aspects of the material model, e.g., the strength model in the ballistic regime and the equation of state (EoS) in the hypervelocity regime. Here, the target geometry is divided into sub-laminates joined by bonded contacts breakable through a combined tensile and shear stress failure criterion.

The models mentioned above are valid for blunt FSP´s from a velocity range of 400 to 6600 m/s. They show considerable shortcomings in simulating pointed projectiles and thick HB26-composites.

This paper will present an optimal solution of this problem with an enhanced model for ultra-high molecular weight polyethylene under impact loading. For the first time, composite armor structures consisting of several layers of fiber-reinforced plastics are simulated for all the current military threats.

III. Methods of Space Discretization

To deal with problems involving the release of a large amount of energy over a very short period of time, e.g., explosions and impacts, there are three approaches: as the problems are highly non-linear and require information regarding material behavior at ultra-high loading rates which is generally not available, most of the work is experimental and thus may cause tremendous expenses. Analytical approaches are possible if the geometries involved are relatively simple and if the loading can be described through boundary conditions, initial conditions or a combination of the two. Numerical solutions are far more general in scope and remove any difficulties associated with geometry [11]. They apply an explicit method and use very small time steps for stable results.

The most commonly used spatial discretization methods are Lagrange, Euler, ALE (a mixture of Lagrange and Euler), and mesh-free methods, such as Smooth Particles Hydrodynamics (SPH) [12].

A. Lagrange

The Lagrange method of space discretization uses a mesh that moves and distorts with the material it models as a result of forces from neighboring elements (meshes are imbedded in material). There is no grid required for the external space, as the conservation of mass is automatically satisfied and material boundaries are clearly defined. This is the most efficient solution methodology with an accurate pressure history definition.

The Lagrange method is most appropriate for representing solids, such as structures and projectiles. If however, there is too much deformation of any element, it results in a very slowly advancing solution and is usually terminated because the smallest dimension of an element results in a time step that is below the threshold level.

B. Euler

The Euler (multi-material) solver utilizes a fixed mesh, allowing materials to flow (advect) from one element to the next (meshes are fixed in space). Therefore, an external space needs to be modeled. Due to the fixed grid, the Euler method avoids problems of mesh distortion and tangling that are prevalent in Lagrange simulations with large flows. The Euler solver is very well-suited for problems involving extreme material movement, such as fluids and gases. To describe solid behavior, additional calculations are required to transport the solid stress tensor and the history of the material through the grid. Euler is generally more computationally intensive than Lagrange and requires a higher resolution (smaller elements) to accurately capture sharp pressure peaks that often occur with shock waves.

C. ALE

The ALE method of space discretization is a hybrid of the Lagrange and Euler methods. It allows redefining the grid continuously in arbitrary and predefined ways as the calculation proceeds, which effectively provides a continuous rezoning facility. Various predefined grid motions can be specified, such as free (Lagrange), fixed (Euler), equipotential, equal spacing, and others. The ALE method can model solids as well as liquids. The advantage of ALE is the ability to reduce and sometimes eliminate difficulties caused by severe mesh distortions encountered by the Lagrange method, thus allowing a calculation to continue efficiently. However, compared to Lagrange, an additional computational step of rezoning is employed to move the grid and remap the solution onto a new grid [13].

D. SPH

The mesh-free Lagrangian method of space discretization (or SPH method) is a particle-based solver and was initially used in astrophysics. The particles are imbedded in material and they are not only interacting mass points but also interpolation points used to calculate the value of physical variables based on the data from neighboring SPH particles, scaled by a weighting function. Because there is no grid defined, distortion and tangling problems are avoided as well. Compared to the Euler method, material boundaries and interfaces in the SPH are rather well defined and material separation is naturally handled. Therefore, the SPH solver is ideally suited for certain types of problems with extensive material damage and separation, such as cracking. This type of response often occurs with brittle materials and hypervelocity impacts. However, mesh-free methods, such as Smooth Particles Hydrodynamics, can be less efficient than mesh-based Lagrangian methods with comparable resolution.

Fig. 1 gives a short overview of the solver technologies mentioned above. The crucial factor is the grid that causes different outcomes.

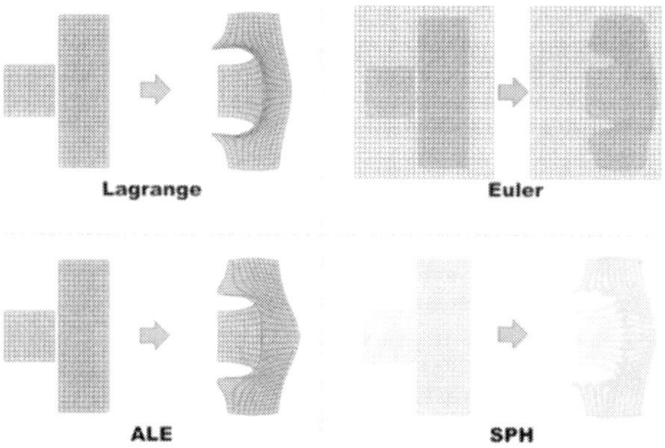

Figure 1. Examples of Lagrange, Euler, ALE, and SPH simulations on an impact problem [14].

The behavior (deflection) of the simple elements is well-known and may be calculated and analyzed using simple equations called shape functions. By applying coupling conditions between the elements at their nodes, the overall stiffness of the structure may be built up and the deflection/distortion of any node – and subsequently of the whole structure – can be calculated approximately [15].

For problems of dynamic fluid-structure interaction and impact, there typically is no single best numerical method which is applicable to all parts of a problem. Techniques to couple types of numerical solvers in a single simulation can allow the use of the most appropriate solver for each domain of the problem.

The goal of this paper is to evaluate a hydrocode, a computational tool for modeling the behavior of continuous media. In its purest sense, a hydrocode is a computer code for modeling fluid flow at all speeds [11]. For that reason a structure will be split into a number of small elements. The elements are connected through their nodes (see Fig. 2).

The behavior (deflection) of the simple elements is well-known and may be calculated and analyzed using simple equations called shape functions. By applying coupling conditions between the elements at their nodes, the overall stiffness of the structure may be built up and the deflection/distortion of any node – and subsequently of the whole structure – can be calculated approximately [16].

Using a CAD-neutral environment that supports bidirectional, direct, and associative interfaces with CAD systems, the geometry can be optimized successively [17].

Figure 2. Example grid.

Therefore, several runs are necessary: from modeling to calculation to the evaluation and subsequent improvement of the model (see Fig. 3).

Bullet-resistant materials are usually tested by using a gun to fire a projectile from a set distance into the material in a set pattern. Levels of protection (see Fig. 4) are based on the ability of the target to stop a specific type of projectile traveling at a specific speed.

IV. Ballistic Trials

Ballistics is an essential component for the evaluation of our results. Here, terminal ballistics is the most important sub-field. It describes the interaction of a projectile with its target. Terminal ballistics is relevant for both small and large caliber projectiles. The task is to analyze and evaluate the impact and its various modes of action. This will provide information on the effect of the projectile and the extinction risk.

Terminal ballistics is the general name for a large number of processes which take place during the high velocity impact of various projectiles/target combinations. There are two related disciplines which deal with launching these projectiles. Interior ballistics concerns their acceleration to the desired velocity, and exterior ballistics deals with their flight dynamics from the launcher to the target.

The science and engineering of impacting bodies have a large range of applications depending on their type and their impact velocities. At very low velocities, these impacts can be limited to the elastic range of response, with practically no damage to the impacted bodies. In contrast, at very high impact velocities these bodies experience gross deformation, local melting, and even total disintegration upon impact. Various scientific and engineering disciplines are devoted to specific areas in this field such as: vehicle impacts, rain erosion, armor and anti-armor design, spacecraft protection against meteorites and the impact of planets by large meteors at extremely high velocities.

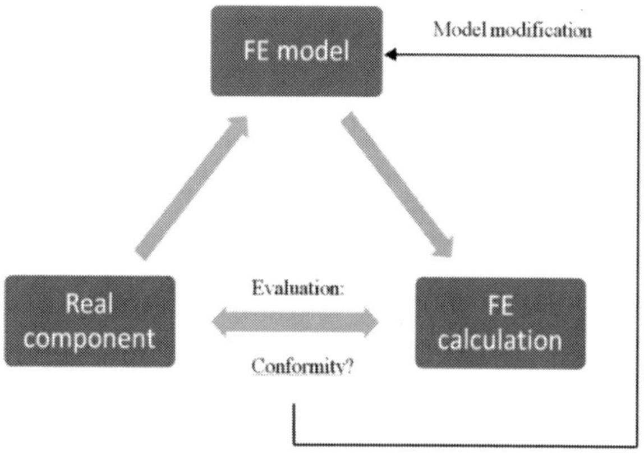

Figure 3. Basically iterative procedure of a FE analysis [15].

In order to follow these different events the researcher has to be acquainted with diverse scientific fields which include: elasticity and plasticity of solids, fracture mechanics and the physics of materials at high pressures and temperatures.

Terminal ballistics is the generic name for the science and engineering of impacts which are of interest to armor and anti-armor engineers. The relevant impact velocities usually range between 0.5 and 2.0 km/s, the so-called ordnance velocity range. These are the velocities at which projectiles are launched against personnel, armored vehicles and buildings, by rifles and guns. The impact velocities of shaped charge jets are within the hypervelocity range of 2.0–8.0 km/s, and their interaction with armor is also of major interest to both armor and anti-armor engineers.

The science of terminal ballistics started with the works of the great mathematician Leonard Euler (1745) and the British engineer Benjamin Robins (1742), who analyzed data for the penetration of steel cannonballs in soil as a function of their impact velocities. In the following two centuries, until the Second World War, the field of terminal ballistics was based on empirically derived relations between the penetration depth and the impact velocity of various projectiles into different targets. The reviews of Hermann and Jones (1961) and Backman and Goldsmith (1978), summarize many of these empirical formulas which were suggested over this period.

During the years of WW-II, scientists in the US and UK have analyzed the penetration process of shaped charge jets and rigid steel projectiles into armor plates, through analytical models which were based on physical considerations. These models identify the main force exerted on the projectile during penetration, which is then inserted in its equation of motion. The aim of these models is to reduce the mathematical description of a complicated three dimensional problem to a simple form which retains the essential physics of the penetration process. This simplification results in either a low dimensional system of ordinary differential equations or a few one-dimensional partial differential equations, which can be easily solved. The models can be tested by controlled experiments, in which the parameters are varied in a systematic way, in order to establish the non-dimensional parameters of the process. With these analytical models data correlation is made easy and extrapolations, to areas beyond the ability of experimental facilities, are possible. On the other hand, these analytical models require some compromise to be made, limiting their use to ideal cases where only a single mechanism is at work. Still, these models have been used successfully in order to account for the data and to reduce the number of the necessary experiments in terminal ballistics. Since the advancements in numerical simulations, the role of analytical models seems to decline as the codes are getting better and more efficient. However, these numerical simulations are often used just to account for experimental data, offering little physical insight for the process. Our strong belief is that analytical modeling is crucial for the field of terminal ballistics in order to understand the physics involved, and to highlight the important parameters which influence these processes.

Predictive numerical simulation of any structural deformation process requires objective constitutive equations including parameters that are derived objectively for the material. Objective, in this context, means that the parameters are valid for the whole spectrum of loading conditions covered by the material model. This includes its applicability to arbitrary domains or geometries without restriction to specific structures. Experimental parameter derivation providing that kind of data can be called material test. The objectivity criterion to the parameters distinguishes the material test from a structural test used for verification or validation purposes.

Given that a projectile strikes a target, compressive waves propagate into both the projectile and the target. Relief waves propagate inward from the lateral free surfaces of the penetrator, cross at the centerline, and generate a high tensile stress. If the impact was normal, we would have a two-dimensional stress state. If the impact was oblique, bending stresses will be generated in the penetrator. When the compressive wave reached the free surface of the target, it would rebound as a tensile wave. The target may fracture at this point. The projectile may change direction if it perforates (usually towards the normal of the target surface).

Because of the differences in target behavior based on the proximity of the distal surface, we must categorize targets into four broad groups. A semi-infinite target is one where there is no influence of distal boundary on penetration. A thick target is one in which the boundary influences penetration after the projectile is some distance into the target. An intermediate thickness target is a target where the boundaries exert influence throughout the impact. Finally, a thin target is one in which stress or deformation gradients are negligible throughout the thickness.

There are several methods by which a target will fail when subjected to an impact. The major variables are the target and penetrator material properties, the impact velocity, the projectile shape (especially the ogive), the geometry of the target supporting structure, and the dimensions of the projectile and target.

In order to develop a numerical model, a ballistic test program is necessary. The ballistic trials are thoroughly documented and analyzed – even fragments must be collected. They provide information about the used armor and the projectile behavior after fire, which must be consistent with the simulation results (see Fig. 5).

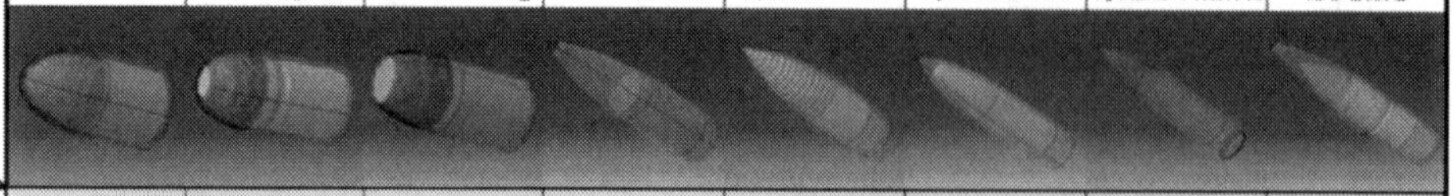

	Protection Level \ Projectile	9 x 19 mm	.357 Magnum	.44 Rem. Mag.	5,56x45 mm	7,62x39 mm	7,62x51 mm	7,62x54 mm R	.50 BMG
1	PM 1 / VR 1								
2	PM 2 / VR 2	$v = 360 \pm 10 \frac{m}{s}$ $E = 518 J$							
3	PM 3 / VR 3	$v = 415 \pm 10 \frac{m}{s}$ $E = 689 J$							
4	PM 4 / VR 4		$v = 430 \pm 10 \frac{m}{s}$ $E = 943 J$	$v = 440 \pm 10 \frac{m}{s}$ $E = 1510 J$					
5	PM 5 / VR 5		$v = 580 \pm 10 \frac{m}{s}$ $E = 1194 J$						
6	PM 6 / VR 6					$v = 720 \pm 10 \frac{m}{s}$ $E = 2074 J$			
7	PM 7 / VR 7 *STANAG Level 1*				$v = 950 \pm 10 \frac{m}{s}$ $E = 1805 J$		$v = 830 \pm 10 \frac{m}{s}$ $E = 3289 J$		
8	PM 8 / VR 8 *STANAG Level 2*					$v = 740 \pm 10 \frac{m}{s}$ $E = 2108 J$			
9	PM 9 / VR 9						$v = 820 \pm 10 \frac{m}{s}$ $E = 3261 J$		
10	PM 10 / VR 10 *STANAG Level 3*							$v = 860 \pm 10 \frac{m}{s}$ $E = 3846 J$	
11	PM 11 *STANAG Level 3*						$v = 930 \pm 10 \frac{m}{s}$ $E = 3633 J$		
12	PM 12						$v = 810 \pm 10 \frac{m}{s}$ $E = 4166 J$		
13	PM 13								$v = 930 \pm 10 \frac{m}{s}$ $E = 18595 J$

Figure 4. The APR 2006 resistance classification and related CAD models [19].

In order to create a data set for the numerical simulations, several experiments have to be performed. Ballistic tests are recorded with high-speed videos and analyzed afterwards. The experimental set-up is shown in Fig. 6.

Testing was undertaken at an indoor ballistic testing facility (see Fig. 7). The target stand provides support behind the target on all four sides. Every ballistic test program includes several trials with different composites. The set-up has to remain unchanged.

The camera system is a PHANTOM v1611 that enables fast image rates up to 646,000 frames per second (fps) at full resolution of 1280 x 800 pixels. The use of a polarizer and a neutral density filter is advisable, so that waves of some polarizations can be blocked while the light of a specific polarization can be passed.

Several targets of different laminate configurations were tested to assess the ballistic limit (V_{50}). The ballistic limit is considered the velocity required for a particular projectile to reliably (at least 50% of the time) penetrate a particular piece of material [20]. After the impact, the projectile is examined regarding any kind of change it might have undergone.

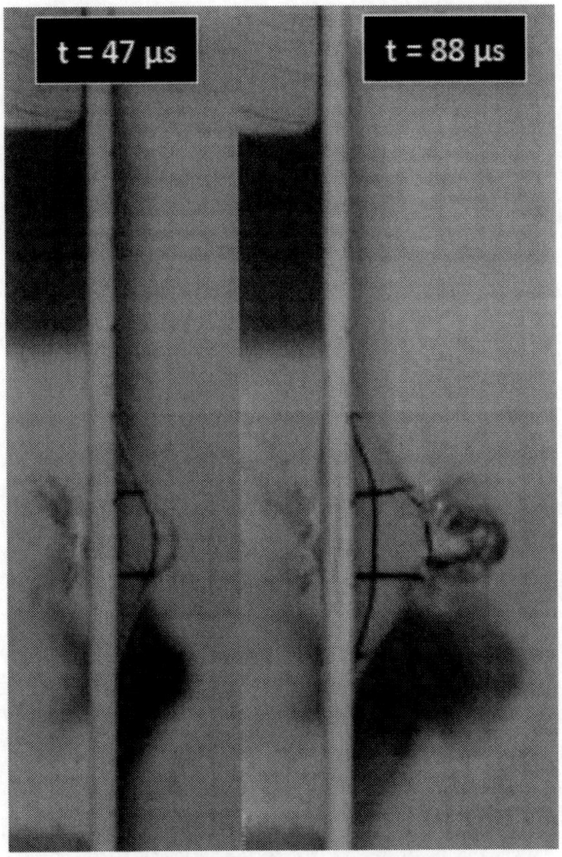

Figure 5. Ballistic tests and the analysis of fragments.

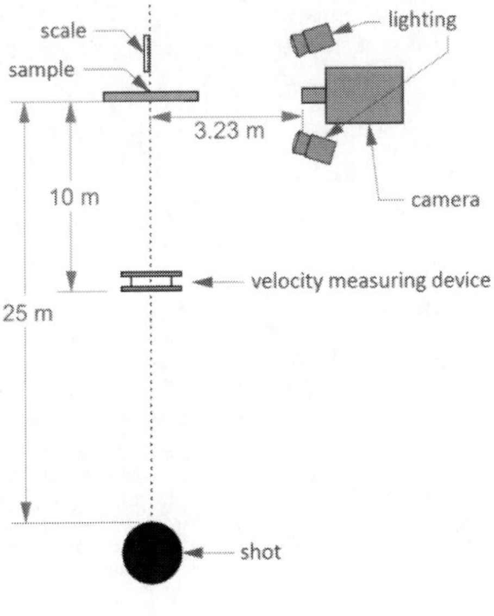

Figure 6. Experimental set-up.

Figure 7. Indoor ballistic testing facility.

The damage propagation is analyzed using the software called COMEF [21], image processing software for highly accurate measuring functions. The measurement takes place via setting measuring points manually on the monitor. Area measurement is made by the free choice of grey tones (0…255). Optionally the object with the largest surface area can be recognized automatically as object. Smaller particles within the same grey tone range as the sample under test are automatically ignored by this filter.

Fig. 8 shows an example of measuring and analyzing damages after impact.

V. Numerical Simulation

The ballistic tests are followed by computational modeling of the experimental set-up. Then, the experiment is reproduced using numerical simulations. Fig. 1 shows a cross-section of the projectile and a CAD model. The geometry and observed response of the laminate to ballistic impact is approximately symmetric to the axis through the bullet impact point.

Numerical simulation of modern armor structures requires the selection of appropriate material models for the constituent materials and the derivation of suitable material model input data. The laminate system studied here is an ultra-high molecular weight polyethylene composite. Lead and copper are also required for the projectiles.

The projectile was divided into different parts - the jacket and the base - which have different properties and even different meshes. These elements have quadratic shape functions and nodes between the element edges. In this way, the computational accuracy, as well as the quality of curved model shapes increases. Using the same mesh density, the application of parabolic elements leads to a higher accuracy compared to linear elements (1st order elements).

A. *Modelling*

In [9], numerical simulations of 15 kg/m^2 Dyneema® HB26 panels impacted by 6 mm diameter aluminum spheres between 2052 m/s to 6591 m/s were shown to provide very good agreement with experimental measurements of the panel ballistic limit and residual velocities, see Fig. 9.

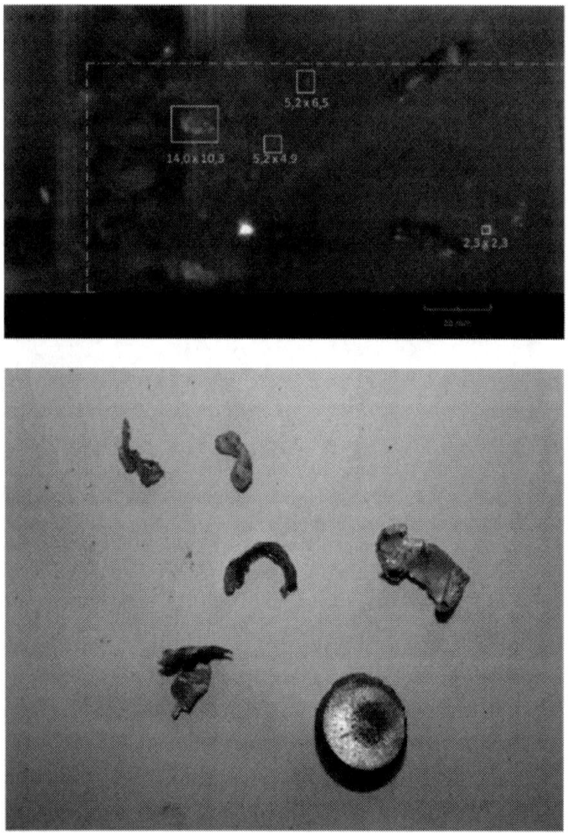

Figure 8. Ballistic tests and the analysis of fragments.

The modelling approach and material parameter set from [8] were applied to simulate impact experiments at velocities in the ballistic regime (here considered as < 1000 m/s). In Fig. 9 the results of modelling impact of 20 mm fragment simulating projectiles (FSPs) against 10 mm thick Dyneema® HB26 are shown. The model shows a significant under prediction of the ballistic limit, 236 m/s compared to 394 m/s.

B. Simulation Results

Relatively newer numerical discretization methods, such as Smoothed Particle Hydrodynamics (SPH), have been proposed that rectifies the issue of grid entanglement. The SPH method has shown good agreement with high velocity impact of metallic targets, better predictions of crack propagation in ceramics and fragmentation of composites under hypervelocity impact (HVI) compared to grid-based Lagrange and Euler methods. Although promising, SPH suffers from consistency and stability issues that lead to lower accuracy and instabilities under tensile perturbation. The latter makes it unsuitable for use with UHMW-PE composite under ballistic impact, because this material derives most of its resistance to penetration when it is loaded in tension. For these types of problems, the grid-based Lagrangian formulation still remains the most feasible for modeling UHMW-PE composite.

3D numerical simulations were performed of the full target and projectile, where both were meshed using 8-node hexahedral elements. The projectile was meshed with 9 elements across the diameter. The target is composed of sub-laminates that are one element thick, separated by a small gap to satisfy the master-slave contact algorithm (external gap in AUTODYN®) and bonded together as previously discussed. The mesh size of the target is approximately equal to the projectile at the impact site. The mesh was then graded towards the edge, increasing in coarseness to reduce the computational load of the model. Since UHMW-PE composite has a very low coefficient of friction, force fit clamping provides little restraint.

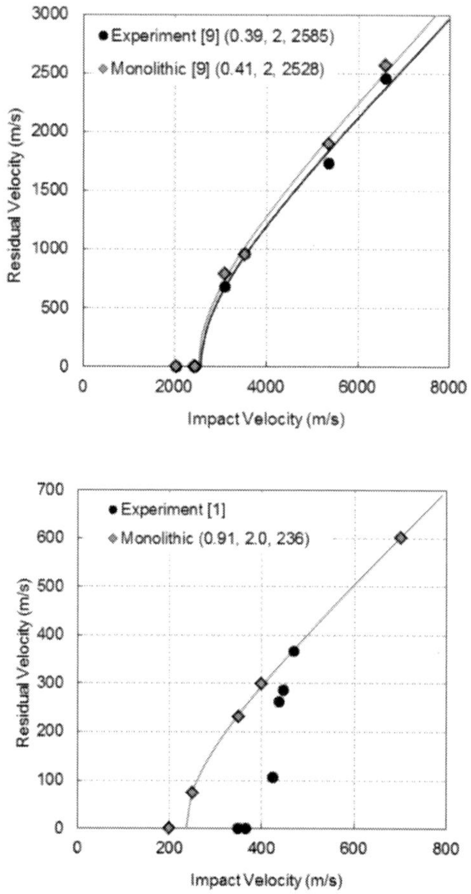

Figure 9. Experimental and numerical impact residual velocity results for impact of 6 mm diameter aluminum spheres against 15 kg/m2 Dyneema® HB26 at normal incidence (left) and impact of 20 mm fragment simulating projectiles against 10 mm thick Dyneema® HB26 at normal incidence (right). Lambert-Jonas parameters (a, p, V_{bl}) are provided in the legend.

High speed video of ballistic impact tests typical showed the action of loosening and moving clamps upon impact. As such no boundary conditions were imposed on the target. The FSP material was modelled as Steel S-7 from the AUTODYN® library described using a linear EoS and the Johnson-Cook strength model [22]. The aluminum sphere was modelled using AL1100-O from the AUTODYN® library that uses a shock EoS and the Steinburg Guinan strength model [23]. The master-slave contact algorithm was used to detect contact between the target and projectile.

The sub-laminate model with shock EoS was applied to the aluminum sphere hypervelocity impact series and 20 mm FSP ballistic impact series presented in Fig. 9, the results of which are shown in Fig. 10. The sub-laminate model is shown to provide a significant improvement in predicting the experimental V_{50} of 394 m/s for the FSP ballistic impacts (377 m/s) compared to the monolithic model (236 m/s).

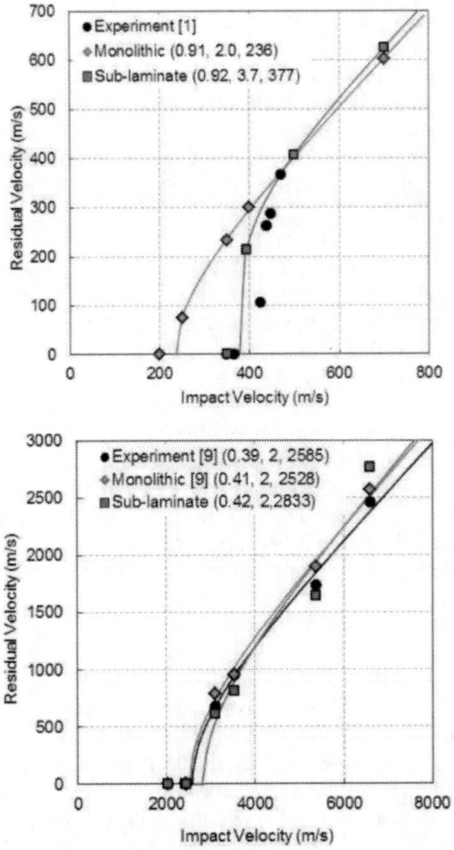

Figure 10. Comparison of the experimental results with the two numerical models for impact of 20 mm fragment simulating projectiles against 10 mm thick Dyneema HB26® at normal incidence (left) , and impact of 6 mm diameter aluminium spheres against 15 kg/m2 Dyneema® HB26 at normal incidence (right). Lambert-Jonas parameters (a, p, Vbl) are provided in the legend.

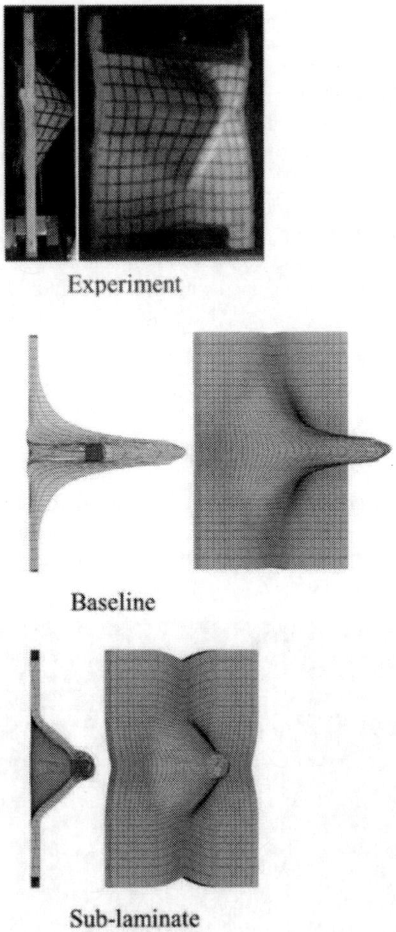

Figure 11. Bulge of a 10 mm target impact by a 20 mm FSP at 365 m/s (experiment) and 350 m/s (simulations), 400 μs after the initial impact.

The ballistic limit and residual velocity predicted with the sub-laminate model for the hypervelocity impact case are shown to be comparable with the original monolithic model. For conditions closer to the ballistic limit, the sub-laminate model is shown to predict increased target resistance (i.e., lower residual velocity). For higher overmatch conditions there is some small variance between the two approaches.

In Fig. 11, a qualitative assessment of the bulge formation is made for the 10 mm panel impacted at 365 m/s (i.e., below the V_{50}) by a 20 mm FSP. Prediction of bulge development is important as it is characteristic of the material wave speed and is also a key measure in defence applications, particularly in personnel protection (i.e., vests and helmets). The sub-laminate model is shown to reproduce the characteristic pyramid bulge shape and drawing of material from the lateral edge. In comparison, the bulge prediction of the baseline model is poor, showing a conical shape with the projectile significantly behind the apex. In the baseline model penetration occurs through premature through-thickness shear failure around the projectile rather than in-plane tension (membrane) which would allow the formation of a pyramidal bulge as the composite is carried along with the projectile. Furthermore, in the baseline model the extremely small through thickness tensile strength (1.07 MPa) in the bulk material leads to early spallation/delamination of the back face. This allows the material on the target back face to fail and be accelerated ahead of the projectile. In the sub-laminate model, these two artifacts are addressed, and so a more representative bulge is formed.

C. Further Validations

The material model developed in [9] and [10] has some shortcomings regarding the simulation of handgun projectiles (see Fig. 12). The ballistic limit was significantly under predicted. Evaluation of the result suggests that the failure mechanisms, which drive performance in the rear section of the target panel (i.e., membrane tension) were not adequately reproduced, suggesting an under-estimate of the material in-plane tensile performance.

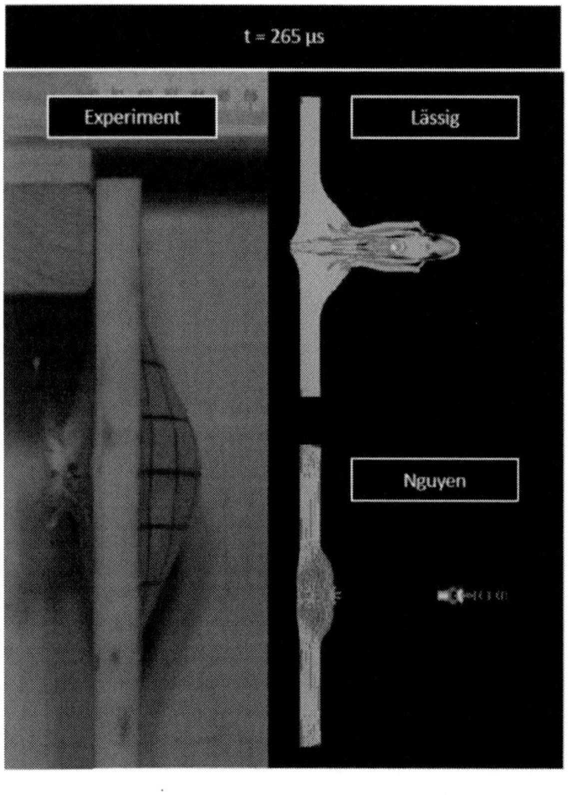

Figure 12. Comparing experimantal results with the previous simulation models of Lässig [8] and Nguyen [9], 265 µs after impact (grey = plastic deformation, green = elastic deformation, orange = material failure); projectile velocity: 674 m/s; target thickness: 16.2 mm (60 layers of HB26).

A major difficulty in the numerical simulation of fibre composites under impact is the detection of failure processes between fibre and matrix elements as well as between the individual laminate layers (delamination). One promising approach is the use of "artificial" inhomogeneities on the macroscale. Here, an alternative simulation model has been developed to overcome these difficulties. Using sub-laminates and inhomogeneities on the macroscale, the model does not match the real microstructure, but allows a more realistic description of the failure processes mentioned above.

Approaches based on the continuum or macroscale present a more practical alternative to solve typical engineering problems. However, the complexity of the constitutive equations and characterization tests necessary to describe an anisotropic material at a macro or continuum level increases significantly.

When considering the micromechanical properties of the orthotropic yield surface with a non-linear hardening description, a non-linear shock equation of state, and a three-dimensional failure criterion supplemented by a linear orthotropic softening description should be taken into account. It is important to consider all relevant mechanisms that occur during ballistic impact, as the quality of the numerical prediction capability strongly depends on a physically accurate description of contributing energy dissipation mechanisms. Therefore, a combination of ballistic experiments and numerical simulations is required. Predictive numerical tools can be extremely useful for enhancing our understanding of ballistic impact events. Models that are able to capture the key mechanical and thermodynamic processes can significantly improve our understanding of the phenomena by allowing time-resolved investigations of virtually every aspect of the impact event. Such high fidelity is immensely difficult, prohibitively expensive or near impossible to achieve with existing experimental measurement techniques.

The thermodynamic response of a material and its ability to carry tensile and shear loads (strength) is typically treated separately within hydrocodes such that the stress tensor can be decomposed into volumetric and deviatoric components. Since the mechanical properties of fibre-reinforced composites are anisotropic (at least at the meso- and macroscale level), the deviatoric and hydrostatic components are coupled. That is deviatoric strains will produce a volumetric dilation and hydrostatic pressure leads to non-uniform strains in the three principal directions.

The strength and failure model was investigated by modeling single elements under normal and shear stresses. It was found that under through-thickness shear stress, the element would fail prematurely below the specified through-thickness shear failure stress. It was found that if the through-thickness tensile strength was increased, failure in through-thickness shear was delayed. This evaluation study shows the importance of the strength, failure and erosion models for predicting performance in the ballistic regime.

Previous material models for fiber-reinforced plastics were adjusted and the concept has been extended to different calibers and projectile velocities. Composite armor plates between 5.5 and 16.2 mm were tested in several ballistic trials and high-speed videos were used to analyze the characteristics of the projectile – before and after the impact.

The simulation results with the modified model are shown in Fig. 13. The deformation of the projectile, e.g., 7.62×39 mm, is in good agreement with the experimental observation. Both delamination and fragmentation can be seen in the numerical simulation.

Compared to the homogeneous continuum model, fractures can be detected easily. Subsequently, the results of experiment and simulation in the case of perforation were compared with reference to the projectile residual velocity. Here, only minor differences were observed.

It should be noted that an explicit modeling of the individual fibres is not an option, since the computational effort would go beyond the scope of modern server systems (see Fig. 14 and Fig. 15).

VI. Conclusions

Coming back to the task of designing structures for vehicles or buildings under dynamic loading conditions like crash, impact or blast, we realize that virtually all fields of application are nowadays supported if not driven by numerical simulation. Along with the rapid development of computer power, utilization of numerical methods as a tool to design structures for all kinds of loading conditions evolved. Simulation of the expected structural response to certain loadings is motivated by the wish

- to optimize the design
- and to better understand the physical processes.

For both intentions the predictive capability of the codes is an indispensable quality. In fact, the predictive capability separates numerical tools from graphical visualization. It means nothing less than the ability to calculate physical processes without experimental results at hand to a sufficient degree of precision.

This work demonstrated how a small number of well-defined experiments can be used to develop, calibrate, and validate solver technologies used for simulating the impact of projectiles on complex armor systems and composite laminate structures.

Existing material models were optimized to reproduce ballistic tests. High-speed videos were used to analyze the characteristics of the projectile – before and after the impact. The simulation results demonstrate the successful use of the coupled multi-solver approach and new modeling techniques. The high level of correlation between the numerical results and the available experimental or observed data demonstrates that the coupled multi-solver approach is an accurate and effective analysis method.

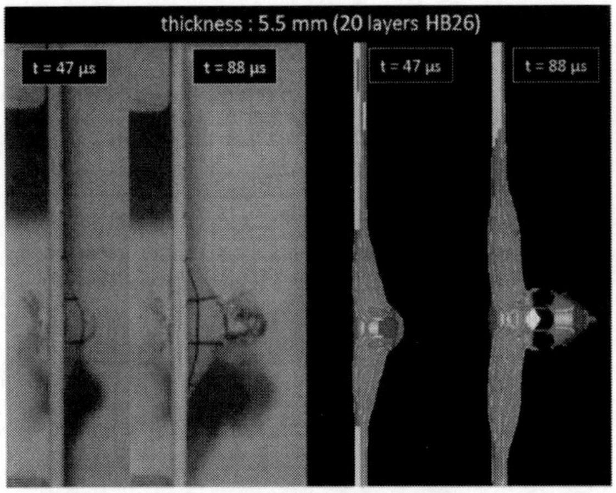

Figure 13. Effect of a 5.5 mm target impact by a 7.62×39 mm bullet at 686 m/s, 47 µs and 88 µs after the initial impact.

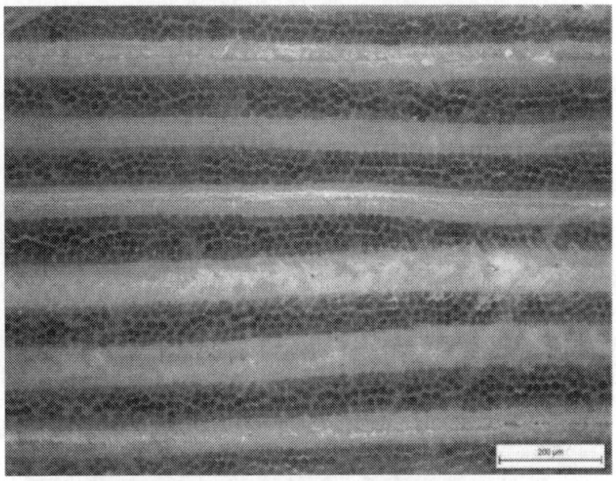

Figure 14. Cross section of a Dyneema® HB26 panel.

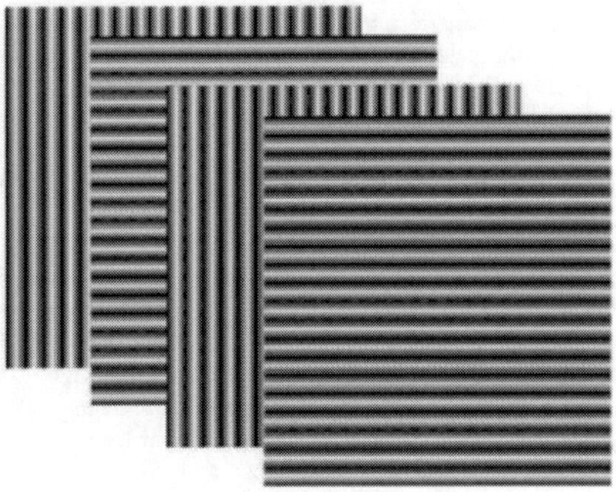

Figure 15. Setup / structure of a Dyneema® HB26 prepreg.

A non-linear orthotropic continuum model was evaluated for UHMW-PE composite across a wide range of impact velocities. Although previously found to provide accurate results for hypervelocity impact of aluminum spheres, the existing model and dataset revealed a significant underestimation of the composite performance under impact conditions driven by through-thickness shear performance (ballistic impact of fragment simulating projectiles). The model was found to exhibit premature through thickness shear failure as a result of directional coupling in the modified Hashin-Tsai failure criterion and the large discrepancy between through-thickness tensile and shear strength of UHME-PE composite. As a result, premature damage and failure was initiated in the through-thickness shear direction leading to decreased ballistic performance. By de-coupling through-thickness tensile failure from the failure criteria and discretizing the laminate into a nominal number of kinematically joined sub-laminates through the thickness, progresses in modelling the ballistic response of the panels was improved.

New concepts and models can be developed and easily tested with the help of modern hydrocodes. The initial design approach of the units and systems has to be as safe and optimal as possible. Therefore, most design concepts are analyzed on the computer.

FEM-based simulations are well-suited for this purpose. Here, a numerical model has been developed, which is capable of predicting the ballistic performance of UHMW-PE armor systems. Thus, estimates based on experience are being more and more replaced by software.

The gained experience is of prime importance for the development of modern armor. By applying the numerical model a large number of potential armor schemes can be evaluated and the understanding of the interaction between laminate components under ballistic impact can be improved.

The most important steps during an FE analysis are the evaluation and interpretation of the outcomes followed by suitable modifications of the model. For that reason, ballistic trials are necessary to validate the simulation results. They are designed to obtain information about

- the velocity and trajectory of the projectile prior to impact,
- changes in configuration of projectile and target due to impact,
- masses, velocities, and trajectories of fragments generated by the impact process.

Ballistic trials can be used as the basis of an iterative optimization process. Numerical simulations are a valuable adjunct to the study of the behavior of metals subjected to high-velocity impact or intense impulsive loading. The combined use of computations, experiments and high-strain-rate material characterization has, in many cases, supplemented the data achievable by experiments alone at considerable savings in both cost and engineering man-hours.

References

[1] A. Ramezani and H. Rothe, "Numerical Simulation and Experimental Model-Validation for Fiber-Reinforced Plastics Under Impact Loading - Using the Example of Ultra-High Molecular Weight Polyethylene," The Eighth International Conference on Advances in System Simulation (SIMUL 2016) IARIA, Aug. 2016, pp. 17-25, ISBN 978-1-61208-442-8.

[2] D. B. Segala and P. V. Cavallaro, "Numerical investigation of energy absorption mechanisms in unidirectional composites subjected to dynamic loading events," in Computational Materials Science 81, pp. 303–312, 2014.

[3] S. Chocron et al., "Modeling unidirectional composites by bundling fibers into strips with experimental determination of shear and compression properties at high pressures," in Composites Science and Technology 101, pp. 32–40, 2014.

[4] C. J. Hayhurst, S. J. Hiermaier, R. A. Clegg, W. Riedel, and M. Lambert, "Development of material models for nextel and kevlar-expoxy for high pressures and strain rates," in International Journal of Impact Engineering 23, pp. 365–376, 1999.

[5] R. A. Clegg, D. M. White, W. Riedel, and W. Harwick, "Hypervelocity impact damage prediction in composites: Part I—material model and characterisation," in International Journal of Impact Engineering 33, pp. 190–200, 2006.

[6] W. Riedel, H. Nahme, D. M. White, and R. A. Clegg, "Hypervelocity impact damage prediction in composites: Part II—experimental investigations and simulations," in International Journal of Impact Engineering 33, pp. 670–80, 2006.

[7] M. Wicklein, S. Ryan, D. M. White, and R. A. Clegg, "Hypervelocity impact on CFRP: Testing, material modelling, and numerical simulation," in International Journal of Impact Engineering 35, pp.1861–1869, 2008.

[8] ANSYS. *AUTODYN Composite Modelling Release 15.0.* [Online]. Available from: http://ansys.com/ 2016.07.08.

[9] T. Lässig et al., "A non-linear orthotropic hydrocode model for ultra-high molecular weight polyethylene in impact simulations," in International Journal of Impact Engineering 75, pp. 110–122, 2015.

[10] L. H. Nguyen et al., "Numerical Modelling of Ultra-High Molecular Weight Polyethylene Composite Under Impact Loading," in Procedia Engineering 103, pp. 436–443, 2015.

[11] J. Zukas, Introduction to hydrocodes, Elsevier Science, 2004.

[12] R. F. Stellingwerf and C. A. Wingate, "Impact Modeling with Smooth Particle Hydrodynamics," International Journal of Impact Engineering, vol. 14, pp. 707–718, Sep. 1993.

[13] X. Quan, N. K. Birnbaum, M. S. Cowler, and B. I. Gerber, "Numerical Simulations of Structural Deformation under Shock and Impact Loads using a Coupled Multi-Solver Approach," 5th Asia-Pacific Conference on Shock and Impact Loads on Structures, Hunan, China, Nov. 2003, pp. 152-161.

[14] ANSYS Inc. Available Solution Methods. [Online]. Available from: http://www.ansys.com/Products/Simulation+Technology/Structural+Analysis/Explicit+Dynamics/Features/Available+Solution+Methods [retrieved: April, 2014]

[15] P. Fröhlich, "FEM Application Basics," Vieweg Verlag, September 2005.

[16] G.-S. Collins, An Introduction to Hydrocode Modeling, Applied Modelling and Computation Group, Imperial College London, 2002.

[17] J. Sarkar, "Computer Aided Design: A Conceptual Approach," CRC Press, December 2014.

[18] H.-B. Woyand, FEM with CATIA V5, J. Schlembach Fachverlag, 2007.

[19] R. Frieß, "General basis for ballistic material, construction and product testing," presented at the Ballistic Day in Ulm, 2008.

[20] D. E. Carlucci and S. S. Jacobson, Ballistics: Theory and Design of guns and ammunition. CRC Press, 2008.

[21] OEG Gesellschaft für Optik, Elektronik & Gerätetechnik mbH. [Online]. Available from: http://www.oeg-messtechnik.de/?p=5&l=1 [retrieved: March, 2015]

[22] G. Johnson and W. Cook, "A constitutive model and data for metals subjected to large strains, high strain rates and high temperatures," in 7th International Symposium on Ballistics, pp. 541–547, 1983.

[23] D. Steinberg, Equation of state and strength properties of selected materials. California, 1996.

Compatibility of Boundary Angular Velocities in the Velocity-based 3D Beam Formulation

Eva Zupan and Dejan Zupan
Faculty of Civil and Geodetic Engineering
University of Ljubljana
Ljubljana, Slovenia
Email: eva.zupan.lj@gmail.com; dejan.zupan@fgg.uni-lj.si

Abstract—**In this paper, a new velocity-based finite element approach for non-linear dynamics of beam-like structures is introduced. In contrast to standard approaches we here base the formulation on velocities and angular velocities expressed in the most suitable basis regarding standard approximation and interpolation techniques. The additivity of angular velocities in local frame description brings several benefits, such as trivial discretization and update procedure for the primary unknowns and improved stability properties of the time integrator. On the other hand, different initial orientations of elements connected together lead to nodal angular velocities that are expressed in different frames and cannot be directly equalized. The compatibility of angular velocities over the finite element boundaries thus needs to be solved. We avoid introducing constraint equations and additional degrees of freedom and introduce a computationally cheap solution instead.**

Keywords–non-linear dynamics; spatial beams; finite-element method; boundary conditions; velocity-based approach; continuity of velocities.

I. Introduction

The total set of equations in solid mechanics consists of non-linear equilibrium, kinematic and constitutive equations that need to be solved for displacements, strains and stresses. Many practical problems in solid mechanics deal with structures that have one dimension larger than the other two, e.g., columns and girders in civil engineering, robotic arms, rotor blades and aircraft wings in mechanical engineering, deoxyribonucleic acid (DNA) molecules in biology and medicine, nanotubes in nanotechnology. Such structures are usually modelled as beams. It is of utmost importance to consider properly the boundary and continuity conditions when proposing a novel finite element (FE) beam model [1]. We focus in this paper on a structure of a velocity based beam element and the computational aspects in satisfying the continuity conditions over the boundaries.

The paper is structured as follows. Section II presents the oveview of the beam formultions, while Section III introduces the governing equations of the Cosserat beam model. In Section IV, we describe a novel numerical solution method for Cosserat beams. The treatment of boundary conditions is presented in Section V. In Section VI, some numerical examples are given. The paper ends with concluding remarks.

II. Beam formulations

For beam-like structures the kinematics of a body becomes simplified but the equations remain non-linear, see, e.g., Antman [2], Reissner [3] and Simo [4]. Additionally, the reduced kinematics introduces the three-dimensional rotations of rigid cross-sections to describe the configuration of a beam. Spatial rotations are often taken to be the primary variables in three-dimensional beam formulations, see, e.g., [4]–[15], despite their demanding mathematical structure. In the solution algorithms for beams many authors reduce the total set of equations in such a way that the configuration variables (displacements and rotations) become the only unknowns of the problem. For numerical solution methods, such reduction means that the configuration variables need to be discretized with respect to space and time. The multiplicative nature of rotations, characterized by non-additivity, orthogonality and non-commutativity, needs to be properly considered in the numerical solution methods to gain a sufficient performance of calculations and accuracy of the results. Such demands highly increase the complexity of algorithms and disable direct applicability of the methods developed for standard Euclidean spaces, see, e.g., [16]–[21].

Mathematically, rotations are linear transformations in three-dimensional Euclidean space and can therefore be represented by 3×3 matrices. However, these nine components have six constraints, which makes a matrix representation of rotations less convenient for numerical implementations. Widely used are the three-parameter representations of which the often chosen "rotational vector" [22] is only one among many possibilities. It is well known that all three-parameter descriptions of rotations posses singularities. To avoid them a four parameter representations were also used, e.g., [23]–[25]. Surprisingly, it was only recently that this ideas were successfully revived, see, e.g., [14], [15], [26]–[29]. In this paper, rotational quaternions will be used as a suitable representation of rotations, but they will not be taken to be the primary unknowns of the problem. From the perspective of total mechanical energy of the system the velocities and angular velocities seem to be more natural quantities.

Thus, the alternative approach employed here exploits computationally simpler angular velocities as the primary quantities for the description of rotational degrees of freedom. Such approach brings several advantages to non-linear beam dynamics:

- when expressed in local bases, the components of angular velocity vector become additive, which enables the use of standard discretization and interpolation techniques;
- the stability of implicit time integrators is improved by taking the derivative of configuration quantities as the iterative unknowns, see Hosea and Shampine [30];
- the time discretization, linearization of equations and the update procedure are much simpler compared to standard beam elements.

Besides its advantages, this new approach brings some novel issues that need to be properly solved. The crucial idea of the finite element method (FEM) lies in subdivision of a larger structure into smaller parts called finite elements. An important part of the solution procedure is the assembly of equations of finite elements into a larger system of equations that describe the problem at the structural level. The simplest assumption used in the assembly procedure is that the elements are rigidly connected so that the displacements and rotations are continuous over the boundaries. When the displacements and rotations are chosen as the primary variables, a simple Boolean identification of degrees of freedom can be used. This yields that velocities and angular velocities are continuous over the finite element boundaries as well, but only when expressed with respect to a fixed basis.

For the sake of computational advantages at the element level, we express the angular velocities with respect to the moving frame. Because of this choice, the simple identification of degrees of freedom that belongs to the joints between elements can no longer be used due to different initial orientations of elements. Thus, the continuity of configuration quantities in a fixed frame leads to a more complicated relation in the local frame. This relation could be introduced at the structural level using the method of Lagrange multipliers, but such an approach would increase the number of degrees of freedom and the computational complexity of the overall algorithm. An elegant and computationally cheap alternative is presented here. Excellent properties of the proposed numerical model are demonstrated by numerical examples.

III. Cosserat Beam Model

Among beam models, the *Cosserat theory of rods*, [2], is widely used. The numerical implementation of the model is usually attributed to Reissner [3] and Simo [4], where it is also called *the geometrically exact beam*. Only a brief description of the model is presented here.

The centroidal line $\left\{\vec{r}\,(x,t)\,,\ x\in[0,L]\,,\ t\geq 0\right\}$ and the family of cross-sections $\{\mathcal{A}\,(x,t)\,,\ x\in[0,L]\,,\ t\geq 0\}$ of the beam are parametrized by the arc-length parameter x and the time t, where L is the length of the beam in its initial position, see Figure 1. We assume that cross-sections are bounded plane regions that preserve their shape and area during deformation.

For the description of beam equations and the quantities therein, we introduce the *local* orthonormal basis

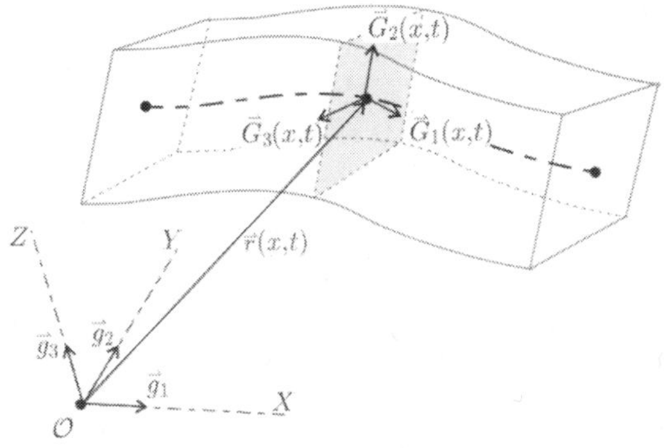

Figure 1. A three-dimensional beam.

$\left\{\vec{G}_1\,(x,t)\,,\vec{G}_2\,(x,t)\,,\vec{G}_3\,(x,t)\right\}$, which defines the orientation of each cross-section, and the *global* orthonormal basis $\left\{\vec{g}_1,\vec{g}_2,\vec{g}_3\right\}$, which is fixed in time and space. A rotation between the global and the local basis, defined by the quaternion multiplication $(\circ)$ reads

$$\vec{G}_i\,(x,t)=\widehat{q}\,(x,t)\circ\vec{g}_i\circ\widehat{q}^*\,(x,t)\,,\qquad i=1,2,3,\tag{1}$$

where $\widehat{q}$ denotes the rotational quaternion and $\widehat{q}^*$ its conjugate. A comprehensive presentation of the quaternion algebra can be found, e.g., in the textbook [31]. For more details on the application of quaternions in beam models please refer to [32] or [15].

Note that any rotational quaternion q has a firm physical meaning. It be presented as the sum of a scalar and a vector,

$$\widehat{q}=\cos\frac{\vartheta}{2}+\sin\frac{\vartheta}{2}\,\vec{n},\qquad \left|\vec{n}\right|=1,\tag{2}$$

where ϑ denotes the angle of rotation and $\vec{n}$ is the unit vector on the axis of rotation.

In what follows abstract vectors will be replaced by component representations. The bold-face letters will be used to represent vector quantities in the component form. The lower case letters will be used when a vector is expressed with respect to the fixed frame and the upper case letters are used for the local basis description. A hat over the letter denotes a four-dimensional vector, a member of the algebra of quaternions. The dependency of quantities on space x and time t will be mostly omitted for better readability.

A. Kinematic compatibility

In Cosserat rod theory the resultant strain measures at the centroid of each cross-section are directly introduced and expressed with kinematic variables by the first order differential equations

$$\mathbf{\Gamma}=\widehat{\mathbf{q}}^*\circ\mathbf{r}'\circ\widehat{\mathbf{q}}+\mathbf{\Gamma}_0,\tag{3}$$

$$\mathbf{K}=2\widehat{\mathbf{q}}^*\circ\widehat{\mathbf{q}}',\tag{4}$$

where $\boldsymbol{\Gamma}$ and $\mathbf{K}$ denote the translational and rotational strain, respectively, both expressed with respect to the local basis. The prime ($'$) denotes the derivative with respect to x. Similarly, when we measure the rate of change of configuration variables with time, we have

$$\mathbf{v} = \dot{\mathbf{r}}, \tag{5}$$

$$\boldsymbol{\Omega} = 2\widehat{\mathbf{q}}^* \circ \dot{\widehat{\mathbf{q}}}, \tag{6}$$

introducing velocity $\mathbf{v}$ in fixed basis and angular velocity $\boldsymbol{\Omega}$ in local basis description, while the dot denotes the time derivative. It is important to observe that strains, velocities, and angular velocities are mutually dependent. Their direct relation is obtained by comparing mixed partial derivatives. After a straightforward derivation, we have

$$\dot{\boldsymbol{\Gamma}} = \widehat{\mathbf{q}}^* \circ \mathbf{v}' \circ \widehat{\mathbf{q}} + (\widehat{\mathbf{q}}^* \circ \mathbf{r}' \circ \widehat{\mathbf{q}}) \times \boldsymbol{\Omega}, \tag{7}$$

$$\dot{\mathbf{K}} = \boldsymbol{\Omega}' + \mathbf{K} \times \boldsymbol{\Omega}. \tag{8}$$

Equations (7)–(8) describe the kinematic compatibility of continuous system, [33], [34]. Its importance is obvious: the relation between the rotational strains and the angular velocities is described without rotational parameters. Since the rotational degrees of freedom are usually highly non-linear when compared to other quantities such modification of kinematic equations can be numerically advantageous.

B. Governing equations

The continuous balance equations of a three-dimensional beam in quaternion notation read:

$$\mathbf{n}' + \tilde{\mathbf{n}} = \rho A \dot{\mathbf{v}}, \tag{9}$$

$$\mathbf{m}' + \mathbf{r}' \times \mathbf{n} + \tilde{\mathbf{m}} = \mathbf{q} \circ \left(\mathbf{J}_\rho \dot{\boldsymbol{\Omega}} + \boldsymbol{\Omega} \times \mathbf{J}_\rho \boldsymbol{\Omega} \right) \circ \widehat{\mathbf{q}}^*. \tag{10}$$

Equation (9) is a standard linear momentum balance equation, while equation (10) represents the angular momentum balance equation in terms of quaternion algebra as it follows from the generalized d'Alembert principle considering the unit norm of rotational quaternion. Here, $\mathbf{n}$ and $\mathbf{m}$ are the resultant force and moment vector of the cross-section expressed in fixed frame, i.e.,

$$\mathbf{n}(x,t) = \widehat{\mathbf{q}}(x,t) \circ \mathbf{N}(x,t) \circ \widehat{\mathbf{q}}^*(x,t), \tag{11}$$

$$\mathbf{m}(x,t) = \widehat{\mathbf{q}}(x,t) \circ \mathbf{M}(x,t) \circ \widehat{\mathbf{q}}^*(x,t), \tag{12}$$

where $\mathbf{N}$ and $\mathbf{M}$ are the same vectors expressed in local basis; ρ is the density of the material; A is the area of the cross-section; $\mathbf{J}_\rho$ is the matrix of mass moments of inertia; $\tilde{\mathbf{n}}$ and $\tilde{\mathbf{m}}$ are vectors of applied distributed force and moment. Together with balance equations the following conditions at the boundaries need to be satisfied:

$$\mathbf{n}(0,t) + \mathbf{f}^0(t) = \mathbf{0}, \tag{13}$$

$$\mathbf{m}(0,t) + \mathbf{h}^0(t) = \mathbf{0}, \tag{14}$$

$$\mathbf{n}(L,t) - \mathbf{f}^L(t) = \mathbf{0}, \tag{15}$$

$$\mathbf{m}(L,t) - \mathbf{h}^L(t) = \mathbf{0}, \tag{16}$$

$\mathbf{f}^0$, $\mathbf{h}^0$, $\mathbf{f}^L$ and $\mathbf{h}^L$ are the external time-dependent point forces and moments at the two boundaries, $x = 0$ and $x = L$.

For constitutive equations various models could be taken, but here we limit ourselves to the simplest case of linear elastic material, where

$$\mathbf{N} = \mathrm{diag}[\ EA \quad GA_2 \quad GA_3\ ]\,\boldsymbol{\Gamma}, \tag{17}$$

$$\mathbf{M} = \mathrm{diag}[\ GI_1 \quad EI_2 \quad EI_3\ ]\,\mathbf{K}. \tag{18}$$

Here, EA/L is the axial stiffness, EI_2 and EI_3 denote the bending stiffness, GI_1/L is the torsional stiffness, GA_2 and GA_3 are the shear stiffnesses.

IV. Numerical solution method

We will solve the balance equations using the method of weighted residuals. Equations (9) and (10) are multiplied by test functions $I_p(x)$, $p = 1, 2, ..., N$, and integrated along the length of the beam:

$$\int_0^L \left[\mathbf{n}' - \tilde{\mathbf{n}} - \rho A \ddot{\mathbf{r}} \right] I_p \, dx = \mathbf{0}, \tag{19}$$

$$\int_0^L \Big[\mathbf{m} - (\mathbf{r}' \times \mathbf{n}) - \tilde{\mathbf{m}} - \widehat{\mathbf{q}} \circ \left(\mathbf{J}_\rho \dot{\boldsymbol{\Omega}} \right) \circ \widehat{\mathbf{q}}^* I_p + \boldsymbol{\Omega} \times \left(\widehat{\mathbf{q}} \circ (\mathbf{J}_\rho \boldsymbol{\Omega}) \circ \widehat{\mathbf{q}}^* \right) \Big] I_p \, dx = \mathbf{0}. \tag{20}$$

The terms $\mathbf{n} I_p$ and $\mathbf{m} I_p$ are integrated by parts, which after considering the boundary conditions (13)–(16) gives:

$$\int_0^L \left[\mathbf{n} I_p' - \tilde{\mathbf{n}} I_p + \rho A \ddot{\mathbf{r}} I_p \right] dx - \delta_p \boldsymbol{f} = \mathbf{0}, \tag{21}$$

$$\int_0^L \Big[\mathbf{m} I_p' - (\mathbf{r}' \times \mathbf{n}) I_p - \tilde{\mathbf{m}} I_p + \widehat{\mathbf{q}} \circ \left(\mathbf{J}_\rho \dot{\boldsymbol{\Omega}} \right) \circ \widehat{\mathbf{q}}^* I_p + \boldsymbol{\omega} \times \left(\widehat{\mathbf{q}} \circ (\mathbf{J}_\rho \boldsymbol{\Omega}) \circ \widehat{\mathbf{q}}^* \right) I_p \Big] dx - \delta_p \boldsymbol{h} = \mathbf{0}. \tag{22}$$

Here

$$\delta_p \mathbf{f} = \begin{cases} \mathbf{f}^0, & p = 1 \\ \mathbf{f}^L, & p = N \\ 0, & \text{otherwise} \end{cases},$$

$$\delta_p \mathbf{h} = \begin{cases} \mathbf{h}^0, & p = 1 \\ \mathbf{h}^L, & p = N \\ 0, & \text{otherwise} \end{cases}.$$

Equations (21)–(22) represent a system of $6N$ algebraic equations that is in general too demanding to be solved analytically. In our approach, we express all the unknown quantities with velocity and angular velocity. The approximative solution in both time and space is then spanned on these two quantities. for completeness the details on discretization will be briefly introduced.

A. Time discretization

For the time discretization, we use the approximation of displacements at t_{n+1} following from the mean value theorem:

$$\mathbf{r}^{[n+1]} = \mathbf{r}^{[n]} + h\frac{\mathbf{v}^{[n]} + \mathbf{v}^{[n+1]}}{2},$$

which yields

$$\mathbf{r}^{[n+1]} = \mathbf{r}^{[n]} + h\overline{\mathbf{v}},$$

where $\overline{\mathbf{v}}$ denotes the average velocity

$$\overline{\mathbf{v}} = \frac{\mathbf{v}^{[n]} + \mathbf{v}^{[n+1]}}{2}$$

and $h = t_{n+1} - t_n$ is the time step of the scheme.

For accelerations we can similarly employ

$$\frac{\mathbf{a}^{[n]} + \mathbf{a}^{[n+1]}}{2} = \frac{\mathbf{v}^{[n+1]} - \mathbf{v}^{[n]}}{h}.$$

After some rearrangement of terms, the scheme for translational degrees of freedom reads

$$\begin{aligned} \mathbf{r}^{[n+1]} &= \mathbf{r}^{[n]} + h\overline{\mathbf{v}}, \\ \mathbf{v}^{[n+1]} &= -\mathbf{v}^{[n]} + 2\overline{\mathbf{v}}, \\ \mathbf{a}^{[n+1]} &= -\mathbf{a}^{[n]} - \frac{4}{h}\mathbf{v}^{[n]} + \frac{4}{h}\overline{\mathbf{v}}. \end{aligned} \tag{23}$$

This scheme can be interpreted as a modification of the classical implicit Newmark scheme, where the average velocity becomes the iterative unknown, see [8] and [35].

A similar approach can be used for rotational degrees of freedom with an important exception stemming from the non-linear relationship between angular velocities and rotational quaternions. The exponential mapping is used to map from incremental angular velocities to incremental rotations. The incremental rotation is then multiplied with the current one. The scheme for rotational degrees of freedom reads

$$\begin{aligned} \widehat{\mathbf{q}}^{[n+1]} &= \widehat{\mathbf{q}}^{[n]} \circ \exp\left(\frac{h}{2}\overline{\mathbf{\Omega}}\right), \\ \mathbf{\Omega}^{[n+1]} &= -\mathbf{\Omega}^{[n]} + 2\overline{\mathbf{\Omega}}, \\ \boldsymbol{\alpha}^{[n+1]} &= -\boldsymbol{\alpha}^{[n]} - \frac{4}{h}\mathbf{\Omega}^{[n]} + \frac{4}{h}\overline{\mathbf{\Omega}}, \end{aligned} \tag{24}$$

where exp denotes the quaternion exponential

$$\exp(\widehat{\mathbf{x}}) = \widehat{\mathbf{1}} + \frac{\widehat{\mathbf{x}}}{1!} + \frac{1}{2!}\widehat{\mathbf{x}} \circ \widehat{\mathbf{x}} + \frac{1}{3!}\widehat{\mathbf{x}} \circ \widehat{\mathbf{x}} \circ \widehat{\mathbf{x}} + \dots \tag{25}$$

The above presented time-discretization scheme describes the assumptions taken regarding displacements, rotations and their time derivatives. For deformable structures time discretization of strain quantities is also needed. We derive the discrete compatibility equations analogously as for the continuous case. This gives

$$\begin{aligned} \mathbf{\Gamma}^{[n+1]} &= \exp^*\left(\frac{h}{2}\overline{\mathbf{\Omega}}\right) \circ \left(\mathbf{\Gamma}^{[n]} - \mathbf{\Gamma}_0\right) \exp\left(\frac{h}{2}\overline{\mathbf{\Omega}}\right) \\ &\quad + h\widehat{\mathbf{q}}^{*[n+1]} \circ \overline{\mathbf{v}}' \circ \widehat{\mathbf{q}}^{[n+1]} + \mathbf{\Gamma}_0, \end{aligned} \tag{26}$$

$$\begin{aligned} \mathbf{K}^{[n+1]} &= \exp^*\left(\frac{h}{2}\overline{\mathbf{\Omega}}\right) \circ \mathbf{K}^{[n]} \circ \exp\left(\frac{h}{2}\overline{\mathbf{\Omega}}\right) \\ &\quad + 2\exp^*\left(\frac{h}{2}\overline{\mathbf{\Omega}}\right) \circ \exp'\left(\frac{h}{2}\overline{\mathbf{\Omega}}\right). \end{aligned} \tag{27}$$

When the governing equations of a beam are evaluated at discrete time t_{n+1} and the schemes (23)–(24) are taken into account, we obtain the system of equations dependent only on the arch-length parameter x. In order to solve these equations at each particular time step we need to introduce the spatial discretization.

B. Spatial discretization

After the time discretization introduced, the average velocities $\overline{\mathbf{v}}$ and $\overline{\mathbf{\Omega}}$ are the only unknown functions along the length of the beam for any particular discrete time. They are replaced by a set of nodal values $\overline{\mathbf{v}}^p$, $\overline{\mathbf{\Omega}}^p$ at discretization points x_p, $p = 1, \dots, N$, with $x_1 = 0$ and $x_N = L$, and interpolated by a set of interpolation functions $I_p(x)$ in-between:

$$\overline{\mathbf{v}}(x) = \sum_{p=1}^{N} I_p(x)\,\overline{\mathbf{v}}^p, \tag{28}$$

$$\overline{\mathbf{\Omega}}(x) = \sum_{p=1}^{N} I_p(x)\,\overline{\mathbf{\Omega}}^p. \tag{29}$$

The same discretization procedure is performed at every finite element of the structure. Thus, boundary nodes x_1 and x_N become members of the global notes important at the structural level, while $x_2,\dots x_{N-1}$ are internal points of the element, often but not necessarily condensed at the elements level. Angular velocities in local basis description are additive quantities and the standard aditive-type interpolation used is in complete accord with the properties of the configuration space.

C. Newton iteration

After time and space discretization, the governing equations (21)–(22) are replaced by a set of nonlinear algebraic equations that need to be solved at each discrete time for all the nodal values. The non-linear equations are solved iteratively using the Newton-Raphson method

$$\mathbf{K}^{[i]}\delta\mathbf{y} = -\mathbf{f}^{[i]}, \tag{30}$$

where $\mathbf{K}^{[i]}$ is the global Jacobian tangent matrix, $\mathbf{f}^{[i]}$ the residual vector of discretized equations (21)–(22), both in iteration i, and $\delta\mathbf{y}$ a vector of corrections of all nodal unknowns

$$\delta\mathbf{y} = \begin{bmatrix} \delta\overline{\mathbf{v}}_1 & \delta\overline{\mathbf{\Omega}}_1 & \cdots & \delta\overline{\mathbf{v}}_M & \delta\overline{\mathbf{\Omega}}_M \end{bmatrix}^T$$

A suitable choice of nodal variables allows the kinematically admissible additive update:

$$\overline{\mathbf{v}}^{[i+1]} = \overline{\mathbf{v}}^{[i]} + \delta\overline{\mathbf{v}}, \tag{31}$$

$$\overline{\boldsymbol{\Omega}}^{[i+1]} = \overline{\boldsymbol{\Omega}}^{[i]} + \delta\overline{\boldsymbol{\Omega}} \tag{32}$$

at each discrete point of the structure. Further details on linearization of equations can be found in [36].

V. Continuity of Boundary Values

Finite elements have equal displacements and rotations at the rigid joints. However, the initial rotations of different elements are not necessarily equal. When the initial orientations differ, we need to distinguish between the initial and the relative rotations. Let us start with two elements having different initial orientations, described by quaternions $\widehat{\mathbf{q}}_0^{\mathrm{I}}$ and $\widehat{\mathbf{q}}_0^{\mathrm{II}}$ at the joint: $\widehat{\mathbf{q}}_0^{\mathrm{I}} \neq \widehat{\mathbf{q}}_0^{\mathrm{II}}$. When the joint is rigid the position vectors are equal, but the total rotations differ

$$\mathbf{r}^{\mathrm{I}} = \mathbf{r}^{\mathrm{II}} \qquad \text{and} \qquad \widehat{\mathbf{q}}^{\mathrm{I}} \neq \widehat{\mathbf{q}}^{\mathrm{II}}, \tag{33}$$

as shown in Figure 2.

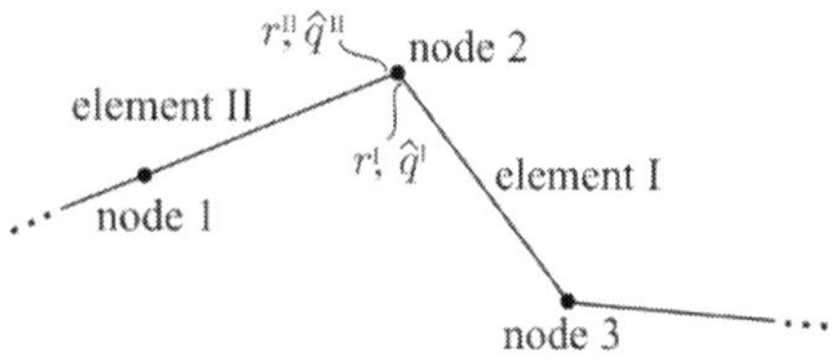

Figure 2. A rigid joint of two differently oriented elements.

The total rotations can be expressed as a composition of initial and relative rotation

$$\widehat{\mathbf{q}}^{\mathrm{I}} = \widehat{\mathbf{q}}_0^{\mathrm{I}} \circ \widehat{\mathbf{k}}^{\mathrm{I}} \qquad \text{and} \qquad \widehat{\mathbf{q}}^{\mathrm{II}} = \widehat{\mathbf{q}}_0^{\mathrm{II}} \circ \widehat{\mathbf{k}}^{\mathrm{II}}, \tag{34}$$

where the relative rotations are equal:

$$\widehat{\mathbf{k}}^{\mathrm{I}} = \widehat{\mathbf{k}}^{\mathrm{II}}. \tag{35}$$

The continuity condition, which could also be called the compatibility of rotations at the element boundaries, thus reads

$$\widehat{\mathbf{q}}^{\mathrm{I}} \circ \widehat{\mathbf{q}}_0^{\mathrm{I}*} = \widehat{\mathbf{q}}^{\mathrm{II}} \circ \widehat{\mathbf{q}}_0^{\mathrm{II}*}.$$

In configuration based approach we usually avoid enforcing this condition by introducing the relative rotational quaternion $\widehat{\mathbf{k}}$ as the nodal variable. For the velocity-based approach, we can similarly observe that

$$\overline{\mathbf{v}}^{\mathrm{I}} = \overline{\mathbf{v}}^{\mathrm{II}} \qquad \text{and} \qquad \overline{\boldsymbol{\Omega}}^{\mathrm{I}} \neq \overline{\boldsymbol{\Omega}}^{\mathrm{II}},$$

as the angular velocities are expressed in different local frames. We will derive the compatibility condition for angular velocities at the joints and propose a similar strategy as for rotational quaternions to avoid the use of Lagrange multipliers method by the substitution of the primary unknowns of Newton's iteration at the structural level. The details are presented in the sequel.

A. Relation between boundary angular velocities

The angular velocity vector expressed in the local frame is defined as

$$\boldsymbol{\Omega} = 2\widehat{\mathbf{q}}^* \circ \dot{\widehat{\mathbf{q}}}, \tag{36}$$

which yields the expressions for the nodal angular velocities of elements I and II at the joint

$$\overline{\boldsymbol{\Omega}}^{\mathrm{I}} = 2\widehat{\mathbf{q}}^{\mathrm{I}*} \circ \dot{\widehat{\mathbf{q}}}^{\mathrm{I}} \qquad \text{and} \qquad \overline{\boldsymbol{\Omega}}^{\mathrm{II}} = 2\widehat{\mathbf{q}}^{\mathrm{II}*} \circ \dot{\widehat{\mathbf{q}}}^{\mathrm{II}}.$$

After considering (34), we have

$$\overline{\boldsymbol{\Omega}}^{\mathrm{I}} = 2\widehat{\mathbf{q}}_0^{\mathrm{I}*} \circ \widehat{\mathbf{k}}^{\mathrm{I}*} \circ \dot{\widehat{\mathbf{k}}}^{\mathrm{I}} \circ \widehat{\mathbf{q}}_0^{\mathrm{I}},$$

$$\overline{\boldsymbol{\Omega}}^{\mathrm{II}} = 2\widehat{\mathbf{q}}_0^{\mathrm{II}*} \circ \widehat{\mathbf{k}}^{\mathrm{II}*} \circ \dot{\widehat{\mathbf{k}}}^{\mathrm{II}} \circ \widehat{\mathbf{q}}_0^{\mathrm{II}}.$$

Since the relative rotation $\widehat{\mathbf{k}}$ is continuous over the boundaries of elements, eq. (35), we are able to express the constraint relation between the boundary angular velocities

$$\widehat{\mathbf{q}}_0^{\mathrm{I}} \circ \overline{\boldsymbol{\Omega}}^{\mathrm{I}} \circ \widehat{\mathbf{q}}_0^{\mathrm{I}*} = \widehat{\mathbf{q}}_0^{\mathrm{II}} \circ \overline{\boldsymbol{\Omega}}^{\mathrm{II}} \circ \widehat{\mathbf{q}}_0^{\mathrm{II}*}. \tag{37}$$

For the clarity of further derivation, it is convenient to express (37) in terms of rotation matrices:

$$\mathbf{R}_0^{\mathrm{I}}\overline{\boldsymbol{\Omega}}^{\mathrm{I}} = \mathbf{R}_0^{\mathrm{II}}\overline{\boldsymbol{\Omega}}^{\mathrm{II}}, \tag{38}$$

where $\mathbf{R}_0^{\mathrm{I}}$ and $\mathbf{R}_0^{\mathrm{II}}$ denote the standard rotation matrices equivalent to quaternion-based rotations expressed with $\widehat{\mathbf{q}}_0^{\mathrm{I}}$ and $\widehat{\mathbf{q}}_0^{\mathrm{II}}$.

B. Algorithmically enforced boundary conditions

A solution of two moment equilibrium equations (22) expressed at the same node, here formally written as

$$\mathcal{M}^{\mathrm{I}}\left(\overline{\boldsymbol{\Omega}}^{\mathrm{I}}\right) = \mathbf{0} \qquad \text{and} \qquad \mathcal{M}^{\mathrm{II}}\left(\overline{\boldsymbol{\Omega}}^{\mathrm{II}}\right) = \mathbf{0}, \tag{39}$$

needs to be found. The solution must also satisfy the algebraic constraint

$$\mathbf{R}_0^{\mathrm{I}}\overline{\boldsymbol{\Omega}}^{\mathrm{I}} - \mathbf{R}_0^{\mathrm{II}}\overline{\boldsymbol{\Omega}}^{\mathrm{II}} = 0. \tag{40}$$

Following the method of Lagrange multipliers the constraint equation is multiplied by a multiplier λ and linearized. The corresponding partial derivatives are then added to the initial variational problem to obtain the weak form of Lagrange function. For the present case it reads

$$\mathcal{M}^{\mathrm{I}}\left(\overline{\boldsymbol{\Omega}}^{\mathrm{I}}\right) + \mathbf{R}_0^{\mathrm{I}}\lambda = \mathbf{0}, \tag{41}$$

$$\mathcal{M}^{\mathrm{II}}\left(\overline{\boldsymbol{\Omega}}^{\mathrm{II}}\right) - \mathbf{R}_0^{\mathrm{II}}\lambda = \mathbf{0}, \tag{42}$$

$$\mathbf{R}_0^{\mathrm{I}}\overline{\boldsymbol{\Omega}}^{\mathrm{I}} - \mathbf{R}_0^{\mathrm{II}}\overline{\boldsymbol{\Omega}}^{\mathrm{II}} = \mathbf{0}. \tag{43}$$

The method thus increases the size of the system and the computational demands. It introduces three additional scalar unknowns and three additional equations for each rigid joint between two elements. To avoid this, we introduce the following change of variables describing the nodal rotation-related unknowns:

$$\overline{\mathbf{\Omega}}_R^{\mathrm{I}} = \mathbf{R}_0^{\mathrm{I}}\overline{\mathbf{\Omega}}^{\mathrm{I}} \quad \text{and} \quad \overline{\mathbf{\Omega}}_R^{\mathrm{II}} = \mathbf{R}_0^{\mathrm{II}}\overline{\mathbf{\Omega}}^{\mathrm{II}}. \tag{44}$$

Based on the substitution of unknowns (44), the method of Lagrange multipliers gives

$$\mathcal{M}^{\mathrm{I}}\left(\mathbf{R}_0^{\mathrm{I}T}\overline{\mathbf{\Omega}}_R^{\mathrm{I}}\right) + \lambda = \mathbf{0}, \tag{45}$$

$$\mathcal{M}^{\mathrm{II}}\left(\mathbf{R}_0^{\mathrm{II}T}\overline{\mathbf{\Omega}}_R^{\mathrm{II}}\right) - \lambda = \mathbf{0}, \tag{46}$$

$$\overline{\mathbf{\Omega}}_R^{\mathrm{I}} - \overline{\mathbf{\Omega}}_R^{\mathrm{II}} = \mathbf{0}. \tag{47}$$

The system (45)–(47) can be easily reduced since the nodal unknowns are now identical: $\overline{\mathbf{\Omega}}_R = \overline{\mathbf{\Omega}}_R^{\mathrm{I}} = \overline{\mathbf{\Omega}}_R^{\mathrm{II}}$. These new variables can be interpreted as the relative angular velocities in a relative local frame. It is important to observe that the equations (45)–(46) represent the moment equilibrium equations, both written with respect to the same fixed basis. This fact allows us to sum the first two equations which directly leads to the reduced moment equilibrium equation at the joint:

$$\mathcal{M}^{\mathrm{I}}\left(\overline{\mathbf{\Omega}}_R\right) + \mathcal{M}^{\mathrm{II}}\left(\overline{\mathbf{\Omega}}_R\right) = 0.$$

Translational degrees of freedom are left unchanged. The vector of nodal unknowns now becomes

$$\mathbf{y}_R = \begin{bmatrix} \overline{\mathbf{v}}_1 & \overline{\mathbf{\Omega}}_{R,1} & \cdots & \overline{\mathbf{v}}_M & \overline{\mathbf{\Omega}}_{R,M} \end{bmatrix}^T,$$

while its iterative correction vector reads

$$\delta\mathbf{y}_R = \begin{bmatrix} \delta\overline{\mathbf{v}}_1 & \delta\overline{\mathbf{\Omega}}_{R,1} & \cdots & \delta\overline{\mathbf{v}}_M & \delta\overline{\mathbf{\Omega}}_{R,M} \end{bmatrix}^T.$$

Note that the corrections of newly introduced variables (44) can still be directly summed up to the current iterative values. This property follows from the distributivity of multiplication of time-constant matrix $\mathbf{R}_0$ with the sum of angular velocity and its update. The original quantities $\overline{\mathbf{\Omega}}^{\mathrm{I}}$ and $\overline{\mathbf{\Omega}}^{\mathrm{II}}$ remain to be the interpolated quantities at the elements level. Hence in each iteration step i the variables $\overline{\mathbf{\Omega}}^{\mathrm{I}}$ and $\overline{\mathbf{\Omega}}^{\mathrm{II}}$ are extracted from $\overline{\mathbf{\Omega}}_R^{\mathrm{I}} = \overline{\mathbf{\Omega}}_R^{\mathrm{II}}$ and applied for further calculations.

In order to adapt a block of the corresponding tangent stiffness matrix at an arbitrary boundary node of a element, we express it with four submatrices appurtenant to translational and rotational degrees of freedom

$$\mathbf{K}_{\mathrm{node}}^{\mathrm{I}} = \begin{bmatrix} \mathbf{K}_{\mathbf{vv}}^{\mathrm{I}} & \mathbf{K}_{\mathbf{v\Omega}}^{\mathrm{I}} \\ \mathbf{K}_{\mathbf{\Omega v}}^{\mathrm{I}} & \mathbf{K}_{\mathbf{\Omega\Omega}}^{\mathrm{I}} \end{bmatrix},$$

$$\mathbf{K}_{\mathrm{node}}^{\mathrm{II}} = \begin{bmatrix} \mathbf{K}_{\mathbf{vv}}^{\mathrm{II}} & \mathbf{K}_{\mathbf{v\Omega}}^{\mathrm{II}} \\ \mathbf{K}_{\mathbf{\Omega v}}^{\mathrm{II}} & \mathbf{K}_{\mathbf{\Omega\Omega}}^{\mathrm{II}} \end{bmatrix},$$

where $\mathbf{K}_{\mathbf{vv}}$ and $\mathbf{K}_{\mathbf{v\Omega}}$ denote the partial derivatives of (21) with respect to velocities and angular velocities, respectively. Similarly, $\mathbf{K}_{\mathbf{\Omega v}}$ and $\mathbf{K}_{\mathbf{\Omega\Omega}}$ denote the partial derivatives of (22). While the matrices $\mathbf{K}_{\mathbf{vv}}$ and $\mathbf{K}_{\mathbf{\Omega v}}$ are left unchanged, the derivatives with respect to angular velocities need to be transformed in accord with the newly introduced variable leading to

$$\tilde{\mathbf{K}}_{\mathrm{node}}^{\mathrm{I}} = \begin{bmatrix} \mathbf{K}_{\mathbf{vv}}^{\mathrm{I}} & \mathbf{K}_{\mathbf{v\Omega}}^{\mathrm{I}}\left(\mathbf{R}_0^{\mathrm{I}}\right)^T \\ \mathbf{K}_{\mathbf{\Omega v}}^{\mathrm{I}} & \mathbf{K}_{\mathbf{\Omega\Omega}}^{\mathrm{I}}\left(\mathbf{R}_0^{\mathrm{I}}\right)^T \end{bmatrix}$$

$$\tilde{\mathbf{K}}_{\mathrm{node}}^{\mathrm{II}} = \begin{bmatrix} \mathbf{K}_{\mathbf{vv}}^{\mathrm{II}} & \mathbf{K}_{\mathbf{v\Omega}}^{\mathrm{II}}\left(\mathbf{R}_0^{\mathrm{II}}\right)^T \\ \mathbf{K}_{\mathbf{\Omega v}}^{\mathrm{II}} & \mathbf{K}_{\mathbf{\Omega\Omega}}^{\mathrm{II}}\left(\mathbf{R}_0^{\mathrm{II}}\right)^T \end{bmatrix}.$$

The above transformation allows the direct summation of nodal tangent matrices within the Boolean identification technique to be admissible for the chosen formulation:

$$\tilde{\mathbf{K}}_{\mathrm{node}} = \tilde{\mathbf{K}}_{\mathrm{node}}^{\mathrm{I}} + \tilde{\mathbf{K}}_{\mathrm{node}}^{\mathrm{II}}.$$

With this procedure only six variables per node are needed and computational complexity is only slightly increased due to transformation of tangent stiffness matrices and the reconstruction of average angular velocities at the element's level from the relative ones at the structural level. This procedure is done by applying a simple time-independent rotation. The main advantage, i.e., the additivity of the iterative and the interpolated unknowns, is preserved. The size of the problem for each element thus remains equal to $6N$, which means that on the structural level we need to solve $6(N \cdot E - n)$ equations, where E denotes the number of elements and n the number of rigid joints. To enforce the boundary conditions, the proposed method requires n additional matrix products of the initial transposed rotation matrix, $\mathbf{R}_0^T$, and the relative angular velocity, $\overline{\mathbf{\Omega}}_R$. As we will show by numerical example, these costs are negligible with respect to the overall numerical procedure.

VI. Numerical Studies

The applicability and excellent performance of the proposed method will be demonstrated by standard benchmark examples for flexible beam-like structures with finite strains where the structure undergoes large displacements and rotations. Equidistant discretization points were chosen for spatial discretization and standard Lagrangian polynomials were taken to be interpolation functions. Integrals were evaluated numerically using the Gaussian quadrature rule. The Newton-Raphson iteration scheme was terminated when the Euclidean norm of the vector of corrections of all primary unknowns was under 10^{-9}. The geometric and material data chosen in the examples are

$$EA = GA_2 = GA_3 = 10^6\ \mathrm{N},$$
$$GI_1 = EI_2 = EI_3 = 10^3\ \mathrm{Nm}^2,$$
$$\rho A = 1\ \mathrm{kg/m}.$$

Other data are provided separately for each example.

A. *Free flight of a beam: the computational performance*

In our first example, we analyse the computational performance of the present approach when solving a problem similar to the one introduced by Simo and Vu-Quoc [18]. The beam is initially inclined and subjected to a piecewise linear point force f_X and point moments h_Y and h_Z at the lower end, as shown in Figure 3. The mass-inertia matrix of the cross-section is taken to be: $\mathbf{J}_\rho = \mathrm{diag}[\ 10 \quad 10 \quad 10\ ]\ \mathrm{kg\,m}$.

For this particular problem, all elements have equal initial orientations. A simple Boolean identification of degrees of freedom is therefore reasonable even if angular velocities in local frame description are the primary unknowns, which is the case in our approach. This allows us to solve the problem in two different ways: i) with Boolean identification and ii) using the proposed algorithm. By doing so, we will be able to compare the computational times and demonstrate the demands of the presented algorithm. Note that the Boolean identification is not appropriate when solving problems, where elements have different initial inclinations, which limits its applicability and generality.

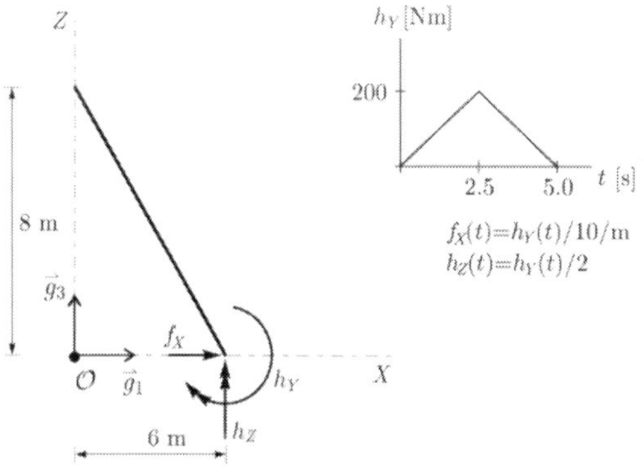

Figure 3. Unsupported beam that is initially straight but inclined.

To compare both methods, a dense mesh of 100 linear elements has been used. For this problem a small number of elements would be sufficient, but by increasing their number the complexity of the overall algorithm raises so the additional demands of the proposed algorithm can be easier observed. Besides that, the computational error of the results becomes negligible with very dense mesh. The average computational times of the same evaluation in seconds are presented in Table I.

TABLE I. COMPUTATIONAL TIMES OF INITIALLY STRAIGHT BEAM.

Method	*initial time step*	*ten time steps*
Boolean identification	3.415	42.820
proposed algorithm	3.508	34.011

We can observe that computational times of the proposed method are only slightly larger after the first time step. However, in the time stepping procedure the proposed algorithm behaves better since the newly introduced relative velocities seem to be more suitable computational unknowns, which leads to a lower number of total iterations needed and, therefore, lower computational times.

B. Large deflections of right-angle cantilever

This classical example introduced by Simo and Vu-Quoc [18] was studied by many authors. A right-angle cantilever beam is subjected to a triangular pulse out-of-plane load at the elbow, see Figure 4. Each part of the cantilever is dicretized with two third-order elements. A dynamic response of the cantilever involves very large magnitudes of displacements and rotations together with finite strains. After removal of the external force, the cantilever undergoes free vibrations and the total mechanical energy of the cantilever should remain constant. Therefore, the stability of the algorithm is here checked through the energy behaviour. The centroidal mass-inertia matrix of the cross-section is diagonal: $\mathbf{J}_\rho = \mathrm{diag}[\ 20 \quad 10 \quad 10\ ]\ \mathrm{kg\,m}$. Originally, the solution was computed on the time interval $[0, 30]$ s with fixed time step 0.25 s, later the interval was extended to $[0, 50]$ s by Jelenić and Crisfield [37] claiming that most of the algorithms encounter numerical stability problems between times 30 s and

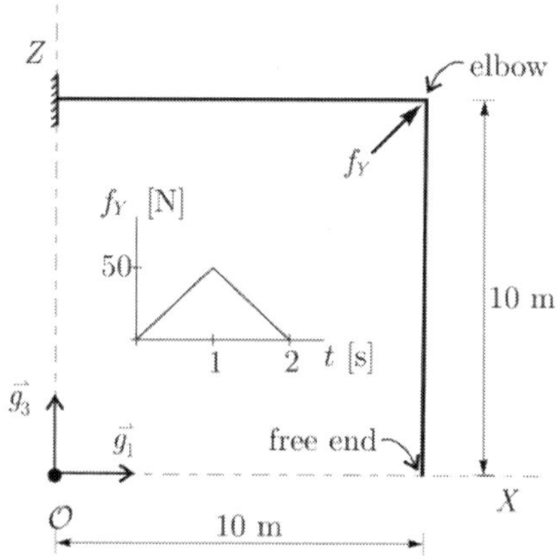

Figure 4. The right-angle cantilever subjected to out-of-plane loading.

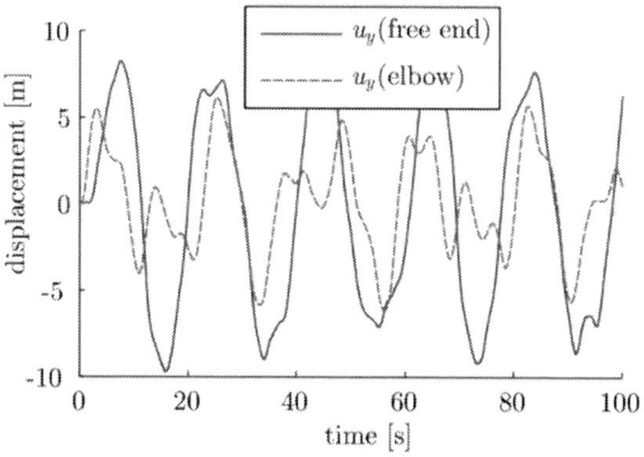

Figure 5. The out-of-plane displacements at free-end and at elbow for the right-angle cantilever.

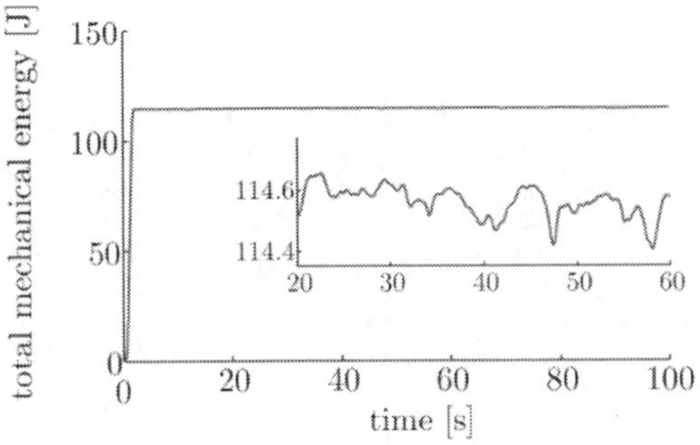

Figure 6. The time history of the total mechanical energy for the right-angle cantilever.

50 s. Here on a longer time interval $[0, 100]$ s solution was obtained without any numerical problems noticed, see Figure 5. However, the time step used had to be reduced by half, $h = 0.125$ s, otherwise the iteration could not achieve the prescribed tolerance condition at time 51.5 s. From Figure 6 we can observe almost constant total mechanical energy after time $t = 5$ s; only slight discrepancy of about 0.2% can be observed, which indicates good stability of calculations. The present results on the time interval $[0, 30]$ s agree well with the results reported by other authors.

C. Large overall motion of a flexible cross-like structure

The large overall motion of completely free "cross" was first presented by Simo et al. [38] to illustrate the performance of the algorithm when calculating the dynamics response of a reticulated structure. The geometry and the applied external out-of plane forces are depicted in Figure 7. The centroidal mass-inertia matrix of the cross-section is taken to be $\mathbf{J}_\rho = \text{diag}[\ 10 \quad 10 \quad 10\ ]\ \text{kg m}$.

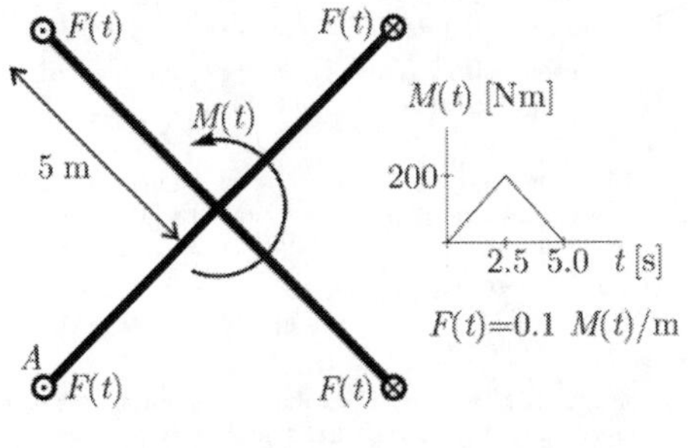

Figure 7. The geometry and the loading of the "cross".

In this example, four finite elements are rigidly connected at the central point sharing the same velocities and the same relative angular velocities. Thus, it is very suitable for the demonstration of the appropriateness of the proposed approach. The solution was computed on a very large time interval $[0, 1000]$ s with time step $h = 0.1$ s. We observed perfect

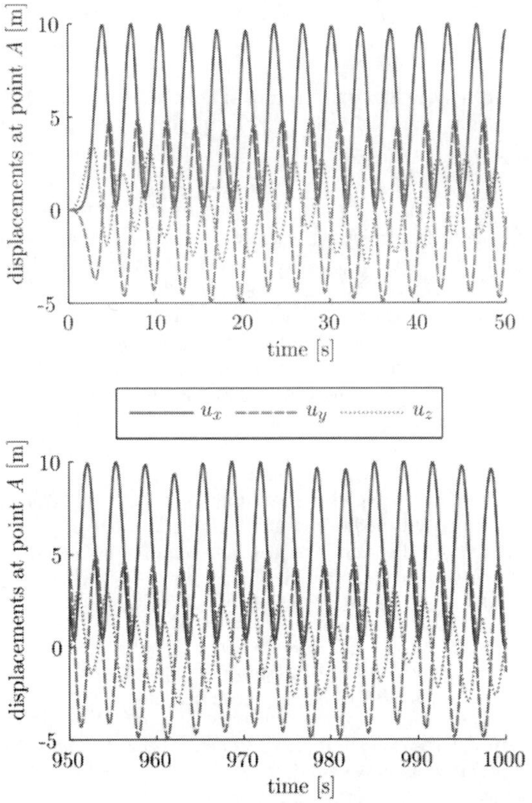

Figure 8. The displacements of the "cross" at point A at the beginning and at the end of calculation.

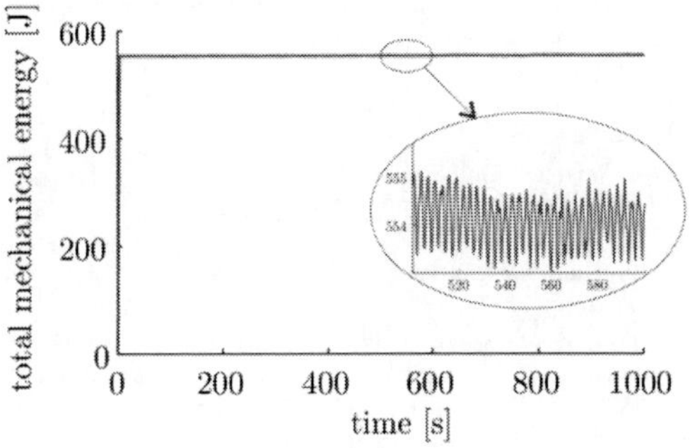

Figure 9. The time history of the total mechanical energy for the "cross".

quadratic convergence of the algorithm during the whole calculation. Because the interval of calculation is so extremely long we present only displacements on short intervals at the beginning and at the end of calculation, see Figure 8.

After removal of external forces at time $t = 5$ s the cross vibrates freely in a periodic-like dynamic pattern and the total mechanical energy is almost constant as expected, see Figure 9. The calculations remain stable even after 10 000 time steps. More detailed results are, to author's best knowledge, not available in literature. However, almost the same response is obtained by finer mesh and/or smaller time step indicating that the computational errors for this problem are small.

VII. CONCLUSION

A novel finite-element approach for the beam dynamics has been presented. The proposed method exploits the benefits of the favourable properties of angular velocity in the local frame description. The computational advantages of the quaternion representation of rotations are preserved, but additionally with the replacement of the primary unknowns we gain the considerable increase of numerical stability and robustness of the model without any other measures needed. The issue of the continuity of the structural unknowns over the element boundaries has been resolved with minimal computational cost. The classical benchmark examples demonstrate the excellent performance of the proposed method. Even for large number of time steps a reliable results were obtained and almost perfect preservation of the total mechanical energy is gained for sufficiently dense meshes and sufficiently small time-step sizes.

ACKNOWLEDGMENT

This work was supported by the Slovenian Research Agency through the research programme P2-0260. The support is gratefully acknowledged.

REFERENCES

[1] E. Zupan and D. Zupan, "On the Implementation of Novel Velocity-based 3D Beam: Compatibility of Angular Velocities Over the FEM Boundaries," ADVCOMP 2016, The Tenth International Conference on Advanced Engineering Computing and Applications in Sciences, pp. 17–22.

[2] S. S. Antman, Nonlinear Problems of Elasticity, 2nd ed. Berlin: Springer, 2005.

[3] E. Reissner, "On finite deformations of space-curved beams," Z. Angew. Math. Phys., vol. 32, no. 6, pp. 734–744, 1981.

[4] J. C. Simo, "A finite strain beam formulation - the three-dimensional dynamic problem. Part I." Comput. Meth. Appl. Mech. Eng., vol. 49, no. 1, pp. 55–70, 1985.

[5] J. M. Battini and C. Pacoste, "Co-rotational beam elements with warping effects in instability problems," Comput. Meth. Appl. Mech. Eng., vol. 191, no. 17-18, pp. 1755–1789, 2002.

[6] O. A. Bauchau and N. J. Theron, "Energy decaying scheme for non-linear beam models," Comput. Meth. Appl. Mech. Eng., vol. 134, no. 1-2, pp. 37–56, 1996.

[7] P. Betsch and P. Steinmann, "Frame-indifferent beam finite elements based upon the geometrically exact beam theory," Int. J. Numer. Methods Eng., vol. 54, no. 12, pp. 1775–1788, 2002.

[8] O. Brüls, A. Cardona, and M. Arnold, "Lie group generalized-alpha time integration of constrained flexible multibody systems," Mech. Mach. Theory, vol. 48, pp. 121–137, 2012.

[9] A. Cardona and M. Géradin, "A beam finite-element non-linear theory with finite rotations," Int. J. Numer. Methods Eng., vol. 26, no. 11, pp. 2403–2438, 1988.

[10] M. A. Crisfield, "A consistent corotational formulation for nonlinear, 3-dimensional, beam-elements," Comput. Meth. Appl. Mech. Eng., vol. 81, no. 2, pp. 131–150, 1990.

[11] L. A. Crivelli and C. A. Felippa, "A 3-dimensional nonlinear Timoshenko beam based on the core-congruential formulation," Int. J. Numer. Methods Eng., vol. 36, no. 21, pp. 3647–3673, 1993.

[12] A. Ibrahimbegovic, "On finite-element implementation of geometrically nonlinear Reissner beam theory - 3-dimensional curved beam elements," Comput. Methods Appl. Mech. Eng., vol. 122, no. 1-2, pp. 11–26, 1995.

[13] G. Jelenić and M. Saje, "A kinematically exact space finite strain beam model - finite-element formulation by generalized virtual work principle," Comput. Methods Appl. Mech. Eng., vol. 120, no. 1-2, pp. 131–161, 1995.

[14] H. Lang, J. Linn, and M. Arnold, "Multi-body dynamics simulation of geometrically exact Cosserat rods," Multibody Syst. Dyn., vol. 25, no. 3, pp. 285–312, 2011.

[15] E. Zupan, M. Saje, and D. Zupan, "The quaternion-based three-dimensional beam theory," Comput. Meth. Appl. Mech. Eng., vol. 198, no. 49-52, pp. 3944–3956, 2009.

[16] P. Crouch and R. Grossman, "Numerical-integration of ordinary differential-equations on manifolds," J. Nonlinear Sci., vol. 3, no. 1, 1993, pp. 1–33.

[17] C. Bottasso and M. Borri, "Integrating finite rotations," Comput. Meth. Appl. Mech. Eng., vol. 164, no. 3-4, 1998, pp. 307–331.

[18] J. C. Simo and L. Vu-Quoc, "On the dynamics in space of rods undergoing large motions - a geometrically exact approach," Comput. Meth. Appl. Mech. Eng., vol. 66, no. 2, 1988, pp. 125–161.

[19] H. Munthe-Kaas, "Runge-Kutta methods on Lie groups," Bit, vol. 38, no. 1, 1998, pp. 92–111.

[20] H. Munthe-Kaas, , "High order Runge-Kutta methods on manifolds," Appl. Numer. Math., vol. 29, no. 1, pp. 115–127, 1999.

[21] A. Zanna, "Collocation and relaxed collocation for the FER and the Magnus expansions," SIAM J. Numer. Anal., vol. 36, no. 4, 1999, pp. 1145–1182.

[22] J. Argyris and V. Poterasu, "Large rotations revisited application of Lie-algebra," Comput. Meth. Appl. Mech. Eng., vol. 103, no. 1-2, pp. 11–42, 1993.

[23] C. Bottasso, "A non-linear beam space-time finite element formulation using quaternion algebra: interpolation of the Lagrange multipliers and the appearance of spurious modes," Comput. Mech., vol. 10, no. 5, pp. 359–368, 1992.

[24] S. Kehrbaum and J. H. Maddocks, "Elastic rods, rigid bodies, quaternions and the last quadrature," Philos. Trans. R. Soc. A-Math. Phys. Eng. Sci., vol. 355, no. 1732, pp. 2117–2136, 1997.

[25] F. McRobie and J. Lasenby, "Simo-Vu Quoc rods using Clifford algebra," Int. J. Numer. Methods Eng., vol. 45, no. 4, pp. 377–398, 1999.

[26] S. Ghosh and D. Roy, "Consistent quaternion interpolation for objective finite element approximation of geometrically exact beam," Comput. Meth. Appl. Mech. Eng., vol. 198, no. 3-4, pp. 555–571, 2008.

[27] H. Lang and M. Arnold, "Numerical aspects in the dynamic simulation of geometrically exact rods," Appl. Numer. Math., vol. 62, no. 10, SI, pp. 1411–1427, 2012.

[28] E. Zupan, M. Saje, and D. Zupan, "Quaternion-based dynamics of geometrically nonlinear spatial beams using the Runge-Kutta method," Finite Elem. Anal. Des., vol. 54, pp. 48–60, 2012.

[29] E. Zupan, M. Saje, and D. Zupan, "Dynamics of spatial beams in quaternion description based on the Newmark integration scheme," Comput. Mech., vol. 51, no. 1, pp. 47–64, 2013.

[30] M. E. Hosea and L. F. Shampine, "Analysis and implementation of TR-BDF2," Appl. Numer. Math., vol. 20, no. 1-2, pp. 21–37, 1996.

[31] J. P. Ward, Quaternions and Cayley Numbers. Dordrecht–Boston–London: Kluwer Academic Publishers, 1997.

[32] H. Lang and J. Linn, "Lagrangian field theory in space-time for geometrically exact Cosserat rods," ITWM, Kaiserslautern, Reports of the ITWM, no. 150, 2003.

[33] S. S. Antman, "Invariant dissipative mechanisms for the spatial motion of rods suggested by artificial viscosity," J. Elast., vol. 70, no. 1-3, pp. 55–64, 2003.

[34] D. Hodges, "Geometrically exact, intrinsic theory for dynamics of curved and twisted anisotropic beams," AIAA J., vol. 41, no. 6, pp. 1131–1137, 2003.

[35] P. Cesarek and D. Zupan, "On the stability of Lie group time integration in multibody dynamics," in The 2nd Joint Conference on Multibody System Dynamics, May 29–June 1, 2012, Stuttgart, Germany. Book of Abstracts, H. M. Götz and P. Ziegler, Eds., pp. 42–43, 2012.

[36] E. Zupan and D. Zupan, "Velocity-based approach in non-linear dynamics of three-dimensional beams with enforced kinematic compatibility," Comput. Meth. Appl. Mech. Eng., vol. 310, pp. 406–428, 2016.

[37] G. Jelenić and M. A. Crisfield, "Geometrically exact 3D beam theory: implementation of a strain-invariant finite element for statics and dynamics," Comput. Meth. Appl. Mech. Eng., vol. 171, no. 1-2, pp. 141–171, 1999.

[38] J. C. Simo, N. Tarnow, and M. Doblare, "Nonlinear dynamics of 3-dimensional rods - exact energy and momentum conserving algorithms," Int. J. Numer. Methods Eng., vol. 38, no. 9, pp. 1431–1473, 1995.

Comparative Analysis of Heuristic Algorithms for Solving Multiextremal Problems

Rudolf Neydorf, Ivan Chernogorov, Victor Polyakh
Orkhan Yarakhmedov, Yulia Goncharova
Department of Software Computer Technology and Automated Systems and Department of Scientific-Technical Translation and Professional Communication
Don State Technical University
Rostov-on-Don, Russia

Email: ran_pro@mail.ru, hintaivr@gmail.com, silvervpolyah@gmail.com, orhashka@gmail.com, jl.goncharova@gmail.com

Dean Vucinic
Vesalius College
Vrije Universiteit Brussel
Brussels, Belgium

Email: dean.vucinic@vub.ac.be

Abstract—**In this paper, 3 of the most popular search optimization algorithms are applied to study the multi-extremal problems, which are more extensive and complex than the single-extremal problems. This study has shown that only the heuristic algorithms can provide an effective solution to solve the multiextremal problems. Among the large group of available algorithms, the 3 methods have demonstrated the best performance, which are: (1) particles swarming modelling method, (2) evolutionary-genetic extrema selection and (3) search technique based on the ant colony method. The previous comparison study, where these approaches have been applied to an overall test environment with the multiextremal Rastrigin functions, has shown already their suitability to solve multiextremal problems. In addition, they are characterized with superior performance properties. Nevertheless, each of the selected heuristic algorithms has demonstrated its own specific search features that allow the detection and identification of both global and local extremes. In this paper, the investigated algorithms have been validated on a larger test functions environment with different types of extremes. The particular attention was given to analyse their individual methods when solving the data-clustering problem. The main conclusion is that each of these methods can find the extremes by satisfying any desired precision and have acceptable performance, when applied to the variety of practical problems.**

Keywords—searching optimization; multi-extremes; genetic algorithm; swarm algorithm; ant algorithm.

I. Introduction

For the current state of the theory of optimization is quite common that most of the known methods are designed to find only the global optima. Many of these methods are highly effective [1][2][3][4]. At the same time, the scope of the optimization methods, and related application areas are continuously expanding, as being part of the most advanced areas in science and technology. In addition, many social and economic projects, military and other applications are almost always faced to the formulation of optimization problems for which more precise solutions are needed.

Many modern practical optimization problems are inherently complicated by counterpoint criterion requirements of the involved optimized object. The expected result - the global optimum - for the selected criteria is not always the best solution to consider, because it incorporate many additional criteria and restrictions. It is well known that such situations arise in the design of complex technological systems when solving transportation and logistics problems among many others. In addition, many objects in their technical and informational nature are prone to multi-extreme property. In particular, these objects and the discrete nature of their respective systems have significant multi-extreme property (ME) [5][6][7][8][9][10] [11][12].

A distinctive approach for solving such problems requires iterative steps to evaluate a large number of options in order to shape and find the solutions. The result of this process is that the developers are forced to apply search engine optimization (SO) [2][3][4].

In the second half of the last century and at the beginning of this century, the theoretical research and the practical application of their results have shown that it is inappropriate to find such methods in the class of so-called deterministic methods, as many attempts in following such approach have resulted to be ineffective. The reason is that these techniques are too sensitive to non-smoothness and other characteristics that are encountered when having continuous dependency, while as well-known, the problems related to the discrete programming lead to the application of the NP-complete algorithms.

Therefore, to solve many practical optimization problems, especially problems of ME, it is appropriate to apply the so-called heuristics methods. These methods, according to the authors, are the most promising for solving the discussed ME problems [6][7][8][9][10][11][12].

A. Formulation of the problem

As mentioned above, the motivation is to apply the most common heuristic SO methods to the environment having more typical, universal and complex ME problem, which has to be solved. The performed research revealed the possibility of finding some or all the extremes by applying the selected methods. For this qualitative evaluation, it is necessary to numerically assess the accuracy of the found extremes values, as well as, the accuracy of their coordinates. Therefore, in the first stage of this research, we suggest the ME test function that might provide a common evaluation environment for validating the selected methods, when solving the proposed ME tasks. In the second stage of this research, the exact heuristic approaches are chosen, in order to determine both the well-known methods of solving ME tasks and their implementation algorithms.

B. *Choosing multiextremal test function with a preliminary analysis of its properties*

The most common and effective test functions for developing and analysing the SO methods are the Rosenbrock, Himmelblau and Rastrigin functions. The Rastrigin function (RF) is the most widely applied ME function between all of them. This universal function is not convex, as already shown in 1974 by Rastrigin [13]. The equation of N function arguments is:

$$f(x) = A \cdot n + \sum_{i=1}^{n} \left[x_i^2 - A \cdot \cos(2 \cdot \pi \cdot x_i) \right], \qquad (1)$$

where: $x=(x_1,\ldots,x_n)^T$ – vector; $A=10$.

The global minimum of this function is at the point (0,0)=0. It is difficult to find a local minimum of this function, because it has many local minimums. The isolation and evaluation of extremes is a complex task.

In Section II, the 3 most popular approaches of finding the set of extreme problems are discussed for the 2-dimensional Rastrigin function. Section III describes the related work. In Section IV, the conclusion of the conducted research is given.

II. Selecting a Group of Heuristic Methods

In this paper, the authors established the 3 most relevant tasks, which are common in practice, when solving various search optimization tasks.

A. *RF using swarming particles method*

The essence and reasons in using the method of swarming particles (MSP) in SO tasks is well known [14][15][16][17][18]. The classic MSP algorithm simulates the real behaviour patterns of insects, birds, fishes, many protozoa, etc. However, ME objects require to know some specific properties of this algorithm.

The authors of [19][20][21] and other members of R. Neudorf team [8][9][10][11][12] have significantly reworked the canonical MSP algorithm. In particular, a new modified version of this algorithm was developed for solving the ME tasks, which is based on a model based on the mechanical principles of the moving particle, and complemented by the mechanisms borrowed from the biological laws, as well as, the method of adaptation mechanisms, being property of the ME task.

The Mechanical Movement Model (MMM) of particles [21] in MSP was significantly modified and refined:

$$X_{ti} = X_{(t-\Delta t)i} + \vec{V}_{(t-\Delta t)i} \cdot \Delta t, \qquad (2)$$

$$\vec{V}_{ti} = \vec{V}_{(t-\Delta t)i} + \vec{A}_{(t-\Delta t)i} \cdot \Delta t, \qquad (3)$$

$$\vec{A}_i = \vec{F}_{pi} + \vec{F}_{tri}, \qquad (4)$$

where: $X_{(t-\Delta t)i}$ – i-th particle previous position; X_{ti} – i-th particle current position; V_{ti} – i-th particle velocity at the current time; $V_{(t-\Delta t)i}$ – i-th particle current velocity; $A_{(t-\Delta t)i}$ – particle previous acceleration in previous time; Δt – integration interval; F_{pi} – acceleration caused by the particles biologically action attractive forces; F_{tri} – slowing under the action of friction forces.

F_{pi} – acceleration caused by the particles biologically action attractive forces includes 3 sub-attractions:

$$\vec{F}_{pi} = \vec{F}_{pi}^{G} + \vec{F}_{pi}^{L} + \vec{F}_{pi}^{C}, \qquad (5)$$

where: F^{G}_{pi} - particle attraction to global extreme; F^{L}_{pi} - particle attraction to the local extreme of particle (the best finding position by particle during its existence); F^{C}_{pi} - particle attraction to the nearest cluster.

The sub-attraction in the described algorithm is based on an analogue of the law of gravitational attraction:

$$\vec{F}_{pi}^{Q} = \frac{\vec{G}^{Q} m_i m_e}{r^2}, \qquad (6)$$

where: $Q \in \{G, L, C\}$, G^Q – the proportionality coefficient (gravity prototype); m_i - the desire measure of ith particle to the selected best particle with bio-similar of m_e mass for the attractive particle (as a "bee flies to the womb"); r - the distance between the current position of the particle and extrema.

In order to eliminate the errors (occurring at r=0 and $r \to 0^+$) the following changes are introduced:

- when the particle is updating the global, local or cluster extreme, it loses one or more sub-attraction, because it is currently located in the best position (global, local or cluster) and thus continues the movement at the expense of the remaining sub-attractions or inertia;
- when the particle is at the point of the current global, local or cluster extreme (r=0). The limitation is naturally set in MM by formula (6):

$$\vec{F}_{pi}^{Q} = \frac{\vec{G}^{Q} m_i m_e}{r^2 + \varepsilon},$$

where ε - setup option, limiting the maximum acceleration, delaying the passage of the actual (and finding) particles from the centre of gravity;

- when the particle moves too close to the global, local or cluster extreme ($r \to 0^+$). The particle gets a great acceleration that causes an increase in resistance of the medium (F_{tri}) and limits the maximum acceleration/speed.

To improve the searching properties, the stochastic blur parameter was introduced:

$$\lambda^{\xi}(\varepsilon) = \lambda \cdot (1 + 2 \cdot \varepsilon(rnd(1) - 0.5)), \quad (7)$$

where: $\lambda^{\xi}(\varepsilon)$ – fluctuating parameter value at each iteration; ε – distorted relative deviation parameter from nominal value; $rnd(1)$ – random number in the range [0, 1].

MSP contains the reflect mechanism. The particles reflect within the boundaries ranges of the selected function. This increases the area under investigation when particles try to "fly" over the treated area.

Initially, the authors had decided to implement a dynamic clustering mechanism, which would allow particles to localized extremes, to further improve the search results, by swarming around the found local and global extremes. However, after preliminary research, authors decided to implement the clustering mechanism that is a combination of the 2 concepts - kinematic and dynamic. The kinematic concept is expressed at each iteration where the positions of all particles together with the previously created clusters points undergo the clustering ("A quasi-equivalence" algorithm [22][23]). This mechanism allows selecting the area of all found global and local extremes (the number of localized extremes may not exceed the number of particles * number of carried out iterations), by selected criteria.

"A Quasi Equivalence" clustering algorithm does not require resulting number of clusters. It can be described by the following equations, which is the matrix of normal similarity measures:

$$\mu_{x_q}(x_i) = 1 - \frac{d(x_q, x_i)}{\max\limits_{k \in [1,Q]} (d(x_q, x_k))}, \quad (8)$$

where: x – is the plurality of elements; Q – is a number of elements in plurality; $(q, i) = \{1, Q\}$; $d(x,y)$ – is a clustering criterion (like Euclidean distance between points or etc.).

The relative similarity measures are defined with:

$$\xi_{x_q}(x_i, x_j) = 1 - \left| \mu_{x_q}(x_i) - \mu_{x_q}(x_j) \right|, \quad (9)$$

where: $(i, j, q) = \{1, Q\}$.

The matrix of similarity measures of the elements plurality:

$$\xi(a,b) = T(\xi_{x_1}(a,b), \ldots, \xi_{x_Q}(a,b)) = \min_{i=1,Q} \xi_{x_i}(a,b), \quad (10)$$

where: $a, b \in X$.

The result matrix:

$$R_{\xi}^{q} = R_{\xi}^{q-1} \circ R_{\xi}, \quad (11)$$

where: S=max, T=min.

The values in the R matrix show whether the pair of points belongs to the R relation, called "quasi-equivalence levels" - a. The choice of a particular level divides the plurality into equivalence classes, which correspond to the separate clusters. Fig. 1 demonstrates the flowchart of "A Quasi Equivalence" clustering.

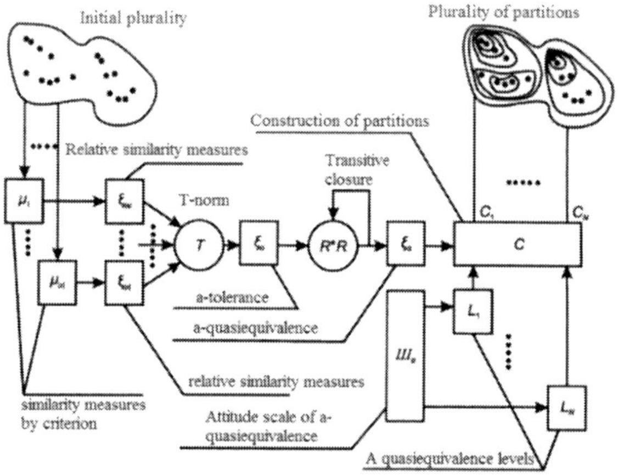

Figure 1. "A quasiequivalence" algorithm flow-chart

The ME MSP modification requires the "A Quasi Equivalence" clustering based on the Euclidean distance between the allocated extremes criteria. After this action, all the points in the considered clusters are deleted, except the extreme point, which allows to dropout the sub-local values.

The dynamic concept consists of the following steps: after the kinematic clustering particles appear with the "attractive force" to the extreme areas of the whole swarm, not only the global extreme, found as the best position for the particle. In this paper, the authors have chosen a strategy of particles attraction to be the centre of the nearby cluster, as it allows them to react instantly to changing situations (the emergence of new areas to find extreme).

To test and debug MSP, the authors have developed the software tool «MMSP» (implemented by I. Chernogorov), which has enhanced functionality. The tool is implemented in C#. Fig. 2 shows the part of MMSP interface (without sub-area, which visualized the selected function, particles and created clusters. The Canvas and Helix library were used to display it. Authors used different libraries, because the 3D scene heavy loads the PC, which is not intended for huge experiments. Fig. 3(a) and 3(b) display the visualization of Guinta function, position and velocity vectors of the particles, and created clusters for 2D and 3D scenes), highlighting the diverse areas to display information.

MMSP workspace is divided into the following sub-areas:

- orange rectangle – MMSP sub-area, is responsible for the initialization of particles, the iteration (in the "step by step" and "automatic" mode) and restarting the computation;
- green rectangle – MMSP sub-area, in which the user selects the desired test function and variable ranges;
- blue rectangle - MMSP sub-area, in which the user sets up the 2D or 3D display mode by selecting the function and/or particles and/or created clusters;
- purple rectangle – MMSP sub-area, is responsible for the customization of MSP parameters;
- pink rectangle – MMSP sub-area, showing the MSP results at current moment: the global extreme computing time of initialization, iteration and clustering, number of the current iteration and the number of test function calls.

The testing modifications effectiveness was carried out for RF in coordinate range $(x,y) \in [-1.5, 1.5]$. In this area, RF has 9 local minimums, including one global. Fig. 4(a), 4(b) and 4(c) show extreme areas localization process with kinematic-dynamic clustering and the creation of the corresponding clusters.

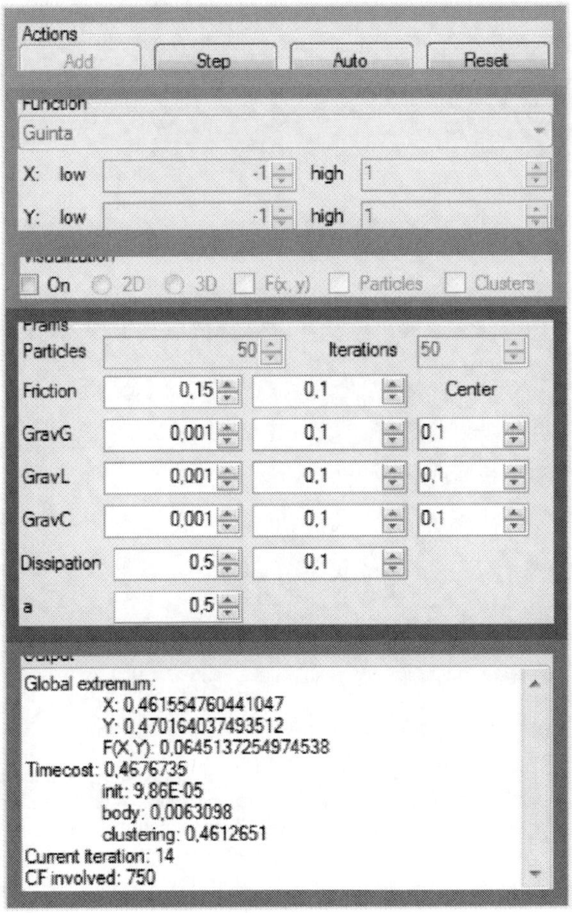

Figure 2. Part of MMSP interface.

a)

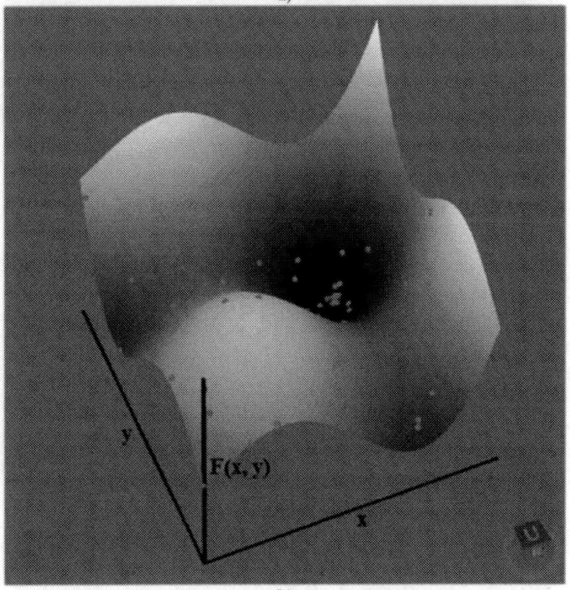

b)

Figure 3. Visualization of the function, particles and clusters in MMSP on (a – 2D scene; b – 3D scene).

Fig. 4(a), 4(b) and 4(c) show that the particles are initially attracted to the resulting cluster, which is located in the global extreme area. This is due to the overall prevalence of the global attraction power over the local forces of attraction. Some peripheral particles might find the local extremes, which are attracted to them, and gathered in clusters. In strict clusters areas, the ME MSP algorithm (in case of having less isolated and significant extremes) is repeated.

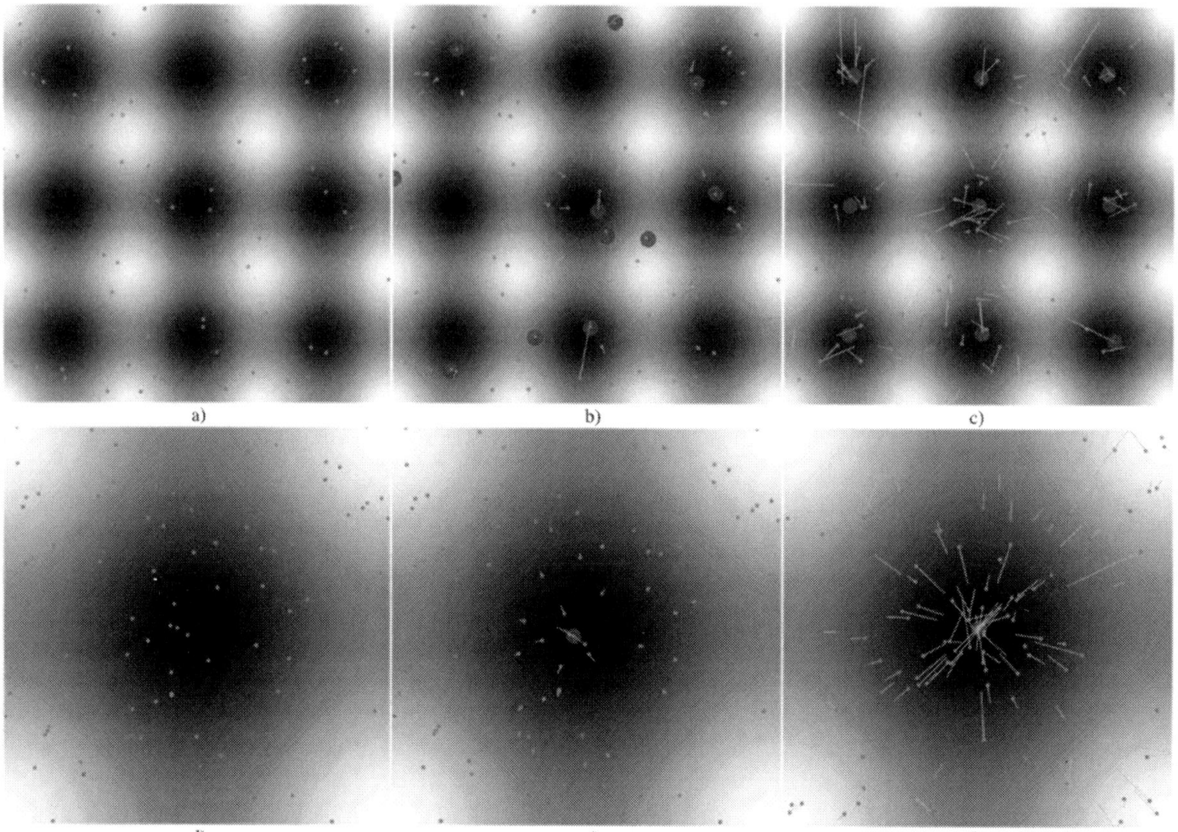

Figure 4. Extremal RF areas localization of (a – the initialization, b – the 1st iteration, c – the 50th iteration). RF local identification of global extreme of (d – the initialization, e – the 1st iteration, f – the 50th iteration)

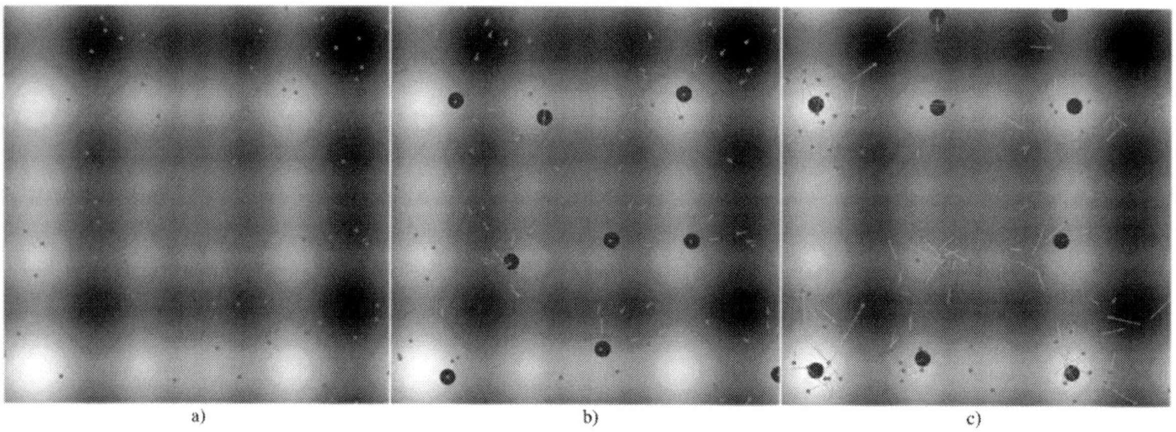

Figure 5. Extremal Schwefel_26 function areas localization of (a – the initialization, b – the 1st iteration, c – the 50th iteration).

This process is iteratively repeated until the desired accuracy of the local and global extreme parameters is achieved. Within the limited time for fulfilling the algorithm of each cluster, a quite stable dynamic equilibrium of particles is set. The calculations, for the modelling activity, make obvious that the average number of the particles is correlated with the value of the extreme. The degree of correlation depends on the ME MSP algorithm settings.

In order to improve the accuracy of any extreme parameters estimation, the repetition of ME MSP algorithm is applied to the contracted areas of the defined clusters. This process can be iteratively repeated until the desired accuracy is achieved, by taking into account all the local and global extremes.

The examples in Fig. 4(d), 4(e) and 4(f) demonstrate the fragments of the iterative identification of the global extreme, which is located at the point [0, 0]. TABLE I shows the results obtained by the localization and additional identification in all areas. The table presents the coordinates $x=x_1$ and $y=x_2$, and the RF values obtained by applying the equation (2). The increase of number of iterations (and the search time) improves the estimated accuracy. Searching tasks carried out on the PC with AMD Phenom II P960 processor and 6Gb of RAM. At the same time, to achieve the described accuracy (localization of all extremes areas and additional identification of 9 areas) took ~ 32 seconds. Thus, we can conclude that ME MSP is an effective tool for solving the ME tasks.

TABLE I. RESULTS OF THE EXPERIMENT

Standard			Extremal evaluation item		
			Coordinates		*Value*
x	*y*	*f (x, y)*	*x*	*Y*	*f (x, y)*
-1	1	2	-1.00007	1.0001	2.000382825
-1	0	1	-1.0001	-0.0004	1.000292529
-1	-1	2	-1.00001	-1.0003	2.000595233
0	1	1	-0.0001	1.00009	1.000177161
0	0	0	-0.0005	0.0002	0.000049304
0	-1	1	-0.0006	-1.0003	1.000659723
1	1	2	1.0005	1.0008	2.002827059
1	0	1	1.0003	-0.002	1.001544741
1	-1	2	1.0003	-1.0004	2.001314045

Additional testing modifications effectiveness was carried out for more asymmetric Schwefel_26 test function [24] in coordinate range $(x,y) \in [-250, 250]$. The equation of N function argument is:

$$f(x) = 418.9829n - \sum_{i=1}^{n} x_i \sin(\sqrt{|x_i|}) . \qquad (12)$$

Search format was changed: extremes – the highest values. Fig. 5(a), 5(b) and 5(c) show MSP work on different stages. To select a larger number of local extremes it is needed to optimize the *a* clustering parameter.

The modification of the kinematic-dynamic clustering mechanism allows reducing the time and increasing the search accuracy. In subsequent papers the authors decided to carry out modification of the clustering mechanism, in the direction of a dynamic paradigm, to give the particles more resemblance to a real prototype, expecting to improve the search results and to reduce the computing clustering time.

B. Features of the evolutionary-genetic algorithm.

In solving the search engine optimization problems [25][26][27], one of the most popular, proven and, therefore, demanded tools is the evolutionary genetic algorithm (EGA). The structure of classical EGA, its respective components, and their processing operators are well known. However, depending on the objective applications, EGA can be characterized by considerable structural parametric features. In particular, the use of EGA for solving ME problems [28][29][30][31], as shown by studies [28][29][30], requires the addition of classical EGA, which application is based on the assessment and extremes selection tools. The evaluation and selection are necessary to identify the type of the extreme (maximum, minimum), and for measuring their size. Furthermore, it is necessary to determine the position of extreme in the factor space, i.e., coordinates.

For the Clustering Algorithm, we develop an approach for the selection of extremes, based on one-sample Student t-test criteria [30][31][32]. The proposed approach involves the implementation of 2 sequential stages: 1 - generation and 2 - evolutionary selection of populations by EGA and subsequent clustering to receive its finishing generations results - the fittest. The obtained results, in the form of quantitative assessments, identified the extremes distributed over the coordinate groups, by checking them in respect to the 0-hypothesis.

The clustering algorithm, implemented in this approach, is a logical comparison of the obtained vectors $\vec{v}_i$ - results of evolutionary individual's selection with the average $\vec{v}_0$ vector for each cluster sample and considers an expectation estimate to find the real extreme. The application of the theoretical positions of 0-hypothesis by using one sample Student t-test takes a decision about the inclusion or non-inclusion of the individual within a cluster sampling. As a result, the clusters are formed from individuals, which structure corresponds to the known necessary and sufficient conditions, for the existence of a local extreme.

Conceptually, these conditions are set to have in each cluster the best individual and the best estimate (estimate of local extreme $\vec{v}_e$) for the sample, and the remaining individuals are forming the extreme neighbourhood. For the neighbouring individuals the sufficient conditions for the extreme $\vec{v}_e$ is to fulfil one of the 2 conditions:

- if $\vec{v}_e$ - maximum, then

$$\forall i \neq e \rightarrow \varphi(\vec{v}_i) < \varphi(\vec{v}_e) , \qquad (13)$$

- if $\vec{v}_e$ - minimum, then

$$\forall i \neq e \rightarrow \varphi(\vec{v}_i) > \varphi(\vec{v}_e) , \qquad (14)$$

where $\varphi(\cdot)$- function for which extremes are sought.

For implementation of the algorithm, in order to be able to estimate one sample, 0-hypothesis requires testing of the toiletries in each formed EGA vector of arguments $\vec{v}$ with each cluster in the finish population.

$$V_k = \{\vec{v}_{ki} \mid i \in [1, n_k]\} . \qquad (15)$$

However, the form of multi-dimensional vector based argument makes it impossible to be directly applied to one sample Student t-test, formulated for the treatment of the scalar arrays.

In connection with this algorithm, the transformation of the vector quantities is implemented for their scalar evaluation. The main vector estimates of cluster V_k are averaged over a cluster sample vector $\vec{v}_0$ and the vector of local extreme evaluating $\vec{v}_e$. The main scalar evaluations of cluster V_k are metric estimation of the discrepancy vectors (the distance between the points in the factor space). A measure of the audited individual proximity between the coordinates of the vector $\vec{v}$ and the cluster is a unit vector of its deviation from $\vec{v}_{k0}$:

$$\Delta v_k = \mid \vec{v} - \vec{v}_{k0} \mid \tag{16}$$

The statistical sampling, which may or may not belong to the $\vec{v}$, with an estimate of the proximity to it (16) is the set of scalar distances estimates of cluster elements (15) from the $\vec{v}_{k0}$

$$\Delta v_k = \{\Delta v_{ki} = \mid \vec{v}_{ki} - \vec{v}_{k0} \mid i \in [1, n_k]\}. \tag{17}$$

The decision of the vector $\vec{v}$ belonging to the set is accepted for the selected confidence level P_k. To determine the supplies of vector $\vec{v}$ to the sample (17), we need to calculate the average based on a sample, as follows:

$$\Delta \bar{v}_k = \frac{1}{n_k} \times \sum_{i=1}^{n_k} \Delta v_{ki}, \tag{18}$$

The following step requires to compute the standard deviation of the vectors that have already been identified in the cluster:

$$S_{\Delta v_k} = \sqrt{\sum_{i=1}^{n_k} (\Delta v_{ki} - \Delta \bar{v}_k)^2}, \tag{19}$$

and compute the standard average with the sample within the deviation cluster

$$S_{\overline{\Delta v_k}} = \frac{S_{\Delta v_k}}{\sqrt{n_k}}. \tag{20}$$

Further on, and according to the calculated values, it is necessary to calculate the experimental value of one-sample Student t-test criteria:

$$t_{ki} = \frac{\mid \Delta v_{ki} - \Delta \bar{v}_k \mid}{S_{\overline{\Delta v_k}}} \tag{21}$$

If the obtained empirical value t_i does not exceed the table value t_p [33] with n degrees of freedom, and can be selected the confidence level P_k in the table, we can assume that $\vec{v}$ belongs to this cluster.

The described algorithm is one of the high quality instruments to study the ME dependencies [33][34]. On its basis, the software tool "EGSO_MET" was developed. The software structure includes 8 separate classes that inherit the standard class Object:

1. Individual class - is used to describe objects such as individual EGA;
2. Cluster class - is used to describe objects such as a cluster;
3. CreatePopulation class - includes methods for creating an initial population of EGA, which consists of a special type of objects;
4. FormPopulation class - contains the methods for the selection and formation of the initial population in EGA based on the user-set parameters;
5. FunctionDeal class - includes methods for calculating the objective function value of the object;
6. EvolutionaryGeneticAlg class - includes methods for simulating crossover and mutation operators in EGA;
7. Student_tTest class - includes methods of clustering obtained with EGA results;
8. MainViewModel class - contains the methods of interaction with the «EGSO_MET» software interface.

A more detailed description of the EGSO_MET interface and structure for each class can be found in [30][31]. This software has an intuitive graphical user interface, which includes a user input settings module, a graphical display of the object in 3-dimensional space and in addition has the statistics gathering module. The instruments used for its reconstruction include:

- Windows Presentation Foundation (WPF) - a system for building the Windows client application with visually appealing possibilities of interaction with the user. The graphics (presentation) subsystem is a part of .NET Framework (since version 3.0), supported with the XAML language.
- Helix toolkit 3D is the graphics framework, based on DirectX engine. It allows you to re-create the elementary 3-dimensional animation.

The input parameters, in addition to the standard input (population size, number of generations, probability of crossover, probability of mutation, the search area, the accuracy, the object under study) have been extended with:

- extremes parameter (minimum / maximum);
- special selection parameter (roulette / casual / tournament);
- parameter of crossover type (single point / two-point);
- parameter of mutation type (one-point / multipoint);
- parameter of breakpoints type.

Intuitive «EGSO_MET» software interface is shown in Fig. 6. On Fig. 6(a) are shown the settings of EGA border parameters, accuracy and extremes type.

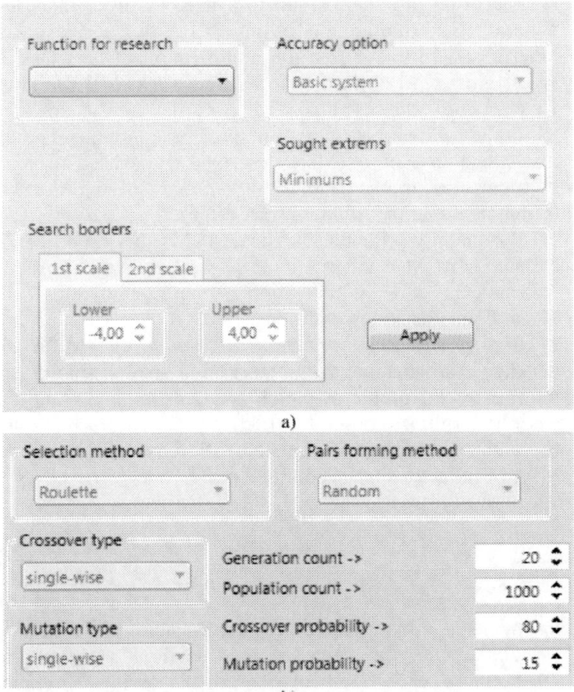

a)

b)

Figure 6. «EGSO_MET» main window settings interface: *a)border settings; b) EGA settings.*

On Fig. 6(a) are shown the settings of EGA border parameters, accuracy and extremes type. On Fig. 6(b) are shown the settings of EGA parameters.

In addition to the tabs of the main window, EGSO_MET software has tabbed settings for the local search options and the tabs for the results to set the global and local search. An example of the displayed results of the global and local searches is shown in Fig. 7.

clusternumber	firstparam	secondparam	functionvalue
1	3.58098	-1.85298	0.00108
2	-3.80655	-3.31459	0.06309
3	2.9888	1.93927	0.07905
4	-2.79521	3.17454	0.07995

Figure 7. «EGSO_MET» obtained results interface.

ME functions research using EGSO_MET software. As example, the modified EGA results of the Himmelblau function research (search minima) and the Shekel function research (maxima search) are presented with the EGSO_MET software described above. It is worth noting that the Himmelblau function study was carried out in the range of [-4, 4], and Shekel function research was carried out in the range [0, 20]. The EGA input parameters are:

- Number of generations = 20;
- Individuals in each generation = 1000;
- Crossover probability = 95%;
- The probability of mutation = 30%;
- The accuracy of the study = 7 digits after the decimal.

In the study of Himmelblau function, 4 clusters are allocated, and the minimums of each cluster can be correlated with Himmelblau function minimums situated in the study area. In the study of Shekel function, 3 clusters are allocated, and peaks of each cluster can be correlated with the Shekel function peaks situated in the study area.

Figure 3 shows the graphs finding sequentially the values of the Himmelblau function, their various coordinates (X and Y) and the corresponding values of the objective function (F (X, Y) $\approx$ 0), which are sorted in the descending order. In Himmelblau function clearly shows that value of the objective function which are close to each other (or in some cases equal to) have significant differences in the coordinate parameters (i.e., parameters of the objective function, providing close to the minimum values are different). This fact confirms that the object has multi-extremes. It should be noted that this property is also inherent to the Shekel function.

In the study of Himmelblau function cluster, the 4 obtained minimum values can be considered for a global extreme, which characterized the local minima of the function, see Fig. 8 (a).

In the study of a Shekel function cluster, see Fig. 8 (b), the 2 obtained extremes are peripheral and their maximum values characterize the local maxima of the Shekel function, and the maximum value of one of the three found with the help of research clusters, characterizes the global Shekel function maximum.

The study of Himmelblau and Shekel functions in finding the global and the local extremes are presented in TABLE II and TABLE III, respectively, with their actual values and their corresponding coordinates.

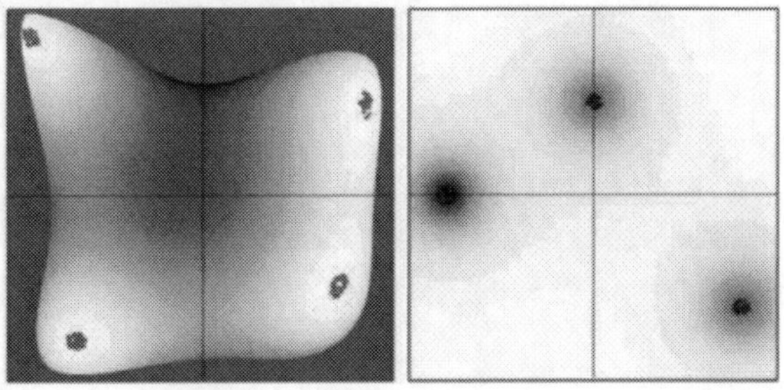

a) b)

Figure 8. Extremes localization areas: *a) selected clusters of Himmelblau function b) selected clusters of Shekel function.*

As seen from TABLE II and TABLE III, the extremes evaluation values and their coordinates are not very accurate. If the obtained values do not satisfy the required accuracy, it has to be followed with a second study of the cluster function. As example, the second research in each cluster area of the Himmelblau function is shown in TABLE IV. The authors have developed the approach for the local search in the extreme areas [31], based on the EGA [29][30], where similar extremes values of the 2nd cluster (Himmelblau function) can be seen in Fig. 9 (a); the best extreme evaluation is highlighted with a red circle. The search was carried out in the area around the highlighted extremes, see Fig. 9 (b).

TABLE II. OBTAINED ON THE FIRST ITERATION RESULTS (CLUSTERS OF HIMMELBLAU FUNCTION)

Himmelblau function					
Standard			*Extremal evaluation item*		
			Coordinates		*Value*
X	*Y*	*f(x,y)*	*X*	*Y*	*f(x,y)*
3.58442	-1.84812	0	3.58931	-1.86579	0.00527
3	2	0	2.98944	2.03233	0.01531
-3.77931	-3.28318	0	-3.76109	-3.25452	0.04045
-2.80511	3.13131	0	-2.79797	3.09164	0.06383

TABLE III. OBTAINED ON THE FIRST ITERATION RESULTS (CLUSTERS OF SHAKEL FUNCTION)

Shekel function					
Standard			*Extremal evaluation item*		
			Coordinates		*Value*
X	*Y*	*f(x,y)*	*X*	*Y*	*f(x,y)*
2	10	1.01439	1.94624	9.87414	0.99575
10	15	0.51646	9.95978	14.99479	0.51612
18	4	0.51646	18.08359	4.03641	0.50665

TABLE IV. EXTREMES LOCALIZATION (SECOND RESEARCH) OF HIMMELBLAU FUNCTION

Values	1st cluster	2nd cluster	3rd cluster	4th cluster
X	3.58518	2.99946	-3.7783	-2.8023
Y	-1.85084	2.00173	-3.28153	3.1294
f(x,y)	0.00012	0.00004	0.00013	0.0004

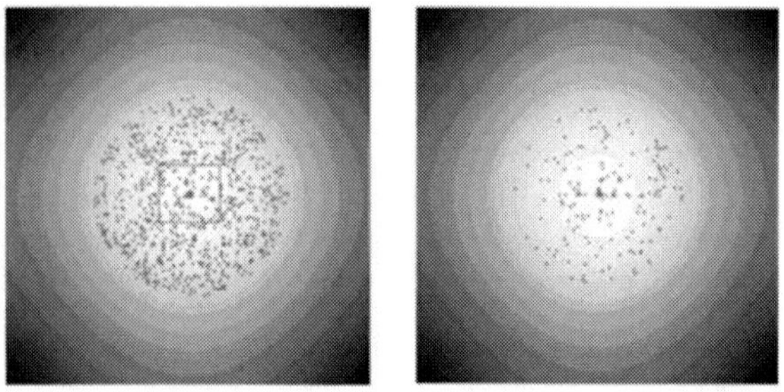

a) b)

Figure 9. Form of clusters in localized area: *a) 100th; b) 110th generation.*

C. *Solving ME problems by ant colony method.*

The "Ant colony method" (ACM) is studied in this section, as the third group of methods that are widely used in solving various optimization problems. A distinctive feature of ACM is that the fundamental behaviour of the real ants is modelled [34][35]. Such behaviour allows the colony to achieve effective results in life, which are often close to optimal solution. As a rule, the ACM is mainly used for the route minimization problems in graph [35][36][37], but, according to studies and to a number of scholars and authors [38][39], these algorithms also show good results in other areas. In this paper, the modification of the classical ACM is used to optimize the reference test ME functions Ursem01 [40] and Styblinski-Tang [41].

In the following section, a method based on the classical implementation of ACM is described. It is used to solve problems on graphs [35], however, for solving the ME problems, some modifications are required.

By analogy with the classical ACM, this modification called MACM, inherited the well-known steps as "placement and initialization", "ants moving" and "breakpoint checking conditions."

Algorithmic and mathematical model of MACM. In general, mathematical and algorithmic model studies the multi-extremal problems which are depending on $\Phi(x)$. It has the arbitrary order n (i.e., x - n - vector), and represented as follows. The field of study $\Phi(x)$ using the MACM in factor space is divided into

$$M = \prod_{i=1}^{n} m_i \qquad (22)$$

fragments – hyper-parallelepipeds, each of which is associated with the value of the function at the centre. Furthermore, each fragment is originally assigned to some small positive pheromone level and a certain number of ants are placed inside the fragment.

Thus, many fragments can be described as a multi-dimensional cellular matrix of the form

$$A = \left(\left(\ldots \left(\left(a_{i_1,i_2} \right)_{i_3,i_4} \right) \ldots \right)_{i_{n-1},i_n} \right), \qquad (23)$$

fulfilling the necessary degree of nesting. The dimension n can be odd. Then the external matrix is column matrix.

The search algorithm implemented in MACO due to [34][35][36][37][40] that every ant in hyper-parallelepiped $a_{i_1,i_2 \ldots i_n}$ evaluates all adjacent hyperparallelepipeds and calculates the probability $P_{i_1,i_2,\ldots i_n}^{i_j \pm 1}$ of transfer expediency according to the (24), where i_i, m_i – the serial number on the fragment location on x_i axis of factor space; Q – the optimization criterion; f – the number of pheromones in a fragment of a particular index; α – the variable pheromone exposure factor on the transition probability of an ant; β - the variable ratio of the intensity variation of the function when passing over the edge.

$$\forall i_1 = \overline{1, m_1}; i_2 = \overline{1, m_2}; \ldots i_n = \overline{1, m_n}; j = \overline{1, n} \rightarrow$$
$$\rightarrow P_{i_1, i_2 \ldots i_n}^{i_j \pm 1} \begin{cases} Q(x_{i_1}, \ldots x_{i_j}, \ldots x_{i_n}) > Q(x_{i_1}, \ldots x_{i_j \pm 1}, \ldots x_{i_n}) \rightarrow \dfrac{\left[f_{i_1, \ldots i_{j \pm 1}, \ldots i_n}\right]^{\alpha} * \left[\Delta Q_{i_1, \ldots i_{j \pm 1}, \ldots i_n}\right]^{-\beta}}{\sum\limits_{j = \overline{1, n}} \sum\limits_{i_k = i_j - 1, i_j + 1} \left\{\left[f_{i_1, \ldots i_k, \ldots i_n}\right]^{\alpha} * \left[\Delta Q_{i_1, \ldots i_k, \ldots i_n}\right]^{-\beta}\right\}} \\ Q(x_{i_1}, \ldots x_{i_j}, \ldots x_{i_n}) < Q(x_{i_1}, \ldots x_{i_j \pm 1}, \ldots x_{i_n}) \rightarrow 0, \end{cases} \quad (24)$$

Model (24) is supplemented by model updates pheromone - the main tool of giving an effective search, inherent only to ACM. Its essence, at each iteration, occurs both the growth and the evaporation of pheromone. Therefore, changing the pheromone stock in each fragment $a_{i_1, i_2 \ldots i_n}$ in one simulation step h is calculated by the following equation of state in discrete form:

$$f_{a_{i_1, i_2 \ldots i_n}}(h+1) = (1-\rho) * f_{a_{i_1, i_2 \ldots i_n}}(h) + \Delta f_{a_{i_1, i_2 \ldots i_n}}(h) \quad (25)$$

where: $\rho \in (0; 9)$ – the variable evaporation coefficient; $f_{a_{i_1, i_2 \ldots i_n}}(h)$ - pheromone content in $a_{i_1, i_2 \ldots i_n}$ hyper-parallelepiped; $\Delta f_{a_{i_1, i_2 \ldots i_n}}(h)$ – the increment on each iteration, calculated according to the formula:

$$\Delta f_{a_{i_1, i_2 \ldots i_n}}(h) = K * \left(Q(x_{i_1}, \ldots x_{i_j \pm 1}, \ldots x_{i_n}) - Q(x_{i_1}, \ldots x_{i_j}, \ldots x_{i_n})\right) \quad (26)$$

where K – the pheromone growth coefficient.

The phenomenon of pheromone evaporation is taken as real property information exchange and causes the ant to confirm or update its results within the search model, thus providing a review of the whole space of possible solutions.

When looking for the minima where $Q\left(x_{i_1}, \ldots x_{i_j}, \ldots x_{i_n}\right) < Q\left(x_{i_1}, \ldots x_{i_j \pm 1}, \ldots x_{i_n}\right)$ is satisfied, transition between fragments is banned. Thus, the breakpoint condition is fulfilled if all the ants are unable to move. As a result, after N iterations ants get fragment with the lowest functions value and localize the minimums.

The software tool Multi-Extreme Optimization of Function by MACM description. On the basis of the described algorithm and model (22)-(26), the software tool (ST) was developed that implements the search of local and global extremes. The ST structure includes 6 independent classes that inherit from the standard class Object:

1. class *Ant* – class that is used to describe objects such as ant;
2. class *Algorithm* – class that is used to describe objects of MACM algorithm;
3. class *Drawing* – class that contains methods for GUI;
4. class *Parameters* – class that contains global parameters;
5. class *Results* – class that is used to generate and output the resultant information;
6. default classes *Form* and *Program* – standard classes that are created by default in the development environment.

ST has an intuitive graphical user interface, which includes a user input settings module, a graphical display of the object, as well as statistics collection and displaying the results modules. To create a modelling module were involved:

- Windows Forms — Application Programming Interface (API), is responsible for the graphical user interface and is part of Microsoft.NET Framework;
- Tao Framework — a library that provides developers with .NET and Mono access to features of popular libraries like OpenGL and SDL.

Fig. 10 shows the software tool graphical user interface (GUI).

The user settings are located on the right side of the the main GUI window, and in the left side of the visual represenattion of the object is dispalyed. The graphical display is based on the Tao framework library using OpenGL. The settings window allows to change all the parameters of the algorithm in an easy way. In the process of implementation, all the information is gathered and displayed on the screen for the visual assessment of the computed optimization results.

To display all localized extremums and their status, a tab with the results is shown in Fig. 11.

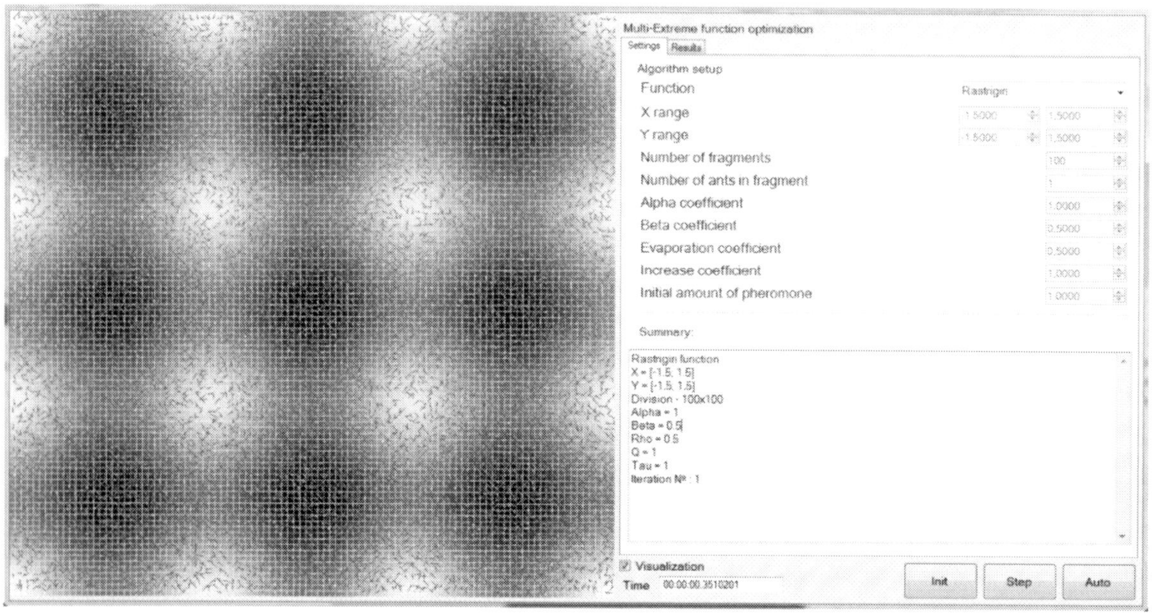

Figure 10. «MEOF_MACM» main GUI

ME functions research using MEOF_MACM. As example, we considered and optimized Ursem01 function and Styblinski-Tang, which plots are presented in Fig. 12.

Research Ursem01 function is performed in the range of x and y [-2;2] coordinates. The selected area is initially divided into fragments with 0.0133 step, and one ant was placed on each fragment. Coefficients $\alpha = 1$, $\beta = 0.7$, $\rho = 0.5$, K = 1 and $\tau = 1$. Fig. 14 shows the individual stages of ST.

The localization results of each extrema are presented in TABLE V.

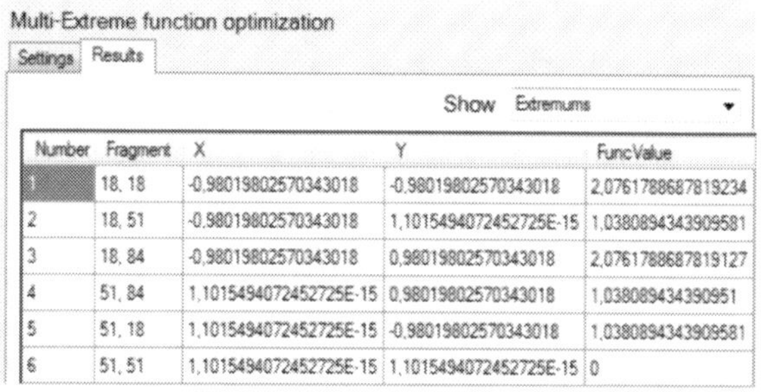
Multi-Extreme function optimization

Settings | Results

Show Extremums

Number	Fragment	X	Y	FuncValue
1	18, 18	-0,98019802570343018	-0,98019802570343018	2,0761788687819234
2	18, 51	-0,98019802570343018	1,1015494072452725E-15	1,0380894343909581
3	18, 84	-0,98019802570343018	0,98019802570343018	2,0761788687819127
4	51, 84	1,1015494072452725E-15	0,98019802570343018	1,038089434390951
5	51, 18	1,1015494072452725E-15	-0,98019802570343018	1,0380894343909581
6	51, 51	1,1015494072452725E-15	1,1015494072452725E-15	0

Figure 11. «MEOF_MACM» result interface

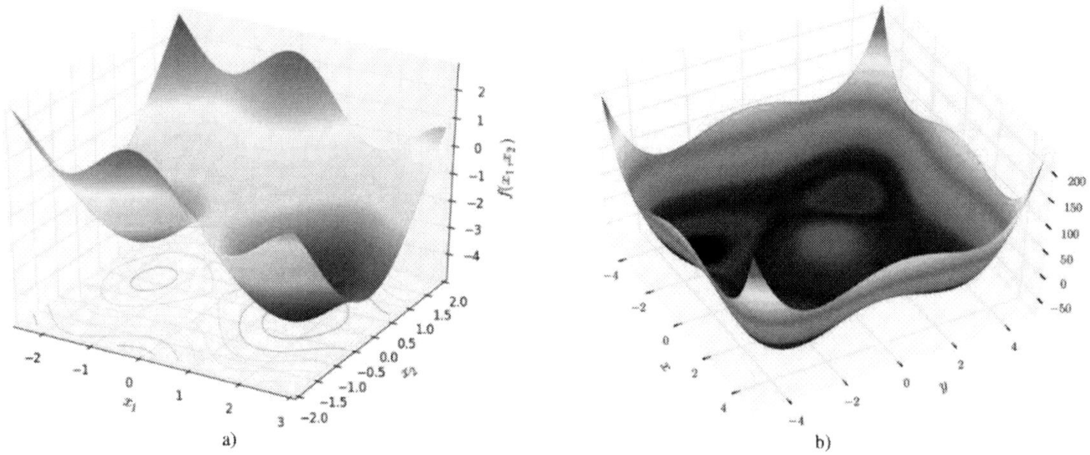

Figure 12. Plots of additional functions to study (a – Ursem01 function plot, b – Styblinski-Tang function plot)

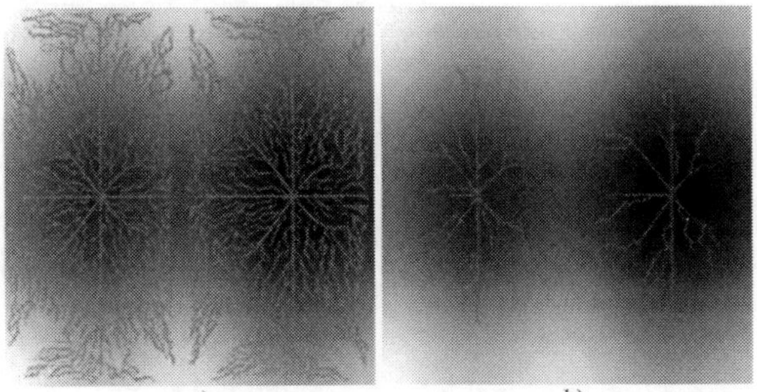

Figure 13. The stages of the localization 300x300 division area (a, b – intermediate results)

TABLE V. LOCALIZED RESULTS (URSEM01 FUNCTION)

Ursem01 function					
Standard			Extremal evaluation item		
X	Y	f(x,y)	Coordinates		Value
			X	Y	f(x,y)
1.69714	0	-4.8168	1.69500	-0.00499	-4.81676
-	-	-	-1.44666	-0.00666	-3.24594

The research on the Styblinski-Tang function is performed in the range [-5; 5] with the partition of the test area by 400x400. Fig. 14 shows the individual stages of ST.

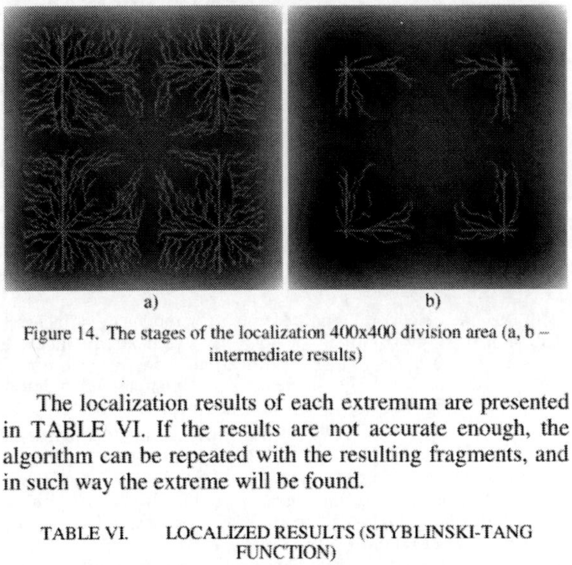

Figure 14. The stages of the localization 400x400 division area (a, b – intermediate results)

The localization results of each extremum are presented in TABLE VI. If the results are not accurate enough, the algorithm can be repeated with the resulting fragments, and in such way the extreme will be found.

TABLE VI. LOCALIZED RESULTS (STYBLINSKI-TANG FUNCTION)

Styblinski-Tang function					
Standard			Extremal evaluation item		
X	Y	f(x,y)	Coordinates		Value
			X	Y	f(x,y)
-2.90353	-2.90353	-39.1659	-2.91249	-2.91249	-39.16477
-	-	-	-2.91249	2.73749	-32.09647
-	-	-	2.73749	-2.91249	-32.09647
-	-	-	2.73749	2.73749	-25.02818

It is worth noting that this algorithm and its software implementation have no special mechanism for clustering. This is due to the fact that the clustering mechanism is incorporated in the mathematical models (22). This approach is characterized by some discreetness. The test area is divided into fragments, thus the resulting agents somehow are combined into groups, which are further referring to a specific function value within the fragment.

D. Computational resources and performance

The search of the extremes by the swarming particles, evolutionary-genetic and ant colony algorithms on 2-dimensional Rastrigin function is carried out on a PC with processor AMD Phenom II P960 with 6 GB of RAM.

To achieve the accuracy 10^{-3}, the time was up to 40 sec. For the additional search within each area, the required computational time was up to 20-50 sec.

III. RELATED WORK

In the design optimization process, we are often confronted with problems facing the ME conditions. Such situation requires several decisions to be taken, which take into consideration several identical or close extremes, and the best choice in-between them has to be used. The classical theory of scheduling gives examples, where several identical optimums and identical sub-optimums, close to them exist. The majority of discrete, integer and combinatory programming problems differs in such property, in particular, when finding solution for graphs. The finite number (though to be very big) of admissible decisions requires considering the ME solutions for the discrete environment optimization. It is important to have a complete solution of the ME task, because the criterion is usually a numerical expression related to the optimized object. However, there are many additional conditions, which can help to choose the extreme, equivalent or close in size, and satisfy both, the numerical criteria estimates and the heuristic ideas. Therefore, the choice of the most effective methods and algorithms, is an extremely important step to find such solution of the ME task.

However, not all of the search methods provide the successful solution for the ME task. It is well known that the determinate methods are sensitive to the sign-variable, so-called "gullied" surfaces, which define the real variables in the factor space. The solution of discrete tasks by such methods leads to the nondeterministic polynomial, in order to be defined for the complete problem in time. The methods of the accidental search are poorly predictable, since it is impossible to control the time expenditure, and even the basic decision, on which heuristic method to apply, when having a real search optimization problem. In particular, in Russia, in the last years, the quite intensive research is conducted to find appropriate solutions for the many optimization problems. Among these methods, it is important to mention the swarming particles algorithm [14][15][16][17][18][19][20][21], the evolutionarily genetic algorithm [25][26][27][28][29][30][31][32][33], and the ant colony algorithm [34][35][36][37][38][39][40][41]. These algorithms were investigated, as the traditional optimization tasks, and in relation to find the solution of the ME tasks. For the last case, they have been significantly modified, by experimenting with different heuristic methods, which research was already conducted by the authors. Therefore, the presented work brings forward a peculiar theoretical result, and trace the roadmap for the future research in this direction.

IV. Conclusion

The application analysis of the 3 heuristic algorithms for solving the ME tasks showed that these methods are efficient, effective, and bring some essential features to the presented solutions.

The specific approaches to solve the task for each of these particular cases is determined through the analysis of the algorithms features; the detection and identification of local extremes, clustering methods and subsequent operations resulting from such analysis. However, in all these cases, the modifications of algorithms is connected with the data clustering necessity, which was found to be essential. In addition, all the methods showed reasonable performance.

To conclude, all the 3 studied methods are considered to be relevant and promising for the future applications. The specific choice of the algorithm tool for solving ME tasks depends on the experience and personal researcher preferences, as well as on the special features of the domain specific research area.

In this paper, the task of finding the set of extremes for 2-dimensional Rastrigin test function was examined. In future research, it is advisable to study the problem of higher dimension (3 or more) in order to assess the impact of algorithms' parameters affecting the time and search accuracy, and to enable algorithms modifications for the mathematical models of any-scale problem dimension.

References

[1] R. Neydorf, I. Chernogorov, V. Polyakh, O. Yarakhmedov, J. Goncharova, and D. Vucinic "Study of Search Optimization Opportunities of Heuristic Algorithms for Solving Multi-Extremal Problems," Proceedings of The X International Conference on Advanced Engineering Computing and Applications in Sciences (ADVCOMP), 2016, pp. 44-51.

[2] S. Boettcher and A. G. Percus, "Extremal optimization: methods derived from co-evolution," Proceedings of the 1999 Genetic and Evolutionary Computation Conference (GECCO), 1999, pp. 825-832.

[3] C. A. Floudas and P. M. Pardalos, "Encyclopedia of optimization, 2nd Edition," Springer, New York: Springer Scince+Business Media, LCC, 2009.

[4] K. B. Jones, "Search engine optimization, 2nd edition," Indianapolis: Wiley Publishing, 2010.

[5] R. Shreves, "Drupal search engine optimization," Birmingham: Packt Publishing LTD, 2012.

[6] I. M. Vinogradov, "Mathematical encyclopedia," Soviet Encyclopedia, vol.4, 1977-1985, pp. 135-140.

[7] R. G. Strongin, "Algorithms for multi-extremal mathematical programming problems," 1992, pp. 357-378.

[8] R. A. Neydorf, A. V. Filippov, and Z. H. Yagubov, "Commute algorithm of biextreme solutions of the homogeneous distribution problem," Herald of DSTU, №5(56), vol.11, 2011, pp. 655-666.

[9] R. A. Neydorf and A. A. Zhikulin, "Research of properties solutions of multi distribution problems," System analysis, management and information processing: Proceedings of the 2nd International Scientific Seminar, Rostov-on-Don: IC DSTU, 2011, pp. 377-380.

[10] R. A. Neydorf and A. A. Dereviankina, "The methodology of solving problems of the modified method of multi swarming particles," Innovation, ecology and resource-saving technologies at the enterprises of mechanical engineering, aviation, transport and agriculture, Proceedings of the IX International Scientific and Technical Conference, Rostov-on-Don: IC DSTU, 2010, pp. 328-330.

[11] R. A. Neydorf and A. A. Dereviankina, "Decision of multi tasks by dividing swarms," Herald of DSTU, №4(47), vol.10, 2010, pp. 492-499.

[12] R. A. Neydorf and A. A. Dereviankina, "The solution of problems of recognition by swarming particle swarm division," News of SFU. Technical science. Special Issue (Intellectual CAD), Taganrog: Publisher TTI SFU, №7(108), 2010, pp. 21-28.

[13] L. A. Rastrigin, "Systems of extremal control," Nauka, Moscow (in Russian), 1974.

[14] R. C. Eberhart and J. Kennedy, "New optimizer, using particle swarm theory," Proceedings of the Sixth International Symposium on Micromachine and Human Science, Nagoya, Japan, 1995, pp. 39-43.

[15] J. Kennedy and R. Eberhart, "Particle swarm optimization," Proceedings of IEEE International Conference on Neural Networks IV, 1995, pp. 1942-1948.

[16] Y. Shi and R. C. Eberhart, "A modified particle swarm optimizer," Proceedings of the IEEE Congress on Evolutionary Computation, Piscataway, New Jersey, 1998, pp. 69-73.

[17] M. Clerc and J. Kennedy, "The particle swarm-explosion, stability, and convergence in a multi-dimensional complex space," IEEE Transactions on Evolutionary Computation, 2002, pp. 58-73.

[18] Mendes, J. Kennedy, and J. Neves, "The fully informed particle swarm: simpler, maybe better," Evolutionary Computation, IEEE Transactions on 8(3), 2004, pp. 204-210.

[19] R. A. Neydorf and I. V. Chernogorov, "Parametric configuration of the algorithm of searching optimization by swarming particles using experimental planning," International Institute of Science "Educatio", №2(9), vol.4, 2015, pp. 44-49.

[20] R. A. Neydorf and I. V. Chernogorov, "Increased functionality of the method of swarming particles by kinematic and dynamic modification of the algorithm of its realization," LTD "Aeterna", International Journal "Innovative science", №6, vol. 1, 2015, pp. 24-28.

[21] R. A. Neydorf and I. V. Chernogorov, "A parametric research of the algorithm of swarming particles in the problem of finding the global extremum," Mathematical methods in technique and technologies – (MMTT-28): Proceedings XXVIII International Scientific Conference, YA.6, Saratov: SSTU, 2015, pp. 75-80.

[22] A. A. Barsegjan, M. S. Kuprijanov and V.V. Stepanenko, "Methods and analysis models of OLAP and Data Mining," Saint Petersburg: BKhV-Peterburg, 2004, 336 p.

[23] https://habrahabr.ru/post/124978 (December 15, 2016).

[24] https://www.sfu.ca/~ssurjano/schwef.html (December 15, 2016).

[25] A. Fraser, "Computer models in genetics," New York: McGraw-Hill, 1970.

[26] D. Goldberg, "Genetic algorithms in search, optimization and machine learning," Addison Wesley, 1989.

[27] H. Mühlenbein, D. Schomisch, and J. Born, "The parallel genetic algorithm as function optimizer," Parallel Computing, vol. 17, 1991, pp. 619-632.

[28] N. A. Barricelli, "Esempi numerici di processi di evoluzione," Methodos, 1954, pp. 45–68.

[29] S. Boettcher, "Extremal optimization - heuristics via co-evolutionary avalanches," Computing in Science & Engineering 2, 2000, pp. 75–82.

[30] S. Boettcher, "Extremal optimization of graph partitioning at the percolation threshold," 1999, pp. 5201–5211.

[31] R. A. Neydorf and V. V. Polyakh, "Method of multisearch using evolutionary genetic algorithm and sample t-test," LTD "Aeterna", International Journal "Innovative science", №3, vol.1, 2015, pp. 135-140.

[32] R. A. Neydorf and V. V. Polyakh, "Study of multi dependencies using an evolutionary genetic method and one sample Student's t-test," Mathematical methods in technique and technologies – (MMTT-28): Proceedings XXVIII International Scientific Conference, YA.6, Saratov: SSTU, 2015, pp. 83-87.

[33] R. A. Neydorf and V. V. Polyakh, "Localization search scopes evolutionary genetic algorithm for solving problems of multi nature," Science.Technology.Production, №6, vol.2, 2015, pp. 18-22.

[34] M. Lovric, "International encyclopedia of statistical science," Springer-Verlag Berlin Heidelberg, 2011.

[35] Bert Holldobler. "The Superorganism: the beauty, legance and strangeness of insect societies"./ Bert Holldobler, Edward O. Wilson. // 2008: W.W. Norton and Company, New York, 576 pp., 110 color and 100 black-and-white illustrations. ISBN-10: 0393067041, ISBN-13: 978-0393067040, Price: Euro 41.99.

[36] R. A. Neydorf and O. T. Yarakhmedov, "Development, optimization and analysis of parameters of classic ant colony algorithm in solving travelling salesman problem on graph," Science. Technologies. Production, №3, vol.2, 2015, pp. 18-22.

[37] A. Kazharov and V. Kureichik, "Ant colony optimization algorithms for solving transportation problems," Journal of Computer and Systems Sciences International, №1, vol.49, 2010, pp. 30–43.

[38] M. Dorigo and L. M. Gambardella, "Ant colony system: a cooperative learning approach to the traveling salesman problem," IEEE Transactions on Evolutionary Computation, №1, vol.1, 1997, pp. 53-66.

[39] X. Liu and H. Fu, "An effective clustering algorithm with ant colony," Journal of Computers, №4, vol.5, 2010, pp. 598-605.

[40] M. D. Toksari, "Ant colony optimization for finding the global minimum," Applied Mathematics and Computation 176, 2006, pp. 308–316.

[41] Jani Rönkkönen, "Continuous Multimodal Global Optimization with Differential Evolution-Based Methods," Ph.D. Thesis, Lappeenranta University of Technology, Lappeenranta, Finland, 2009, [Accessed May, 7, 2015]. [Online].Available:https://www.doria.fi/bitstream/handle/10024/50498/isbn%209789522148520.pdf

[42] Global Optimization Test Functions Index. Retrieved June 2013, from http://infinity77.net/global_optimization/test_functions.html#test-functions-index.

[43] Michael L. Pinedo "Scheduling Theory, Algorithms, and Systems Fourth Edition," ISBN 978-1-4614-1986-0 e-ISBN 978-1-4614-2361-4 DOI 10.1007/978-1-4614-2361-4 Springer New York Dordrecht Heidelberg London Mathematics Subject Classification (2010): Library of Congress Control Number: 68Mxx, 68M20, 90Bxx, 90B35.

[44] https://www.encyclopediaofmath.org/index.php/Discrete_programming (September 29, 2016).

[45] Donald E. Knuth – "The Art of Computer Programming. " vol. 4, Fascicle 0: Introduction to Combinatorial Algorithms and Boolean Functions (vi+240pp, ISBN 0-321-53496-4).

[46] http://www.cs.utsa.edu/~wagner/knuth/ (September 29, 2016).

[47] GRhttp://diestel-graph-theory.com/index.html (September 29, 2016).

[48] Keijo Ruohonen. "Graph theory," (Translation by Janne Tamminen, Kung-Chung Lee and Robert Piché), 2013.

[49] Christopher Griffin, "Graph Theory: Penn State Math 485 Lecture Notes Version" 1.4.2.1 2011-2012.

[50] Paul Van Dooren "Graph Theory and Applications," Université catholique de Louvain Louvain-la-Neuve, Belgium Dublin, August 2009.

iaria journals

www.iariajournals.org

International Journal On Advances in Intelligent Systems
issn: 1942-2679

International Journal On Advances in Internet Technology
issn: 1942-2652

International Journal On Advances in Life Sciences
issn: 1942-2660

International Journal On Advances in Networks and Services
issn: 1942-2644

International Journal On Advances in Security
issn: 1942-2636

International Journal On Advances in Software
issn: 1942-2628

International Journal On Advances in Systems and Measurements
issn: 1942-261x

International Journal On Advances in Telecommunications
issn: 1942-2601